THE
WESTERN LIT
SURVIVAL KIT

THE
WESTERN LIT
SURVIVAL KIT

AN IRREVERENT GUIDE TO THE CLASSICS,
FROM HOMER TO FAULKNER

Sandra Newman

GOTHAM BOOKS

GOTHAM BOOKS
Published by Penguin Group (USA) Inc.
375 Hudson Street, New York, New York 10014, U.S.A.
Penguin Group (Canada), 90 Eglinton Avenue East, Suite 700, Toronto, Ontario M4P 2Y3, Canada
(a division of Pearson Penguin Canada Inc.) · Penguin Books Ltd, 80 Strand, London WC2R 0RL,
England · Penguin Ireland, 25 St Stephen's Green, Dublin 2, Ireland (a division of Penguin Books Ltd) ·
Penguin Group (Australia), 250 Camberwell Road, Camberwell, Victoria 3124, Australia (a division of
Pearson Australia Group Pty Ltd) · Penguin Books India Pvt Ltd, 11 Community Centre, Panchsheel Park,
New Delhi–110 017, India–Penguin Group (NZ), 67 Apollo Drive, Rosedale, Auckland 0632, New Zealand
(a division of Pearson New Zealand Ltd) · Penguin Books (South Africa) (Pty) Ltd, 24 Sturdee Avenue,
Rosebank, Johannesburg 2196, South Africa

Penguin Books Ltd, Registered Offices: 80 Strand, London WC2R 0RL, England

Published by Gotham Books, a member of Penguin Group (USA) Inc.

First printing, January 2012
1 3 5 7 9 10 8 6 4 2

Gotham Books and the skyscraper logo are trademarks of Penguin Group (USA) Inc.

LIBRARY OF CONGRESS CATALOGING-IN-PUBLICATION DATA

Newman, Sandra, 1965–
The western lit survival kit : an irreverent guide to the classics, from Homer to Faulkner /
Sandra Newman.
p. cm.
ISBN 978-1-59240-694-4
1. Best books. 2. Literature. 3. Criticism. I. Title.
Z1035.9.N55 2012
011'.73—dc23   2011032730

Printed in the United States of America
Set in Adobe Caslon Pro
Designed by Elke Sigal

Acknowledgments

This book might never have been written were it not for my sometime writing partner/sometime roommate Howard Mittelmark, who suggested the project and helped shape it from the start. I am grateful for his comments and contributions throughout, particularly in the medieval and American sections. Nonetheless, all errors remain mine. (Except one! If you think you know which error is Howard's, send in your answer. If you win, you'll receive a limited edition, leather-bound collection of all of our very best errors.)

CONTENTS

THE
WESTERN LIT SURVIVAL KIT

Introduction

In the 1920s, educators like Mortimer Adler started the Great Books programs, while imprints like Everyman's Library made the classics available to everyone at reasonable prices. It was an ambitious crusade to bring literature to the people, and was phenomenally successful in achieving one thing. From then on, not just English majors, but everybody else could feel guilty about not reading the Great Books. Meanwhile, universal education gave young people the opportunity to associate literature with suffering as early as high school. By the time they reached college, they already knew that *Sister Carrie* was impenetrable, turgid, and boring, and that whatever language Shakespeare spoke, it wasn't English. Tainted by association, literature had all the appeal of Bible studies.

Recently, publishers have turned to spoon-feeding (*Ulysses for Dummies—Extra-Dumb Edition*); fear (*1001 Books to Read or You'll Die!!!!*); and quirk (*How Proust Can Change Alain de Botton's Income*) with some success. Even people who don't want to read the Great Books will read *about* the Great Books. In fact, reading about the Great Books is now a votive act, like buying a gym membership although you never go, or separating your recyclables before jumping in the SUV.

There's just one thing wrong with this. Literature is a pleasure. It should be emotionally satisfying, intellectually thrilling, and just plain fun. And if it isn't, you shouldn't feel bad about not reading it.

This book treats Western lit like an amusement park. It offers a guide to the rides, suggesting which ones are fun for all ages, which are impossibly dull for all ages, and which might take a lot out of you but offer an experience you simply can't get anywhere else.

For readers who have already ingested a generous sampling from the Great Books, this book will offer a unifying perspective, fresh insights, and cheap jokes at the expense of your favorite and least favorite authors. For the reader approaching Western literature for the first time (or for the second time, having been badly burned in school), this book will help you judge which authors are really worth attempting.

Each individual work is assigned ratings from one to ten in the areas of Importance, Accessibility, and Fun. I have tried to make these as objective as possible. This means that they are subjective assessments of what the average reader will feel. Of course, you may be a person who ripped through Joyce effortlessly, or who thought *The Scarlet Letter* was a laugh riot. Please do not be upset if you stumble over anomalies. Instead, sit back and congratulate yourself: dude, you are no average reader.

A note: "Fun" does not mean "Quality." *Paradise Lost* is a work of acknowledged genius. It is also about as much fun as being trapped in a freezer. In the Fun rating, I've tried to incorporate various possible sources of fun, such as the loveliness of poetry and the page-turning quality of fiction. However, it all boils down to assessing the entertainment value of a work—not the deathless masterpieceness.

For the purposes of this book, Western literature is what you traditionally learn about when you go to college to study literature. This book will not redress imbalances or redefine the canon. It will concentrate on works considered important in the English-speaking world, passing by Büchner and Mickiewicz and every single Albanian who ever lived without a second glance. Or a first glance.

Among other matters, the present author, like almost everyone else, would be happier if Western literature were not quite as white and male as it is. Like almost everyone else, however, there is nothing I can do about it, except try not to let it bother me, and drink. C'est la vie, which as everyone knows, is not a bowl of cherries. And if it were, in past centuries, white men would have eaten all of them, while the rest of us would have had to wash the bowl. Still, when they were full of all that healthy cherry energy, those white guys wrote some pretty good books.

CHAPTER I

Greece: Cradle of Greek Civilization

The term "classical literature" refers to the works of the ancient Greeks and Romans, which were written during classical antiquity—between about 900 B.C. and A.D. 400. All Western literature ultimately originates from these Greeks and Romans, although it often takes a detour through the English and a bottle of whisky. For centuries, learning Greek and Latin was considered part of any serious education. Many of the writers we will meet in the coming pages learned these dead languages at ages as young as five. Now they are dead themselves. Was it worth it? We may never know.

Nowadays, people read only a handful of all-star Greek and Latin works, and almost no one reads them in the original language. We strongly recommend reading these works—in English. It will make you look smart out of all proportion to how hard it is. Even though somebody else has done the really hard work of translating from the Greek, you can sit back and take the credit. Do not make the mistake of learning Greek, however, since this takes you past "smart" into "disturbing asexual presence."

THE INSTANT CLASSIC

Please note: while "classical literature" refers to ancient Greek and Latin works, "the classics" has come to signify any works worth studying, even if they were written in the seventies by Puerto Ricans. Do not mistake "classical literature" for "the classics"—and be especially careful not to confuse either with an "instant classic."

"Instant classic" is an oxymoron only seen in the quotes printed on the back covers of books. What does it mean? Well, usually, it means the person quoted is a bought-and-sold lackey of the publishing industry. Sometimes, though, it means he is the author's boyfriend.

Greece: The Fundamentals

In ancient Greece, material which nowadays would form the basis for a novel or screenplay was always rendered in poetry. In fact, political speeches were written in poetry, philosophy was written in poetry, and sports coverage was written in poetry. I would like to be able to tell you that poetry was written in prose, but alas! Poetry also was written in poetry.

Another difference: poetry at this time was always sung, not read. A poet like Sappho composed the music to her works and sang them publicly. Homer was also a singer-songwriter. The lyre was the acoustic guitar of its day. This is the origin of the term "lyric poetry"—poetry sung to the accompaniment of a lyre. Certain songs were performed by groups of hot young boys or girls, who danced as they sang—much like the Pussycat Dolls of today. This was not considered cheesy then. Apparently the gods liked it.

Even after the Greeks learned to read and write, they preferred hearing singers to reading poetry—just like us!

SOUND SMART!

In any conversation about classical literature, it is smart to interject, with a worldly smile, "Of course, homosexuality was considered normal in ancient Greece." Since everyone already knows this, it's crucial to speak quickly, before anyone can beat you to the punch. If someone else does say it first, wink and say, "When in Rome . . ."

HOMER (POSSIBLY 8TH CENTURY B.C.)

Who was Homer?

Homer, if he existed, was probably a traveling minstrel, exchanging an evening's entertainment for food, lodging, and tips. In fact, some scholars speculate that the second half of the *Odyssey* is so prolonged because Homer had found a host who had a good cook, and he wanted to squeeze out a few extra days of hospitality.

An interesting fact about Homer, the greatest writer of antiquity, is that he almost certainly couldn't read or write. This would have passed unnoticed, though, since neither could anyone else. A larger question is whether Homer was a person, never mind could he read. Nowadays, many people doubt there was a man called Homer, who single-handedly composed the *Iliad* and the *Odyssey*.

The main theories are:

- Innumerable poets sang versions of these stories, which were copied and reworked over generations. Because the poems were too long to reliably memorize, some of the material was made up on the spot. The poems we have are the result of freezing the text at the point where the Greeks began to write things down. "Homer" was a name traditionally associated with the songs, but even if he existed, the songs had changed many times since his death.
- The *Iliad* and the *Odyssey* were written by two different people, who probably knew each other well; like a master and his disciple, or a father and son, or two cowboys who were secretly in love.
- Homer was a woman, a theory proposed by Samuel Butler, author of *The Way of All Flesh*. So few people believe this that more people have read *The Way of All Flesh*.
- Mainly, though, Homer was blind. The ancient Greeks believed this, and it's plausible since blindness was common among bards in oral traditions worldwide. Since a blind man was ill-suited to being a farmer, hunter, or shepherd, he became a musician. This is also in the great tradition of blues men like Blind Lemon Jefferson and Blind Willie McTell and Gropes Joe Washhouse and Al "Needs Glasses to Read" Possombone.
- That Homer was Homer's clone, sent back in time from the future to prevent the galactic war with the Bacteroid Legions in 2045, is one thing no one has suggested. That doesn't stop it being true.

The *Iliad*

In ancient Greece, poetry was thought to be inspired by one of nine "Muses," who were the goddesses of the arts. Thus, the *Iliad* begins with an invocation: "Sing, Muse, of the wrath of Achilles." This line is by far the most famous in the book, because it is as far as most people get. Therefore, "Sing, Muse, of the wrath of Achilles" is a good thing to quote when the *Iliad* comes up in conversation. (Oh, it will. Don't get complacent.)

While quoting, adopt a dreamy look, as if recalling many pleasant hours spent in a persimmon bower drunk on heavenly verse.

Before the tale begins, Helen of Troy has run away from her husband, Menelaus, with a good-looking devil, Paris. Therefore, the whole Greek fleet lays siege to Troy for ten years, the greatest effort and manpower ever devoted to stalking.

In those good old days when civilization was still just a bad dream, successful armies dragged off all the women of the conquered nation as slaves, for purposes of sex and/or as labor, much as the French do today. This bulk enslavement also made the conquered soldiers crazy, before they were slain en masse. (As a general note, all Homer's heroes were illiterates who considered rape and genocide normal. Generations of European boys were raised on Homer. Just saying.) Once caught, the newly enslaved girls were parceled out, with the best girl going to the head of the army and the second-best going to the neck of the army, and so on, until the penny-ante soldiers were getting girls who looked like Salman Rushdie, had sleep apnea, and could not carry a tune.

As our story opens, the top king of the Greeks, Agamemnon, has a problem. His new top-pick slave girl, Chryseis, is the daughter of Chryse, a priest of the god Apollo. Feeling dissed by this, Apollo has been slaying Greeks by the bucketload. Chryseis has to be sent home to get Apollo off everyone's back. King Agamemnon pouts and makes a big fuss and tells his best fighter, Achilles, that he's going to take his slave girl, Briseis, to replace Chryseis.

Achilles makes an even bigger fuss, saying if that's the way it's going to be, he isn't fighting anymore, and don't come crying to him, because without Achilles, the Greeks are helpless weaklings who can't even barely do anything.

"Yeah, whatever," says Agamemnon.

Achilles storms off to his tent, bursts into tears, and tells the whole awful story to his mother, a river nymph named Thetis.

She responds, "Oh, God, why did I ever have children?"

Achilles tells her, "Go ask Zeus to punish the whole Greek army until they beg me to come back." (NB: As a group, Homer's heroes displayed the emotional development of third graders.)

To make a long story short, Thetis does it, and Zeus listens to her because she's one of his favorite people, even though, as he says, "My wife is going to kill me if she finds out."

For many, many pages thereafter, Zeus punishes the entire Greek army with defeat after defeat, despite their superior numbers and firepower, and despite the fact that he hypocritically continues to accept their sacrifices while laughing behind his hand. (Hey! Is that what happened in Vietnam? Looks fishy!)

In general, the *Iliad* consists of one fight after another. A typical scene has a hero spearing the eyeball of his dying foe and lofting it to the skies to deliver a speech that amounts to "Ha ha! Take that!" Blood gushes, intestines spill, brains spatter forth, and the victor crows like a James Bond villain. At one time, the *Iliad* must have combined the joys of an action film with those of a slasher pic. For some readers, it still does. For others, it's uncannily like reading the same paragraph over and over and over and over.

Spoiler: By the end, the Trojan prince Hector has single-handedly butchered most of the Greeks, while Achilles sits in his tent with his arms crossed. When Achilles' best friend, Patroklos, is killed, though, Achilles at last goes out and kills Hector. The last third of the book consists largely of funerals and weeping, including long descriptions of the athletic competitions traditional at Greek funerals. This was the Greeks' favorite part of the *Iliad*, corresponding to our modern "sports pages."

MANY-ADJECTIVED HOMER

You can scarcely leaf through any introduction to the *Iliad* or the *Odyssey* without encountering an explanation of epithets.

Epithets are short descriptors added to a character's name, before or after, as in "gray-eyed Athene" or "Diomedes, breaker of horses." The likelihood is that they were originally devised to be put in at the last moment to make up the requisite number of beats in a line. Some epithets are particular to one person or god, like "Zeus of the aegis" or "laughing Aphrodite." Some are more generic, and some are so all-purpose that they amount to "Mr. Achilles" and "Ms. Athene." Almost any man can be "spear-famed" or "of the great war cry," for instance; while all Greek women were apparently "lovely-haired" without exception. The Homer-era singer could pad a line with one of these whenever he was caught short—much in the way today's politicians use meaningless phrases like "my fellow Americans," "in this great country of ours," and "I will not raise taxes."

The Odyssey

At the beginning of the *Odyssey*, the Trojan War is over finally, and all the spear-famed heroes of the great war cry have gone home. But ten years later, Odysseus still hasn't made it back from Troy to his native Ithaca. Reasonably enough, the Ithacans have decided he is dead. Odysseus's house has filled up with more than a hundred men who want to marry his wife, Penelope, and become king in his stead.

For reasons that are never explained, Penelope feeds and houses these one-hundred-plus men for years rather than say, "No thanks, I won't marry you." It's also unclear why marrying Penelope would make someone king, since this is not how kingship works anywhere else in Homer, or in Greek history. Some scholars have argued that this plot detail is evidence for a previous matriarchal society. Either that or it's the eighth century B.C. equivalent of a wacky sitcom premise.

Another aspect of Greek literature that seems far-fetched today is the way gods constantly meddled in human affairs. Nor did the gods meddle for any higher purpose, rewarding the just and chastising the wrongdoer, as we might expect. Generally it was for petty reasons, like vanity, or jealousy, or because somebody cute asked them. They often accomplished their meddling by taking the form of your next-door neighbor, who would then be suddenly full of "helpful" advice. Zeus was notorious for taking on the form of just about anything he could think of in order to get girls to sleep with him—a bull, a swan, a shower of gold. Apparently it never occurred to him that girls might want to sleep with someone who looks like a Greek god.

Roughly half of the *Odyssey* tells the story of Odysseus's trip home, during which all of his men are killed. The other half tells how he kills all of the suitors in his house with the help of his teenaged son Telemachus. He is accompanied every step of the way by the goddess Athena, who tells him what to do, kills his enemies, makes him invisible one moment and irresistibly gorgeous the next. It goes beyond deus ex machina to "deus, get a life already."

Although the *Odyssey* is more of a page-turner than the *Iliad*, it still takes some time to get going. Homer warms up by sending Telemachus out into the world to look for his father. The narrative high point of this episode occurs when he meets some people and has dinner with them.

In Books 5 through 12, Odysseus is at the court of King Alcinous, where he recounts all of his adventures to date. These are the stories everyone has heard of, even if they don't know where they come from. Innumerable movies and books have retold them, because they remain pretty good stories, and also because the writers of the movies and books want people to know that they've read the *Odyssey*.

Perhaps the best known is the story of the Sirens. On his way home, Odysseus must sail past the Sirens, whose beautiful singing lures men to their doom on the treacherous, rocky coast. Odysseus is too smart to fall for that and has his men stop their ears with wax. Odysseus wants to hear the Sirens, though, and has the men lash him to the mast while leaving his ears unwaxed. This is the first known occurrence in history of the concept of the designated driver.

Odysseus also has a run-in with a Cyclops; there is an episode in which Circe, a witch, turns his men into swine; and a trip to the Underworld, where he interviews various fallen heroes. In the course of this, all his men are brutally killed, while Odysseus himself is horribly, tragically forced to sleep with beautiful women. We can guess already which character Homer identified with.

This becomes still clearer in the second half of the *Odyssey*, in which Odysseus arrives home to find the brutish suitors in his home. Athena disguises him as an aged vagrant, for no particular reason, and he spends nine books wandering around the court begging for scraps and being treated like crap by aristocrats, uncannily like what Homer himself would have been going through even as he composed the poem!

The story ends when Odysseus, aided by Athena and his son, kills the hundred-plus bad guys. This scene plays out exactly as it would in a Hollywood action movie. The bad guys have amazingly poor aim, and the good guys never miss, all the while performing superhuman feats of acrobatic skill while tossing off snappy one-liners. In Homer, though, all this is happening for the very good reason that one of the good guys is an all-powerful god.

Odysseus in Latin is Ulysses, which is pronounced "Ulysses."

	Importance	Accessibility	Fun
The *Iliad*	8	3	6
The *Odyssey*	10	5	7

HESIOD (7TH CENTURY B.C., IN ALL LIKELIHOOD)

The Greeks traditionally thought that Homer and Hesiod were contemporaries. In fact, Hesiod probably lived somewhat after Homer. All we know for sure is that both of them lived before people started knowing exactly when people lived. In Greek literature circles, this is known as the Epic Age.

Although much of Hesiod's poetry is about mythology, he keeps coming back to the present day, and talking about himself, unlike Homer. Also, while Homer is the poet of the aristocrat, Hesiod is the poet of the working classes. The final difference between the two is that you don't have to read Hesiod.

What you need to know about Hesiod

1. Pronounced "Heh-see-odd," emphasis on heh. Or however you want.
2. Wrote *Theogony*, about the origins of the gods.
3. Also wrote *Works and Days*, a long almanac poem of wise sayings and random agricultural advice: when to plow, what wood to choose for the plow, how to winnow your yeomen and hemp your scumble. *Works and Days* is addressed to Hesiod's brother, Perses, not because Hesiod loved Perses, but because Perses stole the family inheritance by bribing corrupt officials, and Hesiod never got over it. *Works and Days* therefore includes a lot of trash talk about Perses and the officials concerned. "You gigantic idiot" is a typical style of address Hesiod uses for Perses.
4. Only known Greek poet from the time of Homer who did not write Homer.
5. For an ancient Greek, pretty fun—and much, much shorter than Homer.

	Importance	Accessibility	Fun
Theogony	3	6	6
Works and Days	3	6	7

THE LYRIC AGE

As noted earlier, the time of Homer and Hesiod is known as the Epic Age, or "We're not sure when it was." It is followed in Greek literature by the Lyric Age, which spans the seventh and sixth centuries B.C. (Keep in mind these are backwards centuries, so that the eighth century came before the seventh, the seventh came before the sixth, and flowers were sucked down into the ground, rain fell upward, and you would be getting younger while reading the *Iliad*.)

Most of what you need to know about Greek lyric poets is Sappho (late seventh to early sixth century B.C.). In a time when women were still acceptable birthday presents, Sappho's status was unprecedented. There were other female poets at the time, but none were remotely as important.

Sappho is important not only as a great poet, but as the original Lesbian from Lesbos. History tells that she had a husband, but from the poems extant, he does not seem to have made a strong impression. Sappho from beginning to end is eating her heart out for some girl.

We only have one complete poem by Sappho. The rest is from papyrus that has rotted, leaving only phrases here and there; or from short quotes in other Greek writers' books. All poetry from the lyric period is more personal in tone than Homer, but Sappho is an extreme case; almost every line she wrote is clearly love poetry. Even the one-word fragments tend to be words like "skin."

The remaining poets of the Lyric Age are no longer much read, largely because most of their work is lost, and there isn't much to read. An exception is Pindar (late sixth to mid fifth century). Pindar wrote all kinds of poetry, but by pure chance, all that survives are the songs he wrote to celebrate the victories of athletes at Olympics-style sporting events. At these games, the athlete's family would commission a victory ode, which would be sung and danced by a chorus of young boys from the athlete's hometown; basically cheerleaders. Though Pindar's odes are glorified cheers, they're considered some of the most beautiful poems in any language. In English translation, however, it's impossible to see why.

	Importance	Accessibility	Fun
Sappho	9	7	7
Pindar	4	2	1

Ancient Greek Tragedy: The Fundamentals

Unlike contemporary drama, Greek tragedy is about suffering, not story. Therefore a remarkable percentage of it consists of characters bitching and moaning about their problems rather than doing anything to entertain the audience. It is like dating a writer.

In Athens, plays were only performed at big religious festivals in honor of Dionysus, god of theater. Like many Greek religious occasions, these were competitions. Each day a trilogy of tragedies was performed, followed by a low-comedy "satyr" play, all by the same playwright.

The actors were all male and wore masks throughout. There was a chorus, which danced as well as sang. (In our terms, all Greek tragedies would be musicals.) Generally, the chorus's role was to act as a sort of all-singing, all-dancing vox populi, commenting on the action. In the satyr plays, the chorus were dressed as satyrs, wore large strap-on phalluses, and engaged in sophomoric, filthy jeering. In one fragment that has survived, the hero Perseus, as an infant, gives a satyr a hand job. Nowadays, Greek tragedies are generally performed without music, without dancing, and without strap-on dildos, making them what specialists call "very long." If you get a chance to see a Greek tragedy performed, by all means go, and bring a book.

Although there were many, many Greek playwrights, only three wrote works that have survived: Aeschylus (525–456 B.C.), Sophocles (496–406 B.C.), and Euripides (480–406 B.C.). The big three playwrights were all contemporaries, Aeschylus being roughly thirty years older than Sophocles and forty years older than Euripides. Aeschylus is known for being upright and pious. (Of course, in Greece, piety included genocide and sex slaves, so the bar was set pretty low.) Sophocles was known as modest, law-abiding, nice; typical middle child stuff. Pre-1900, Euripides was known for writing outrageously lascivious and violent female characters. Post-1900, Euripides is known for his psychological realism.

Below we give brief descriptions of the tragedies that are most important to know.

PROMETHEUS BOUND
Aeschylus

The people of Aeschylus's time believed that as soon as the gods created mankind, they realized we were a complete disaster. Zeus intended to destroy us and start over. But another god, Prometheus, got involved and gave mankind fire, agriculture, etc. Due to Prometheus's pernicious meddling, Zeus could not destroy human beings. This was extremely frustrating, since Zeus would have been looking forward to destroying us a lot.

To vent his frustration, Zeus had Prometheus manacled to a rock, stabbed through the chest, buried underground for hundreds of years, then brought to the surface, where an eagle tore his flesh off all day long and ate his liver. Being immortal, Prometheus was totally screwed.

In Aeschylus's version, Prometheus bitches about his punishment, says what a great guy he is, blames everyone else, and refuses to apologize, swearing that Zeus will get his. "How I will gloat then, ha ha!" In a long, unconnected scene, probably added for page length, Io appears and bitches about being turned into a cow (long story). Io was probably originally played by one man in a cow mask, not, disappointingly, by two men in a cow costume.

THE ORESTEIA
Aeschylus

The *Oresteia* is a trilogy consisting of *Agamemnon*, *The Libation Bearers*, and the *Eumenides*.

In the first play, the king of Mycenae, Agamemnon, returns home from the war with his new slave, Cassandra, a daughter of the Trojan king. His wife, Clytemnestra, is overjoyed, because his return finally gives her the opportunity to stab him to death. She kills Cassandra for good measure and displays the two corpses in a bathtub while ranting about how Agamemnon sacrificed their daughter Iphigenia to the gods before going to war. "The bastard deserves it five times over, ha ha, take that," etc.

In the second play, Orestes, the only son of Agamemnon and Clytemnestra, comes home and kills Clytemnestra to avenge his father. In the third play, Orestes is punished for this act by being driven mad by vengeance gods called the Furies. At last the goddess Athena gets sick of all the fuss and does the deus ex machina thing. Poof! For no reason, the Furies give up their vengeful ways and change their name to the Kindly Ones. Still, don't try anything funny in Texas.

DEUS EX MACHINA

In Greek drama, a play would often end with a god appearing out of nowhere to influence events and provide a happy ending. The actor playing the god would be lowered to the stage mechanically. Therefore the practice is known as deus ex machina, or "god from the machine." Critics from Aristotle on have been pointing out that this is totally stupid. Writers from Aeschylus on have ignored them, secure in the knowledge that people are suckers for special effects.

OEDIPUS REX / OEDIPUS AT COLONUS / ANTIGONE
Sophocles

When Oedipus is born, his parents, Laius and Jocasta, the king and queen of Thebes, are warned by an oracle that their son will someday murder his father. Sick already of being parents, they give the baby to a servant to be killed.

Who can tell us what their mistake was?

The baby was right there, in their hands! Just kill the baby! It's not rocket science!

But, no, they don't kill the baby. They give him to a servant, who obviously leaves him somewhere and walks off, whistling a tune. Obviously the baby is rescued by a shepherd and passed on to a conveniently childless royal couple, who obviously raise him as their own. Well, some people just bring it on themselves.

When he is full-grown, Oedipus goes to an oracle and learns that he is destined to kill his father and sleep with his mother. Stricken, he leaves home and vows never to return. On the road, he meets you-know-who. Oedipus and Laius argue about the right of way, and in a fit of road rage, Oedipus kills his father. He then goes on to Thebes, where he frees the town from the curse of the Sphinx and is rewarded by being married to the queen, Jocasta. They have four children. Years pass.

Into this happy scene, the gods send down a plague to punish the Thebans for not avenging the murder of Laius. Oedipus calls for a big manhunt to seek out the murderer.

Savor the irony!

To make a long story short, Oedipus eventually finds out that he himself is the murderer, and that the MILF he has been sleeping with is really his M. Jocasta hangs herself and Oedipus gouges out his own eyes. Then he goes into exile, leaving behind his two sons, Polyneices and Eteocles, and his daughters Antigone and Ismene. End of *Oedipus Rex*.

In the second play, *Oedipus at Colonus*, blind beggar Oedipus, led by his now teenaged daughter Antigone, comes to the outskirts of Athens and sits on a rock. For the remainder of the play, various people come and try to get him to leave the rock. They kidnap his children, war breaks out over this, etc. Oedipus will not leave. Finally he dies of old age.

The third play, *Antigone*, opens a few years later. Oedipus's grown-up sons have had a civil war with each other over the kingship of Thebes. It's a waste of time, because they both get killed. Their uncle Creon now rules the city. He decides that Polyneices, who led the rebel forces in the civil war, can't be given a proper burial. He will instead be exposed for the birds to eat, or the dogs, or whoever is hungry.

Polyneices' sister Antigone refuses to accept this. She goes and buries her brother on the sly.

Creon responds in the usual measured Greek fashion by having Antigone walled up alive in a cave. Unluckily for him, his son Haemon, who is also Antigone's fiancé, has himself buried in the cave with his sweetheart. After some time left alone with the chorus, who are extremely critical of this (in song and dance, don't forget), Creon crumbles and admits he overreacted. He goes back to the cave, only to find his son and Antigone dead. Hearing the news, his wife also kills herself. Creon repents as the play ends. Still, don't try anything funny in Texas.

THE OEDIPAL-INDUSTRIAL COMPLEX

Sigmund Freud famously opined that all boys want to sleep with their mothers and kill their fathers. He called this the Oedipus complex, spawning an entire industry in which people lie on couches trying to make their dreams sound interesting. In these heady years, eminent doctors tried to cure schizophrenics by talking to them. The favored way of saving a marriage was to brood about your toilet training.

In later generations, people began to wonder why boys never do sleep with their mothers, never try to sleep with their mothers, and feel sick at the thought of it. This effectively rid us of Freudianism, along with its attendant ills of psychoanalysis, bad Surrealist film, and being reminded Mom has a vagina.

MEDEA
Euripides

The hero Jason has accomplished his heroic feats largely through the help of his wife, Medea. Now that Jason is a big success, the king of Corinth offers Jason the hand of his daughter Glauke in marriage. Jason dumps Medea immediately, although they have two sons, and it is very unfair. He has apparently forgotten that Medea is a powerful witch, the granddaughter of the sun god, and humorless. What ensues is straight out of *I Spit on Your Grave*.

First, Medea sends Glauke a poisoned robe and tiara. Glauke dies horribly. Glauke's father, embracing her as she dies, is also poisoned and killed. That was so much fun that Medea stabs her own sons to death. Then she gets her grandfather the sun to send her a winged chariot as a getaway car. The play concludes with a long scene in which Medea hovers over the stage with the gory corpses of the children draped across the chariot while Jason rages ineffectually below—anticipating the modern custody battle.

Because so much of the play is taken up with repetitive ranting, all this murder is surprisingly dull; it's like watching blood dry.

	Importance	Accessibility	Fun
Prometheus Bound	5	4	4
Oresteia	8	3	7
Oedipus Rex	9	6	7
Oedipus at Colonus	2	2	2
Antigone	6	6	5
Medea	6	6	5

ATHENIAN OLD COMEDY

In the early years of Greek drama, satyr plays, attached to tragedy trilogies, were the only comic relief. But by the time of Euripides, there were also freestanding comedies. These included the smut and slapstick of the satyr plays, but added a framework of blistering political satire.

For our purposes, Old Comedy = Aristophanes, since no other writer's works have been preserved. Aristophanes (446–386 b.c.) is a deadly cocktail of bawdiness, toilet humor, political satire, and men being hit with sticks. In his plays, what all these ingredients have in common is that they're not funny. While Aristophanes can be surprisingly contemporary and clever, it is always in a way that adroitly avoids humor. (Some people claim to find Aristophanes funny. Best to avoid these people. Whatever they may claim, they are probably actors involved in a production of Aristophanes.)

Unlike the tragedies or satyr plays, Old Comedy dealt with current events and mocked the celebrities of the day. Because all upstanding citizens attended theater performances (which were important religious festivals, after all), those satirized were sitting in the audience. A famous instance of this was Aristophanes' *The Clouds*, which viciously ridiculed the teachings of Socrates. Socrates attended the play. At the end, he stood up and bowed, smiling, to the audience. They all laughed and applauded him warmly. These same people later made him drink poison.

The best-known of Aristophanes' plays is *Lysistrata*, written toward the end of the Peloponnesian War. Here, the women of the warring nations all refuse to sleep with their husbands until they make peace. Hijinks ensue. You have probably heard of this one because antiwar theater companies are continually performing updated versions, each of them trying some gimmick, like setting it in thirties Chicago, or using Balinese shadow puppets, or incorporating footage of bonobos, all in the hope that no one will notice it still isn't funny.

	Importance	Accessibility	Fun
Lysistrata	6	5	4
The Clouds	5	5	3
The Frogs	4	5	4

NEW COMEDY

Old Comedy flourished from around 480 to 440 B.C. It was then replaced by Middle Comedy, which finally led to New Comedy, starting after the death of Alexander the Great in 323 B.C. and continuing until the Greeks gave up pretending to laugh at the jokes. No complete plays of Middle Comedy have been discovered, which saves us the trouble of not going to them. Many New Comedy plays, however, have been tragically preserved.

While Old Comedy, with its political satire, often feels like a bad *SNL* skit, New Comedy is more like a bad sitcom. It has no political content, and the jokes revolve around stock characters like the Angry Old Man and the Boastful Soldier. These will typically be involved in a misunderstanding about a Girl. It is every bit as funny as Old Comedy, or wood.

Menander (342–291 B.C.) is the best-known New Comedy playwright. Until recently, we only had long extracts of his work; there were no complete plays. The best preserved works were *The Grouch*, *The Woman from Samos*, and *Who Are We Kidding, You're Never Going to Read These*. Recently a complete play by Menander, *Dyskolos*, has been discovered. It is out there; we have warned you. It's only a matter of time before someone attempts to mount a funny production.

CHAPTER 2

Rome: When the World Was Ruled by Italians

Roman literature has fallen out of fashion. At one time, all educated people sprinkled their conversation with Latin and could describe all Julius Caesar's campaigns without breaking a sweat. In the modern world, this has dwindled to a fuzzy idea that carpe diem is the fish of the day, Opus Dei run the Post Office, and that habeas corpus was good, when we had it, because it meant you couldn't go to prison if you were dead. Now if someone accuses us of making an ad hominem argument, we can deflate them utterly by calling them elitist. In fact, the only thing most people are sure about Rome is that Catholic girls are easy.

It's time to halt this trend. Everybody is saying it: Rome is just like America, and therefore its literature is more relevant than ever. Of course, there are some superficial differences. The Romans wore ghost costumes to work and made decisions of state by looking at cow guts. On the other hand, they, like us, bankrupted their government with foreign wars fought by mercenaries, while the citizens moved heaven and earth to evade the draft, taxes, and telltale signs of aging. Romans shared our basic frivolity: there was no smut too low for them, and no complaint too trivial. They loved sarcasm, gossip, and actors. In fact, by the time of the Silver Age, Romans are not just Americans, but actually New Yorkers.

Many of the writers we will meet later on, from John Milton to James Joyce, quote Latin freely in their works and make offhand references to Roman generals and early Christian fathers. Contemporary readers navigate these passages with a combination of strategies, including footnotes, skipping forward in disgust, Wikipedia, and Pabst Blue Ribbon. A quick fix is to treat all Latin quotes as meaning that Catholic girls are easy. They don't, but it may cheer you through the dryer passages of *Paradise Lost*.

ROME MADE SIMPLE

Rome as a political entity existed for more than a thousand years, going from kingdom to republic to empire to hot mess. The great writing all belongs to the imperial period. In fact, the Golden Age of Roman literature is also known as the Augustan Age, for Caesar Augustus, who was Rome's first emperor. He was followed by a batch of barking mad tyrants who liked to roast people in giant brass bulls, be worshipped as gods, and go to war with Libya. Still somehow, a Silver Age followed, which limped along until it ran into the brick wall of Christianity.

Roman Christianity produced Saint Augustine, then closed its eyes, held its nose, and jumped into the Dark Ages. Soon the empire was in tatters; war and rapine spread through the land. If you look at this series of events with an impartial mind, the conclusion is unavoidable: this is what awaits America if we begin to produce good books. Remember: those who do not understand history are doomed to repeat it. However, they won't know they're repeating it, so at least it won't spoil the surprise.

CATULLUS,
INVENTOR OF THE GIRLFRIEND (84–54 B.C.)

It is generally accepted that the ancient Greeks were better writers than the Romans. They were also better philosophers, better scientists, better historians, and nicer people. But one thing the Greeks could not do was relationships. The Greek idea of a mature relationship involved a thirteen-year-old boy and the exchange of money. The few Greeks who found this troubling (i.e., Plato) suggested that one should give up sex altogether and just hold hands with the thirteen-year-old boy while talking about the Ideal. In general, the Greeks were terrific and all, but just don't marry one.

So it is with great relief that we come to the poetry of Catullus. He is a trailblazer not because his poetry is new in form, but because he has a long-term girlfriend. He wrote hundreds of poems about this girlfriend, to whom he was apparently devoted for his entire short life.

The lady in question—one Clodia Metelli—is called Lesbia in the poems, in honor of Sappho. Don't get the wrong idea: she was not a lesbian. In fact, to Catullus's chagrin, she practiced her heterosexuality with most of the notable men of the time. Her spotty morals were publicly ridiculed in a famous oration of Cicero's, "Pro Caelius." Though the oration is fun to read, Cicero apparently slept with her too.

Catullus's example was followed by various other singers of love with strong-minded, wayward girlfriends—notably Propertius (girlfriend Cynthia) and Tibullus (girlfriend Delia).

Keep in mind: these are girlfriends, never wives. It takes another fifteen hundred years before the poets marry the girlfriend. This is still roughly the amount of time you will wait for a poet to marry you.

	Importance	Accessibility	Fun
Catullus (poems in various editions)	7	7	6
Propertius	5	7	6
Tibullus	3	7	5

VIRGIL (70–19 B.C.)

There is not much to say about Virgil's life. This is partly because we don't know much about it, and partly because nothing happened to him. Apparently, he spent his life writing books in a room by himself. Biographical tradition depicts him as shy, sickly, and gay. However, these biographers may simply have been speculating based on the fact that he wrote poetry.

In the Middle Ages, people thought Virgil had the gift of prophecy. This was based on the belief that his Fourth Eclogue predicted the nativity of Christ, which was based on make-believe. Virgil's poetry itself was therefore used to predict the future. People would ask a question and then select a line of Virgil at random. This helped keep Virgil in print until the late medieval invention of the Magic 8 Ball.

Virgil had a second run at fame when he became one of the main characters in Dante's *Divine Comedy*. So we say good-bye to Virgil now with a light heart, knowing we will see him in hell.

POETRY AS PR

Virgil's big break came when he was picked up by Maecenas, a cultural minister who served Caesar Augustus by sponsoring poets to glorify his reign. Since Augustus was a dictator who crushed Roman democracy with pitiless violence, this was questionable ethically. Except, nobody cares anymore. Scholars are much more focused on the fact that Maecenas gave the poet Horace a whole farm.

Until recently, a rich patron of the arts was sometimes called a Maecenas. This was meant as flattery, though it is really the same as calling someone a Goebbels. Luckily, 99.99 percent of patrons of the arts didn't know what the allusion meant, and the other .01 percent was Goebbels.

Virgil's Eclogues (aka Bucolics)

(The title of this collection of pastoral poems is variously translated. Feel free to make up your own title that sounds even more like a gastric condition.)

Pastoral poetry, as exemplified by Virgil's *Eclogues*, takes place in a world in which shepherds sing songs about their loves, the gods of the wood sometimes come out and sing along, and no one ever has to herd sheep. The tradition began with the Greek poet called Theocritus, whom we failed to mention in the ancient Greek section because we have read him.

For centuries, the field of pastoral poetry was rich, beloved, and respected. In the pages of this book, you will meet with many more examples of this genre. Today, it's impossible to understand why people were so fascinated by descriptions of the sun-blessed goats in the fields, or the wooing of Nivea by Kleenex, or the whistling competition between the god Pan and a thicket. Possibly natural selection has weeded out humans who connect sheep with romance.

Apart from the (not really) prediction of Christ's birth in Eclogue #4, the *Eclogues* are mainly notable for popularizing Arcadia as the place where all things pastoral happened. Theocritus initiated Arcadia as a setting, but his Arcadia was the real, unremarkable, Greek province. Virgil's *Eclogues* invented a fantasy version, which impressed people so deeply that there are now twenty-one Arcadias in the U.S., two in Australia, and one each in the Ukraine, Canada, South Africa, and Mars.

The Georgics

This is a book of farming advice, written in gorgeous verse. If you have any feeling at all for nature or for poetry, you will be moved by the *Georgics'* descriptions of the Italian countryside, and of stars, cows, and gods. If you are, on the other hand, deaf to the glories of verse, the *Georgics* is still the go-to guide for how to run a farm into the ground.

Virgil's advice varies from the obvious—"Plant in spring!"—to the asinine. Charmingly, he is under the impression that bees are ruled by a king, and that they gather their young in their mouths from leaves. If you want new bees, you should make a hut and put the rotting carcass of a calf inside. In no time, bees will gather. We assume that Virgil was only citing then-current beliefs about the natural world, as Ovid does when he casually mentions that weasels give birth from their mouths. (Well, have you ever seen a weasel giving birth? Let's give Ovid the benefit of the doubt.)

The Aeneid

This is not only Virgil's masterpiece, it was long considered the greatest master-piece ever, ever. Virgil modeled it on Homer's epics, and the medievals basically considered it a New, Improved Homer. The most famous section of the *Aeneid* concerns the romance of Dido and Aeneas, which later became a common topic of Renaissance painting.

When the story begins, Dido, the queen of Carthage, has sworn eternal fi-delity to her dead husband. Even when Aeneas appears on her shores, asking for help, and is smokin' hot, she is determined to remain chaste. She is too busy founding Carthage, anyway. She is a career girl now, blah blah.

Tough luck, Dido. Aeneas's mother is actually Venus, the goddess of love. Venus sends her other little boy, Cupid, down to put the old love hex on Dido. Next thing you know, Queen Dido is in a cave with Aeneas, "sheltering from a storm." When Aeneas leaves her cave, Dido is in love.

Unfortunately, Aeneas has to go found Rome, which he is not considerate enough to found next door to Carthage. Even more inconsiderately, instead of discussing these plans with Dido, Aeneas slips out to his ship when she isn't looking. When she spots his sails heading out to sea, the heartbroken Dido tricks her sister into building a big pyre, saying she wants to burn everything that re-minds her of Aeneas. Then she goes to the top of the pyre and kills herself with a sword. There is no need to move the corpse or anything; all they need is a match. At least somebody is considerate around here.

In the next book, Aeneas descends into the underworld, where he sees Dido, but she isn't talking to him. She turns her face away and goes off with her dead husband. So poignant! Then Aeneas goes off to conquer Italy and never thinks about her again. Cue six books of tearing out people's eyeballs and boasting in a rain of spears.

The *Aeneid* ends smack in the middle of a scene, with the death of arch-enemy Turnus. The scholarly consensus is that Virgil intended to add a neat ending, but sadly dropped dead himself. As it stands, the non-ending carries an existential pang; we are cheated of closure, left in the middle of a battlefield without any sense of what all this carnage means. It also gives the reader a mental image of Virgil face-down on the last stanza of the *Aeneid* with a pen in his hand.

	Importance	Accessibility	Fun
The *Eclogues*	5	2	0
The *Georgics*	5	4	6
The *Aeneid*	10	5	8

OVID (43 B.C.–A.D.17)

Ovid is that rarest of gems: an ancient author whose jokes are funny. While Virgil is the severe, imposing Great Poet, Ovid is the frivolous aesthete, a man who spent his life drinking, writing smut, and making fun of Virgil.

His funniest book was *The Art of Love*, history's most popular collection of sex tips. A great success in Rome, it later became the great one-handed read of the Middle Ages. A copy was confiscated by U.S. Customs as porn as late as 1930.

The book approves any underhanded trickery, if it gets you laid. Ovid advises that you never see your mistress on her birthday, because it will be expensive. If you are broke, put up with insults, or else you won't get sex. If you are rich, throw away this book, because you will always get sex. A fair-minded debaucher, he also gives women advice in how to deceive their lovers, and advocates that they try a range of both older and younger men, for piquancy. Ovid really throws caution to the wind, however, when he tells men that no always means yes. (Of course, since we don't speak Latin, we cannot swear that this is wrong. It would also explain some puzzling things about the Catholic Church.)

Much of Ovid's advice is devastatingly practical. Some sections specify conversational gambits and choreograph the seducer's flirting. The book even gives beauty tips. Blondes should wear gray; long-faced girls should part their hair in the middle. Men should get rid of nostril hairs, but shaving the legs is going too far—all as true today as it was in the time of Jesus.

GOD'S GIFTS

The Art of Love was actually written on and around Jesus's birthday—between 1 B.C. and A.D. 1. Even as the Magi were wending their way to Bethlehem, Ovid was advising dudes to screw their girlfriend's maid.

The Metamorphoses

Fun fun fun though *The Art of Love* is, Ovid's acknowledged masterpiece is his *Metamorphoses*. This epic-length poem is really a collection of linked short stories, in all of which someone turns into something else. In fact, after a hundred pages of the *Metamorphoses*, one begins to feel that the only reaction to any event is to turn into a plant or animal. Running away from a rapist? Turn into a laurel tree. Had sex with Daddy and now feel dirty? Make that a myrrh tree. Whenever things look grim, the hero turns into a weasel. (Hint: don't try this at home. Nothing will happen.) Since the average Greco-Roman myth starts with Jupiter turning into a swan/bull/shower of gold, goes through a patch where his latest flame is a heifer, and ends with her becoming a constellation, Ovid was spoiled for choice. Just a few short centuries later, he would have been stuck with one short story about a box of wafers and a bottle of red turning into Jesus Christ.

Ovid was a great storyteller, and the stories are brilliantly entertaining. The book is also a fun way to brush up on your Greek/Roman myths. In fact, broad reading of Western literature shows that most writers learned their myths from the *Metamorphoses*, just as they learned about fidelity from *The Art of Love*.

The final transformation in the book is that of Augustus Caesar into a god—a repellent piece of flattery that really makes you think twice about this Ovid. There is a good chance, though, that the whole thing was a sarcastic joke. Almost immediately afterward, Ovid was exiled to Tomis, better known today as Fucking Romania. The more commonly cited reason for this exile was the immorality of *The Art of Love*—Augustus was on an ill-fated crusade to clean up public morals (especially his sister Julia's, which were getting embarrassingly public; there is also speculation that Ovid was part of Julia's public.) Ovid spent his ten years of exile desperately flattering Caesar, whining and begging to be allowed to leave Romania. Despite this, the thick-skinned Romanians have adopted Ovid as "The First Romanian Poet." Ovidiu is a common first name for Romanian boys. This seems more reasonable when you consider that, while Ovid hated Romanians, he probably also fathered a slew of them.

	Importance	Accessibility	Fun
The *Metamorphoses*	10	8	8
The *Art of Love*	8	9	9

HORACE (65–8 B.C.)

Yes, the man who got the farm from Maecenas. Keeping in mind that the farm came with slaves to do the work, this was really the ancient Roman equivalent of university tenure.

The son of a freed slave, Horace is the most down-to-earth of Roman authors. He chased slave girls and boys instead of having a newfangled "girlfriend." A true heartland conservative, he revered Maecenas, Augustus Caesar, and his father, and extolled country ways in his works.

The early poems, his *Epodes* and *Satires*, are caustic, nasty send-ups of Roman society. They depict Rome in all its glory and misbehavior—it's sort of like watching *The Tudors*, if the makers of *The Tudors* were Tudors. The post-farm *Odes* are much lovelier, if less fun. For their exquisite artistry, they have served as models for countless poets, who have therefore produced millions of poems startlingly like Horace's. These were imitated in their turn, and similar poems continue to appear in new books published by university presses. Horace's *Odes* are so much like contemporary poetry, in fact, that most people will find them boring.

A NOTE ON NAMING

In Roman literature, something called a satire isn't always meant to be funny. For instance, Horace wrote both serious and comic "satires." Horace himself called these pieces *sermones*, which confusingly means "conversations," not sermons.

To simplify matters: in classical literature, we find satires, odes, elegies, carmina, etc. All these words mean "poem." Any serious attempt to differentiate between them will begin in pedantry and end with people forgetting to tell you that everybody's going out for drinks later.

Horace quotes:

(Just in case you were wondering where these common phrases come from.)

Dulce et decorum est pro patria mori. "It is sweet and proper to die for your country." Nowadays, please note, it's fine to just send a check.

Carpe diem. "Fish of the day."

Aurea mediocritas. "The golden mean." Also acceptable when used by psychics to say someone's aura is only so-so.

	Importance	Accessibility	Fun
Epodes and *Satires*	4	8	6
Odes	6	7	4

POETRY AFTER CHRIST BUT BEFORE CHRISTIANITY: THE SILVER AGE

In these years, Romans became more dissolute. Emperors were often sadistic whack jobs. Democracy faded from memory. Nero fiddled, Rome burned. Literary responses varied in tone, but all shared the quality of being Not Golden. Some Silver Agers:

Martial (A.D. 42–102): a poet famous for his scathing epigrams—the short comic poems that were also a popular form of Roman graffiti. A sample of his concise cattiness:

> You're beautiful, oh yes, and young, and rich
> But since you tell us so, you're just a bitch.

Juvenal (A.D. 60–140): wrote satires composed of vitriol leavened with bile. Boiled down: Everything was better in our fathers' days. Today's Roman men are debauched girlie-men who make noise when I'm trying to sleep. If there's anything worse than a Roman man, it's a Roman woman. Worst of all, a dirty foreigner.

Lucan (A.D. 39–65): wrote the *Pharsalia*, about the Civil War between Julius Caesar and the defenders of the Republic. Lucan was a friend of Nero's and, like most friends of Nero's, was eventually asked to kill himself, the privileged method of execution at the time.

Seneca (A.D. 4–65): was Nero's tutor. Wrote hopelessly turgid plays and sanctimonious essays, then was asked to kill himself. Anyone who has read one of Seneca's essays will allow that this Nero might not be all bad. Anyone stuck watching one of his plays will consider suicide without Nero's help.

Lucian (A.D. 125–180): wrote satires that were massively influential. He is now completely, totally, forgotten. Notable for writing the first science fiction, *A True Story*, which was a very untrue story about trips to the moon and Venus, wars between planets, etc. Also wrote the first send-up of Christianity, *The Passing of Peregrinus*. You can still get Lucian's works, only nobody does.

When the Novel Was Novel

Many writers say that the novel originated in the medieval romance, gradually evolving into its current form over centuries, flourishing for a time, then petering out with Jonathan Franzen.

Unfortunately for this theory, there were novels in ancient Rome. These continued to be read in the Middle Ages—when the novel was supposedly originating and evolving. Well, so much for that theory! Better luck next time, other writers!

We can divide the Greco-Roman novel into two broad categories. There are trashy romances about lovers who are separated and then reunited—like Longus's *Daphnis and Chloe* or Heliodorus's *Aethiopica*. And then there are filthy, scurrilous satires, of which the two most important are the *Satyricon* of Petronius and *The Golden Ass* of Apuleius.

No one is certain who the author of the *Satyricon* was. Apparently, in Rome, every Tom, Dick, and Harry was named Petronius. However, most scholars believe it was Gaius Petronius Arbiter, a courtier of Nero and renowned voluptuary. He was, in fact, the master of orgies for Nero, consulted in all matters of taste.

All good things come to an end, and all friends of Nero came to the same end: having fallen out of favor, Petronius was asked to kill himself. The story goes, Petronius took days to commit suicide. He opened his veins, then bound them up again, then opened them again, all the while eating lavish meals and chatting wittily to his friends. He also took the time to write to Nero—not a plea for mercy, but a compendium of all the Emperor's vices, naming the names of all the people, male and female, Nero had debauched.

The *Satyricon* is a suitable monument to this man's life. Very few scenes of the book survive in their entirety; the remaining scraps are garbled, goofy, and tirelessly X-rated. There is a long scene, for instance, where the hero and his boytoy

Giton are sexually abused for hours by female devotees of Priapus. Since it has many missing sections, the effect is like having passed out drunk at an orgy, and waking every couple of hours to find that the debauchery shows no sign of abating.

Apuleius's *Golden Ass* (aka *Metamorphoses*) has come down to us whole. Its hero is fascinated by magic; with his dabbling, he turns himself into a donkey. In this guise, he goes through various owners, ranging from thieves to runaway slaves to a woman enamored with his donkey self. Every ten pages of this book contain four stories, a sexual encounter, and a scene of gratuitous violence. Meanwhile, we get a tour of the generally miserable lives and morals of the Roman Empire's lower classes. Apuleius, incidentally, had the job of arranging gladiatorial competitions for the city of Carthage and was once prosecuted for practicing black magic. Really, you can't buy that kind of publicity.

THE CONFESSIONS OF ST. AUGUSTINE

Augustine of Hippo (354–430) was one of the first great African writers. Born on the border of modern-day Algeria, he was probably an ethnic Berber. (Hippo, by the way, was the place in Northern Africa where he had his bishopric; disappointingly, he was not the forerunner of Tarzan of Ape.)

His *Confessions* are a deadly cocktail of Christian theology and the misery memoir. Here he goes through his life and methodically wallows in guilt for every single thing he has ever done. Page after page, Augustine flagellates himself for sins such as stealing pears from a neighbor's tree, not listening to his mother, or watching a spider weave a web when he should have been contemplating God.

The thing he feels most guilty for is having been slow to embrace Catholicism: as a youth, he was a Manichaean. Manichaeans were cultish, off-brand Christians who believed, for instance, that people did not sin. An evil spirit sinned through them. Therefore they did not need to wallow in guilt for finding spiders interesting. Instead, they could go out and have a good time.

Augustine's most concrete sin was that he had a girlfriend. (To make this sound more sinful, she is usually called a "concubine.") It was a relationship modern people would find unexceptionable. He remained with her for more than a decade and had a son with her, whom he deeply loved and raised with care. On the other hand, when he decided to marry, he dumped her for a more respectable girl with money.

Today, a person might feel bad about dumping the girlfriend, or about the fact that the new fiancée was eight. This never crossed Augustine's mind. He felt bad about wanting sex with girls at all. The only right answer, to a fourth-century Christian, was down-the-line celibacy. But poor Augustine! Sex was his absolute favorite thing! Hence his much-cited cri de coeur: "Lord, give me chastity and continence, but not yet!"

At last, in one of his nightly long nights of the soul, Augustine heard a voice saying, "Take up and read." Although this voice might have meant any book, the luckless Augustine grabbed the New Testament. "Blah blah blah, put on the Lord Jesus Christ," he read. All doubt vanished, and he was converted.

At one time, people all over Europe responded to all this with: "You took the words right out of my mouth!" Augustine's *Confessions*, in fact, are like a time capsule packed with the inner life of the Dark Ages. Today, many readers still identify with Augustine's loves, sorrows, and ethical dilemmas. It is a very rare bird, however, who still identifies with his joyless Christianity. In fact, it is a pterodactyl. If you have no interest in theology, go ahead and skip the most godly bits. Wherever God is addressed as "you," this is a red flag. We propose that these "you" parts were actually meant to be read only by God.

SAINT, SCHMAINT

Not wishing to second-guess some infallible pope, but Augustine of Hippo was no saint. No visions, no miracles, no moral perfection: no saint. Clearly he got the halo purely for being famous. This is taking canonization down to the level of the naming of airports. Of course, no idea could be more appealing to the contemporary mind. One hopes future popes will extend this treatment to luminaries like Saint Snooki of Jersey, Saint A-Rod of the Yankees, and Saint Lady of Gaga.

	Importance	Accessibility	Fun
Confessions	9	5	5

CHAPTER 3

The Middle Ages and Points Between

Europe breathed a collective sigh of relief with the coming of the medieval period. Many had worried that with the end of antiquity they would be plunged directly into the Renaissance, forced to rediscover the Greeks before they had managed to forget them. Others had taken the predictions of the Bible to heart and believed that the End Times were due any minute. So you can just imagine everybody's relief when they realized it was the Middle Ages.

The Medieval period lasted approximately one thousand years, during which many things happened. The Catholic Church spread Christianity throughout Europe. Islam tried to spread Islam throughout Europe but was unsuccessful, until now. Vikings raided and pillaged the coasts, while feudal fiefdoms gradually joined into nations. Millions leapt to join the latest fad, bubonic plague.

After centuries of Rome's thriving literary culture, Europe was taken over by Germanic tribes like the Ostrogoths, the Visigoths, and, of course, the Original Recipe Goths, none of whom wrote things down. These were oral cultures, and occasionally downright anal cultures. Everyone forgot how to read and write, except for a handful of monks. These monks wrote and copied manuscripts, mainly about God and damnation, creating a further disincentive for anyone else to learn to read.

Here are some of the greatest hits of a thousand years of middleness.

BEOWULF

(FIRST WRITTEN DOWN SOMETIME BETWEEN 700 AND 900)

Beowulf is the first great work of English literature. Nonetheless, it begins with a people called Spear-Danes (what we would nowadays call "Danes with spears"). It goes on to introduce more Danes, as well as Swedes, Frisians, and Geats, along with a number of monsters. It does not contain a single Englishman, nor does it take place in England. It is really expatriate Viking lit, and it is only a matter of time before the Danes come to claim it, like the Greeks with the Elgin marbles.

It's written in Old English, the language of the Anglo-Saxons. The Anglo-Saxon style of poetry is alliterative verse: The first two beats of the line usually shared a consonant sound with either one or two of the beats in the second half of the line. Confused? That's what examples are for.

Here are the first two lines:

Old English

Hwæt! We Gardena   *in geardagum,*
theodcyninga,   *thrym gefrunon,*
hu tha æthelingas   *ellen fremedon.*

New Improved English

Listen! We have heard *of the glorious Spear-Danes*
in the old days   *the king of tribes*
how noble princes   *had great courage.*

Notice how manly it is. Anglo-Saxon poetry was usually about warriors, and sometimes even written by warriors. At the time, composing poetry was considered a manly skill. In fact, in the Norse pantheon common to the Germanic people, Odin was in charge of both battle and poetry (the gods back then were often shorthanded and had to double up).

After the first of many historical digressions, the story begins with Hrothgar building his great hall, Heorot. Between the noise of construction and all the drunken gathering and singing that follows, crabby neighbor Grendel is irked. Before you think of your own noisy neighbors and sympathize: Grendel is a horrible misshapen giant, descended from Cain, and very poorly socialized. Rather than simply complain, Grendel attacks and eats Hrothgar's followers. Nobody can stop him, although the noise complaints do cease.

Now Beowulf—the strongest man alive, the greatest warrior, the cat's pajamas, the bee's knees—hears of Hrothgar's troubles and travels to Denmark with his men. That night, Grendel arrives, and after a mighty hand-to-hand battle, Beowulf rips Grendel's arm from his shoulder. Grendel scuttles away to his swampy lake to die.

Unfortunately, the following night, Grendel's mother, whom nobody had thought to mention before, comes to exact revenge, and also to retrieve Grendel's arm. She kills Hrothgar's best friend and advisor, and then storms off, arm in arm.

In the morning, they all troop off to the magic hellish lake where Grendel lived with his mother (ha, what a loser). Beowulf dives in and swims most of the day to reach the bottom. He grapples with sea monsters, then follows the mother into her underwater cavern and slays her with a giant sword she keeps lying around. The lesson this teaches is often overlooked: monsters who keep a loaded sword in the lair for self-defense are much more likely to be killed by intruders.

There are other Old English poems from the period, likewise anonymous, but they are not the first great work of English literature, so they are read almost entirely by people who read obscure things for a living. The best known—like *The Wanderer*, the story of a thane who mourns his dead king and so drifts leaderless through the world—reflect both the fatalistic worldview found in *Beowulf* and a growing mystical Christian perspective.

The Dream of the Rood actually includes the story of the crucifixion from the point of view of the cross. Although anonymous, *The Dream of the Rood* has sometimes been attributed to Caedmon, the first English poet whose name we know. An unlettered shepherd, Caedmon got his songwriting skills when God came to him in a dream, presumably a weird dream featuring a talking cross.

	Importance	*Accessibility*	*Fun*
Beowulf	9	5	8
Other Anglo-Saxon poetry	2	4	3

THE SONG OF ROLAND

(EARLIEST WRITTEN VERSION, MID-12TH CENTURY)

Chansons de geste are a genre of narrative poem written in Old French, beginning in the eleventh century. They celebrate the heroic adventures of Charlemagne and the knights of his court, fighting nobly in the name of Christ. Some draw on historic events but many become very fanciful, involving all manner of magical creatures. As time goes on, these beasts proliferate while reality vanishes, a process familiar to people who watch Fox News.

The oldest and best known of the *chansons de geste* is *The Song of Roland*, the founding work of French literature. Roland is based on an actual battle of the late eighth century in which the rearguard of Charlemagne's army was attacked by locals in the Pyrenees.

Through the magic of storytelling, Charlemagne's unsuccessful campaign is turned into a string of glorious victories and his attackers become infidel Muslims. Today we call this propaganda, and as propaganda, *Roland* exhibits a breathtaking shamelessness. "Christians are right and pagans are wrong," Roland announces. Try that these days.

In the key battle scene, our hero Roland, along with twenty thousand knights, is swamped by four hundred thousand Muslims. Oh, no! There's still hope, though: Roland has only to blow his olifant, a horn made of an elephant's tusk, and Charlemagne will come to him with the main army.

So does Roland blow the olifant? He does not. It would be a dishonor to his name and his family. Roland and his buddies kill thousands. Despite the mightiness of their blows—they do not just cleave an enemy in two, they cleave the enemy and the horse he sits on in two—they are soon facing defeat. Finally, Roland blows the olifant, so loud and hard that blood comes out of his ears. It is a fatal blow! Roland crawls away to die from tooting his own horn.

When Charlemagne arrives, the pusillanimous Muslims flee, but the emperor will have his revenge. God stops the sun in the sky to give Charlemagne enough daylight to pursue and kill all the scummy pagans. In defeat, the Muslims turn on their own gods. Yes, gods plural: *Roland*'s Muslims don't worship Allah, but Mahomet, Apollo, and somebody named Tergament. So they curse the statue of Apollo, pull the jewels from the statue of Tergament, and throw Mahomet to the pigs and the dogs, to do whatever it is pigs and dogs do to idols.

Roland is a glimpse into the Western mind at a time when new ideals of chivalry were spreading throughout Europe. They taught the highborn and wealthy a new gentility that would become the mark of their class—and also that everyone different from them was a scheming, lying pagan, and God wanted them dead.

	Importance	Accessibility	Fun
The Song of Roland	7	6	4

THE MATTER OF BRITAIN

Collectively, the medieval tales of Charlemagne and his court are known as the Matter of France. Stories about King Arthur and his knights are called the Matter of Britain. Unlike Charlemagne, Arthur is almost certainly a fictional character. If there is a historical figure vaguely lurking behind the stories, he was a Celtic warrior who fought the invading Anglo-Saxons—which would mean that the national hero of the English made his reputation killing their ancestors.

The Arthurian boom began when Geoffrey of Monmouth wrote *Historia Regum Brittanniae*, the History of the Kings of Britain, in the early twelfth century. The book set off a vogue for Arthur stories all across Europe. At tournaments, knights would sometimes dress as their favorite Arthurian figures and joust in character. That's right: mind-bogglingly, Ren Fairs actually predate the Renaissance.

Among the most important Arthur writers was the French courtier Chrétien de Troyes. He wrote five influential Arthurian romances in the late twelfth century, among them *Perceval, le conte du grail*, which introduced Camelot and the Holy Grail. De Troyes's most influential work, though, was *Lancelot, le chevalier de la Charrette*, the Knight of the Cart, about the love of Lancelot and queen Guinevere. This relationship was an example of "courtly love" or, as we would call it today, cheating.

In *The Knight of the Cart*, Guinevere has been kidnapped by Maleagent (which, just saying, is the French equivalent of naming your bad guy Badguy). Lancelot faces many dangers in his quest to rescue Guinevere, while walking around in a daze because he can't stop thinking about her. And—although he defeats his opponents and crosses the perilous Sword Bridge for her, and apostrophizes his love to a single hair of Guinevere's found in a comb—when he reaches her, she gives him the cold shoulder. Apparently, his love wasn't perfect enough.

See, on the way to find her, a dwarf in a cart offered to show Lancelot the way, but only if Lancelot would get in the cart. At the time, de Troyes explains, there was no greater dishonor for a knight than to ride in a cart, because criminals were transported in carts. This might seem stupid to us, because it is. Still, *autres temps, autres bone-headed moeurs*. Lancelot makes up his mind to get in the cart—after two steps of hesitation. Guinevere holds those two steps against him. She eventually gets over it, though, and they get down to some courtly love.

For English speakers, the Arthur stories are known primarily through Sir

Thomas Mallory's mammoth epic *Le Morte d'Arthur*. This starts slow by modern standards, but really picks up after the first eight hundred pages.

	Importance	Accessibility	Fun
Le Morte d'Arthur	6	4	5
The Knight of the Cart	4	6	4

PETER ABÈLARD (1079–1142) AND HÉLOÏSE D'ARGENTEUIL (1101–1164)

Peter Abèlard was a star among scholars, who excelled at the public lectures and debates that were the heart of medieval intellectual life. Flocks of students came to his lectures, idolized him, and even got into street fights defending his theses.

His downfall came in the form of his private student Héloïse. As well as being a gifted scholar, she was a pretty nineteen-year-old. Soon Abèlard was schooling her with an undefended thesis, and Héloïse duly gave birth to a son. Abèlard named the boy Astrolabe, and the two were secretly married.

Happy ending? No. When Héloïse's uncle Fulbert found out, he hired men to capture Abèlard and castrate him, preventing him from having any more children and giving them names like Astrolabe. Many have heard of this episode, and remember it with a shudder. Fewer people, however, remember that our friend Abèlard then had two of the hired thugs castrated and blinded.

This story of love gone wrong takes up roughly the first third of Abèlard's autobiography, *The History of My Misfortunes*. As the book continues, the disfigured and embittered Abèlard travels through Europe, making enemies wherever he goes. He attributes his unpopularity either to envy or to the fact that his sanctity makes other people feel inferior. Meanwhile, he writes at length about how brilliant he is, until the reader is thinking, "Uncle Fulbert should have finished the job."

Meanwhile, Héloïse had become a nun and then a prioress. When she read Abèlard's autobiography, she couldn't resist and wrote to him; he wrote back. Their letters chart the strange afterlife of this relationship. Abèlard confesses that he pressed Héloïse to become a nun out of jealousy, thinking that "after the revenge taken on me, you would only be safe [from other men] in a convent." He had even bribed the other nuns to tell Héloïse how much they liked being nuns. Still, he exhorts her to turn to God and forget about love.

Of course, he is a forty-something castrato, while she is a twenty-something girl with all her working parts. Although she really tries the "turning to God" thing, Héloïse's letters are essentially passionate love letters. "Even . . . at the altar, I carry the memory of our love, and far from lamenting having been seduced by pleasures, I sigh for having lost them." This falls on deaf ears and empty trousers.

	Importance	Accessibility	Fun
The History of My Misfortunes	3	6	5
Letters	6	6	5

ROMAN DE LA ROSE / ROMANCE OF THE ROSE
(BEGUN IN 1225, COMPLETED 1278)

The *Romance of the Rose* was a huge bestseller in its day and massively, stunningly, brain-damagingly, influential. It was the iconic work of medieval allegory and the primer for courtly love.

The story: A young man falls asleep and dreams that he finds the Garden of Pleasure. A lady called Idleness lets him in. Once he is there, the God of Love shoots him with five arrows, all of which enter his eye and wound him in the heart. As a result, he falls in love with a rose. (Yes, the flower. Not a woman named Rose, or a rosy-cheeked girl. A plant.) He then has to deal with a series of allegorical people—Fair Welcome, False Seeming, Constrained Abstinence, etc.—before he can have the shrub of his dreams.

The glory of this book is its prolific weirdness. The God of Love is dressed entirely in flowers and birds. When Nature explains the weather, it involves satyrs, nymphs, and the clouds putting on different outfits. In the Garden of Pleasure, one of the attractions is rabbits "engaged in more than forty different games."

When the young man finally takes possession of the rose, the following allegorical passage wraps up the book: "I was forced to break the bark a little, for I knew no other way to obtain the thing I so desired. I can tell you that when I had shaken the bud, I scattered a little seed there. This was when I had touched the inside of the rose-bud and explored all its little leaves, for I longed, and it seemed good to me, to probe its very depths. . . . The rose-bud swelled and expanded."

Then the young man wakes up. THE END.

Books written entirely about long, involved dreams were common in the Middle Ages. No one objected to this; it was then believed that most dreams were meaningful. Now science has taught us that this isn't even true of things that happen when you're awake.

	Importance	Accessibility	Fun
Romance of the Rose	8	3	3

OLD AGE, TRUTHFULNESS, AND HUSBAND WALK INTO A BAR

For those to whom this is new, an allegory is a story in which each character represents an idea. The character usually has the name of that idea—say, Slander. Then Slander goes around behaving as slander would if it had a body, talking as slander would if it talked, wearing the clothes it would if it wore clothes, ordering the burrito slander would order if they'd had Mexican restaurants in medieval France.

Allegory can sometimes be confusing because abstractions are personified with no rhyme or reason—Slander, Venus, and Friend are all acceptable allegorical characters. But it is mainly confusing because critics aren't willing to come out and say that this has no system and it makes no sense.

Allegorical characters typically love to make long speeches explaining who they are. They also like to face off against each other—say, Despair is pitted against Christian, or Chastity against Fair Countenance. For a medieval person, this was just as much fun as watching Superman fight Batman, or Godzilla fight Mothra. For us, it is as much fun as sleet.

GEOFFREY CHAUCER (1343–1400)

Despite solidly middle-class origins, Chaucer became a cosmopolitan and a courtier. He traveled to France and Italy as a diplomat, served in Parliament, and fought in various campaigns, presumably (given the period) in shining armor. But the biographical detail that sticks with most readers is that, in reward for his service, Edward III granted him a gallon of wine every day for life.

Chaucer is best known for his game-changing masterpiece *The Canterbury Tales*. Some scholars have even claimed that Chaucer actually invented the English language in order to write this book. This is not the case, but it is still considered acceptable to teach it to schoolchildren. (We like this kind of thing in the Western Lit business; it gives university professors something to debunk later on.)

The Canterbury Tales was always Chaucer's most popular book, but in the Middle Ages, Troilus and Criseyde was the most admired. It's a courtly love story set in Troy and has some charming moments, but these are almost lost in a trackless waste of courtly love clichés. These well-turned clichés were the thing that made a book high literature to the medievals. Happily, there is now no reason to read Troilus and Criseyde, unless you have an itch to read it that cannot be scratched. But, really, if the itch can be scratched by scratching, scratch.

Chaucer was the first poet buried in Poets' Corner at Westminster Abbey. Of course, it wasn't known as Poets' Corner then; it was known as "that corner where we put Chaucer." A popular legend says that if you go to Westminster Abbey and put your ear to the ground over Chaucer's grave, you will be crouching in Westminster Abbey with your butt in the air. Then you will look like an idiot.

The Canterbury Tales

Here, a group of pilgrims travel together to Canterbury, telling stories to pass the time. It is Boccaccio's Decameron without the plague (see page 48).

When he planned the tales, Chaucer intended to write four stories for every pilgrim. He never completed even the first round. This was not because he died too young, but because he found it tough to finish things. Even individual stories are often dropped in the middle. This may reflect the moment Chaucer finished his day's gallon of wine and passed out.

Schoolchildren are sometimes told that The Canterbury Tales was the first novel, right after being taught that Chaucer invented the English language. This first-novel theory has two flaws. First, the novel had already existed for more than a thousand years. Second, it isn't a novel. A stick is more like a novel, because a stick is not written in verse. But if you don't mind that it wasn't the first, or a novel, there is nothing to stop you telling schoolchildren that The Canterbury Tales was the first novel. Also remember to tell them that if they sit too close to the television, they will become radioactive.

While devout literati may trudge through every tale, first-time readers should pick and choose. You can start by trying these:

The general prologue is terrific if you have any interest in the Middle Ages. If you don't, you may get it here, so it's still worth reading the general prologue. Also, those who like cheese and those who don't like cheese should read the general prologue. If there's anyone left over, they should read the general prologue. It's a short, digestible version of a genre called estates satire, which involves ridiculing every profession in turn, and includes some of Chaucer's best writing.

"The Miller's Tale" is about a carpenter's wife with a body "as graceful and slender as a weasel's." When an amorous lodger grabs her by the "queynte," she falls instantly in love. Featuring an obscene prank by the lady which remains disgusting to this day.

The prologue to "The Wife of Bath" is famous for its account of medieval marriage. The wife tells how she married five times, for money and lust, and got each husband to obey her without question. "The Wife of Bath's Tale" begins with a knight's unceremonious rape of a chance-met maiden. To escape being punished with death, he has to answer the question "What does a woman want most?" He goes through some changes before he gets the answer right: women want to be obeyed without question.

"The Summoner's Tale" is a scurrilous tale about friars. Its prologue explains where friars are kept in hell (a clue: Satan lifts his tail to let them fly out). The main tale is even more juvenile. Tip: don't read while eating.

In "The Pardoner's Tale," three drunks set out to murder Death, furious at him for killing their friend. Directed by an old man to the place of Death, they discover a heap of gold. They forget about Death immediately, little guessing that they have found him. This is often cited as the source for *The Treasure of the Sierra Madre*, only not by the author of *The Treasure of the Sierra Madre*.

	Importance	Accessibility	Fun
Troilus and Criseyde	4	3	4
The Canterbury Tales	10	6	9

MIDDLE ENGLISH

You could be forgiven for supposing that Middle English is what they speak in Middle Earth. It has a rumpy-tumpy-tiddley-tom quality that makes you imagine a race of hobbits succumbing to the Black Death, fighting the Battle of Agincourt, and telling *The Canterbury Tales*. Despite this, it is worthwhile trying to read the *Tales* in Middle English, in an annotated version. Much of the language is immediately recognizable, and it becomes more so as you get used to it. There's no shame in failing, but if you succeed, it's an immersive medieval experience, a unique form of escapism, and a mother lode of bragging points.

SIR GAWAIN AND THE GREEN KNIGHT
(LATE 14TH CENTURY)

Sir Gawain and the Green Knight begins with King Arthur's best and brightest gathered for a holiday feast. They are interrupted by a giant green knight who questions their manliness and offers a challenge: the beheading game. Try to chop off my head, he says. If I live, in a year I will chop off yours. Gawain rises, the giant kneels, Gawain swings an axe. Boom, the giant's head rolls under the table. Collective sigh of relief. Then the giant stands and retrieves his head. Wouldn't you know it!

A year later, Gawain's honor requires that he seek out the Green Knight and submit to the axe. After much wandering, he comes upon a castle whose master, Lord Bertilak, can direct him to the Green Knight. Bertilak invites Gawain to relax for a few days before moving on. He further proposes they play a Christmas game. You'd think Gawain would be wary of games by now, but intelligence was never emphasized as a knightly quality.

The new game works like this. Every evening, after Bertilak is back from hunting, the two will exchange whatever they got that day. Great! This game is easy! Trouble is, while Bertilak is out hunting, Gawain daily finds himself fending off the advances of Lady Bertilak. As chivalrously as he can, he turns her down, but he does accept a gift from her, a green girdle, which magically makes the wearer invulnerable to harm. Given his impending beheading, Gawain is in a chivalric pickle. . . .

By far the most entertaining of the tales of chivalry, this is great out of all proportion to its little fame.

	Importance	Accessibility	Fun
Sir Gawain and the Green Knight 3		9	10

OH NO—DANTE! (1265–1321)

La Vita Nuova

When he was nine years old, Dante Alighieri fell in love with his eight-year-old neighbor, Beatrice Portinari. How adorable! However, Dante loved this Beatrice for the rest of his life, long after it had stopped being cute. He even immortalized her as his guide to heaven in his *Divine Comedy*. (Of course, if he was right about paradise, she would be immortalized in paradise without his help, but let's not split hairs, at least until we need more hairs.)

La Vita Nuova is a collection of the poems Dante wrote about his love, with connecting prose that puts the poems into their autobiographical context. The relationship went nowhere for two reasons. First, whenever Dante came near Beatrice, he had a fainting spell from the sublime perfection of her wondrousness. Second, after falling in love with her at eight, he didn't see her again for nine years; by then, she was married to Simone del Bardi, the scion of an old banking family.

Dante reports that Beatrice was a beacon of perfect virtue, but it's not clear how he knew. They never had a single conversation. He also never mentions anything she did or said. He doesn't say if she was fat or thin, happy or sad, or if she was a golden retriever. As much as "consensus scholarship" wants to ignore it, the possibility exists that we are dealing with a golden retriever.

In his later essay "Convivio," Dante refers to the tradition of interpreting writings on four levels: the literal, the allegorical, the moral, and the anagogical. So, on the literal level, this is the story of Dante's love for Beatrice. Looking deeper, Beatrice is a symbol for an aspect of God. Look deeper still, and she represents a vast, secretive, Thomas Pynchon–esque conspiracy, already active in fourteenth-century Florence but still controlling our world today, as witnessed by those creepy nineties "We're Beatrice" TV commercials. And finally, a golden retriever.

FUN FACT

Beatrice Portinari's tomb has become a favorite place to leave letters asking for luck in love. We assume the letters are written by girls who want poets to write about how beautiful they are, from a distance, while they marry a banker.

The Divine Comedy

The concept has stunning universal appeal—a tour of heaven and hell! The details, however, are daringly parochial. Everyone immediately notices that Dante's hell is packed with Florentines. Dante knows a surprising number of the people here personally; the others are villains du jour, the Bernie Madoffs and Osama bin Ladens of the fourteenth century. Purgatory is similar, while paradise has two kinds of people: saints and Dante's neighbors. Thanks to this, many editions of *The Divine Comedy* have more notes than text.

Before we go on: Dante really is a genius. Even in the dreariest wastes of the *Purgatorio*, there are passages that are fascinating and beautiful. He can make the most phantasmagorical scenes feel real, and he was a brilliant philosopher as well as a great poet. But he was also a humorless prig, and now we're going to make fun of him.

Inferno

When people talk about Dante, they almost always mean Dante's *Inferno*. A seething mass of burning, freezing, dismembered, disfigured neighbors of Dante, this vision of hell was so successful that Western civilization's default hell is based on it.

The poem is presented as autobiography. We are meant to believe that Dante himself is lost in a forest when he bumps into the ghost of the poet Virgil. Virgil has been sent by Beatrice Portinari to guide Dante through hell. Conveniently, this forest contains the mouth of hell, so they don't have far to walk.

In Dante's cosmology, heaven, hell, and purgatory are all physical places. Although the spirits of the dead are not material, the places are. Hell is a pit in the earth, descending in nine tiers, or "circles." In each circle, a different sin is punished—theoretically. Actually, Dante wasn't very strict about keeping his circles straight. While the first few circles each contain only one sin, with one torture, the system soon spins out of control. The penultimate circle (fraud) includes ten sub-sins: pimping, flattery, fortune-telling, theft, etc.. The cooler sins have their own custom-designed tortures, but some of the dull sins have to share a torture.

At first, Dante is inclined to feel sorry for the people suffering excruciating pain forever, often for sins like being sullen, pigging their food, or lending money at too high a rate of interest. Virgil, however, frowns on Dante's compassion. This is how God wants it, and God is always right. Soon Dante wises up and is happily shoving damned souls down into boiling rivers of blood and jeering at their agony.

Here are a few of hell's highlights:

- The gates of hell have a scary inscription, which ends: "Abandon all hope, ye who enter here." This line is perennially popular. People have used it to describe everything from the Japanese DMV to Connecticut to the Time Warner Cable Customer Service helpline. It also shows up as a device on welcome mats and novelty underpants, and posting this slogan anywhere in an office is always a big crowd-pleaser.

- People who take their own lives appear in hell as trees and bushes. Harpies perch among them and feed on their leaves. Blood trickles from the broken twigs, and voices issue from the split wood. "Ow!" says Kurt Cobain. "That smarts!" cries Sylvia Plath. When Judgment Day comes, the suicides will retrieve their bodies; each body will hang from a noose tied to the tree that houses its soul.

- The thieves are variously persecuted by reptiles (some are attacked by six-legged reptiles that merge with them and produce a lizard-man) and snakes, upon whose bite they spontaneously combust. Here Dante is obviously running out of sensible tortures. He has already used up bugs, fire, boiling pitch, boiling blood, tearing with prongs, flaying . . .

- But he still has ice in his back pocket. On the bottom floor of hell, Satan is up to his armpits in a lake of ice in which sinners are frozen. Satan's six wings flap, keeping the ice cold. He has three faces; one black, one red, and one yellow. Because this is where treachery is punished, each face is chomping on a traitor: Judas, Brutus, or Cassius. Customers of Time Warner Cable will find no surprises here.

PLANNING YOUR VISIT TO HELL

As long as you take your time with the *Inferno*, it's not difficult. Read the notes. Entertain yourself by figuring out which circle you would be sent to. If you can't find any such circles, pause in your reading to commit some sins. Pause in your reading to phone your friends and tell them you're reading Dante's *Inferno*.

One tip: when you read the notes to the *Inferno*, you will find many references to Florentine political factions called the Ghibellines and Guelphs, and to both Black and White Guelphs. It is not important to understand the disputes between these factions. In fact, there was seemingly no good reason for their mutual animosity. One major Guelph bloodbath was triggered by a snowball fight. While Guelphs were supposed to support the pope and Ghibellines the Holy Roman Emperor, this could suddenly change, depending on who was pope, who was emperor, and who was watching.

Happily, all you need to know is that they opposed each other. You can think of them as the Star-Bellied Sneetches and the Plain-Bellied Sneetches, or as the Yankees and the Red Sox, and you're done.

Purgatorio

In the *Purgatorio*, Dante starts with a less compelling concept, gets bogged down in details, and repeatedly disgresses about his own hobby horses. In short, it's a typical disappointing sequel.

Purgatory, for Dante, is a mountain which is the only land in the Southern Hemisphere. It is round at its base and has several tiers; like hell turned inside out. Dante and Virgil, together again, trudge up Mount Purgatory, where they encounter people who aren't as bad as the ones in hell and who are suffering less, in less interesting surroundings. The people in the bottom circle can't even start suffering yet. They are just sitting around on a hillside for centuries, waiting, bored out of their skulls. Above this are seven circles, furnished with petty miseries designed to cleanse away the Seven Deadly Sins. The avaricious, for instance, have to lie flat on their bellies, staring at the ground, because they loved earthly things. Most of the people in purgatory are punished by doing something tedious, which is a little hard on the reader, who has done nothing wrong.

At the top, Dante and Virgil find the Garden of Eden, where a long, baffling allegory is acted out, involving a griffin, a chariot, and the inevitable pretty girls. Reading this section of the *Purgatorio* will purge you of the sin of wakefulness.

Paradiso

Dante's paradise is based on the Ptolemaic model of the universe, which all sensible people then believed. In this model, Earth was at the center of a series of spheres. Each sphere enclosed the last, like the layers of an onion. Heavenly bodies were attached to these spheres and defined them.

So to get to heaven, Dante flutters up from the tip of Mount Purgatory, into the crystalline sphere of the moon. From here, it is a short zoom to Mercury, etc.

Dante is now guided by Beatrice, because Virgil never accepted Christ and therefore can't even visit heaven. Virgil doesn't know how lucky he is.

In heaven, the perfected souls have nothing better to do than form themselves into huge crosses or roses. In the sphere of Jupiter, they actually spell out words. Then the M turns into a giant eagle, and the souls sing hymns while they make the eagle wings flap. For Dante, our heavenly reward is similar to a role in the opening ceremonies of the Beijing Olympics.

When they are not forming words, the blessed souls deliver sermons and give nonsense explanations of the phases of the moon. By the end, the light show includes the Virgin Mary, the Apostles, and even Jesus. It does not include a sense of humor, fun, interest, friendship, sex, food, or anything else that people like.

We are meant to imagine that, once we are perfected, we will like this antiseptic wasteland. The blessed keep insisting they're deliriously happy, and that God is right about everything. It's a mix of North Korea, your first office job, and a Busby Berkeley number. To make a long story short, it's hell.

THE BOREDOM THRESHOLD

It's a curious fact that the more challenging a work of literature is, the more likely the reader is to fall asleep facedown in its pages. Conversely, even the most scornful reader of Dan Brown effortlessly stays awake through his books. One might think that when you gave your brain a lot of challenging knots to untie, it would be more engaged and fascinated than when it is announcing triumphantly that one plus one is two. Alas, that is so not the case.

Paradoxically, the most interesting works of literature are often also the most boring. This is because, as you give your brain more and more things to do, the chances of giving it something it doesn't feel like doing increase exponentially. Eventually, the grumpy brain shuts itself off, leaving you drooling into the pages of *The Divine Comedy*, while the brain waltzes off to have a dream about having sex with the person who lent you the copy—and who will now never sleep with you when she gets back her drool-laden book, with the comment that, um, you liked page one. The brain, let's face it, doesn't care about us.

Do not cave in to the demands of this organ. It is only jealous because we are better-looking than it is. Ask yourself: who is boss around here? Answer yourself: I, I am boss. Remember, if you let the brain get the upper hand, other organs may follow its lead, ultimately ending in a situation where you can't sleep with anyone, or go to the bathroom.

Also, some day, the brain will thank you, because reading boring-interesting literature will make it faster and stronger, and more able to reference Dante when it is trying to get the upper hand on other brains. Or, actually, the brain won't thank you, because that's what these ungrateful brains are like. But never mind, soon we will be able to replace them with computers, at which time, furthermore, *The Divine Comedy* will be a painless twenty-second download.

	Importance	Accessibility	Fun
La Vita Nuova	4	4	4
Inferno	10	6	8
Purgatorio	6	5	5
Paradiso	6	4	5

CHAPTER 4

The Renaissance: Back to the Future

As every child knows, the word "renaissance" means "reupholstery" in French. It also refers to the period after the Middle Ages when people started to think the Middle Ages were over.

It was a time of religious upheaval. People woke one morning and said to one another: "Hang on. What if the pope's not Catholic?" Martin Luther published his *Ninety-five Theses*, attacking abuses in the church, and triggered an era of religious questioning, with questions like "Do you confess now?" and "How can he stand all this pain?" on everyone's lips.

It was also the time of the Renaissance man. A figure like Leonardo da Vinci was not only a great artist, but also a great scientist and a terrific cook, boldly speculating in his notebooks about the possibility of a four-cheese pizza. Science blossomed. Using a telescope, Galileo observed that the Earth moved around the sun, and that his neighbor Donna was all woman. It was a new dawn in how we looked at dawn, and Donna.

Writing was changed forever by the invention of movable type. No longer would monks laboriously copy out manuscripts one at a time; no longer would bestsellers trumpet, "Over three copies sold!" The new publishing industry would free writers from pandering to wealthy patrons and allow them to achieve the proud indigence that is now the hallmark of their profession.

Below we meet some of the amazing minds that typified Renaissance verve and elegance, and also some people who just wrote books.

A ROSE BY ANY OTHER NAME WOULD SMELL LIKE JARGON

Among literary historians, the name of the Renaissance has recently changed. It is now the "Early Modern Era," to reflect the new belief that the rebirth of classical knowledge was not its crucial feature, and to allow academics to snicker at dinosaurs who still say "Renaissance." I cling to the old nomenclature on the grounds that the word "Renaissance" is classy (French!). Also, dinosaurs are cool. Finally, "Early Modern Era" makes me think of modern furniture. I don't need any mental images of Cervantes in an Eames chair. Finally, take a closer look, and you'll notice that "Early Modern Era" is an anagram of "*Le moray de narre*," which means nothing in French. That should silence my critics.

You will notice that some of the figures described in this section were actually contemporaries of writers discussed in the previous section. Not only is the terminology for the era a moving target, so is the era. There are no precise dates for the Renaissance, so writers from the thirteenth to the fifteenth centuries are assigned to the Middle Ages or the Renaissance based on scientific measures like how Renaissancey they feel. I have used the Pusillanimous System, choosing categories by watching what everyone else is doing, copying it, and smiling apologetically.

FRANCESCO PETRARCA, AKA PETRARCH (1304–1374)

Most scholars agree that Petrarch inaugurated the Renaissance, that he was the father of Humanism, and that his sonnets are so deathlessly beautiful, even reading them can give you no idea how beautiful they are. He was the first humanist, the first Renaissance man, the first historicist, and the first man to be first. In short, there has been a lot of hype.

While he wrote many philosophical works, Petrarch is now mainly remembered for *Il Canzoniere*, a sequence of girlfriend poems to a woman named Laura. Petrarch never had a conversation with Laura. He didn't even want to sleep with her, despite his love, since she was married, and that would be wrong. His poems to her, though, became the standard for Western love poetry for the next three hundred years. Poets throughout Europe learned Italian in order to read *Il Canzoniere*.

Still, Petrarch was no closer to doing it with Laura. He just hung around until she died, and then wrote more poems, about how much her death upset him.

Unless you can read Italian, there's no good reason to read *Il Canzoniere*. The highly formal poems can't be translated into English without massive, point-defeating changes—it's like trying to make a dog out of parts from cats. They are short, highly formulaic poems about the lover's feelings; and while the sweetness of the language and the lofty ideas are still charming, a modern reader may think they would benefit by the writer actually meeting his girlfriend, once.

	Importance	Accessibility	Fun
Il Canzoniere	10	7	3

WHY JOHNNY CAN'T DO ANYTHING BUT READ

In the Middle/Dark Ages, university study had consisted of the *trivium* (rhetoric, logic, grammar) and the *quadrivium* (arithmetic, music, geometry, astronomy). Renaissance humanists like Petrarch replaced this with the *studia humanitatis*. They threw out arithmetic, music, geometry, astronomy, and logic. They kept the super-useful grammar and rhetoric, and added history, poetry, and moral philosophy. Basically, sounding good was favored over actually doing anything. The effects resound down to this day, in the form of a million graduates in the "humanities" who think food will just fall into their mouths.

The saving grace of humanism was that when people stopped learning science by reading theories that had been wrong for hundreds of years, they began performing experiments. With scholastic logic gone, just plain logic swept through a generation of thinkers. Astronomers gave up studying charts of the spheres and at last looked up. Finally, someone played music you could dance to. Petrarch got credit for this, because he was the first man to discredit the last generation of thinkers. This freed up a lot of credit, and Petrarch was standing there with a bucket. For the invention of this tactic alone, he deserves to be honored as an innovator.

THE DECAMERON, GIOVANNI BOCCACCIO (1313–1375)

Plague has come to Florence. Ten glossy-looking rich kids flee to a country house, where they while away the time by telling stories. Every day a theme is chosen, and each person tells a story on that theme. The adventure lasts ten days, resulting in one hundred tales.

The stories are brief—two to four pages—and most are of the naughty friar type. In a typical tale, a fourteen-year-old pagan girl hears of Christianity and sneaks off into the wilderness to find God. She meets a monk, who volunteers to teach her how to "put the devil back into hell." The first time they try it, it hurts her, but pretty soon she comes to enjoy it. In the end, the monk becomes a shadow of his former self because she is constantly pestering him to put his devil into her hell. There are occasional romances about shipwrecked princesses and the like, but Boccaccio's basic formula is a lusty woman plus a lusty cleric, with an optional jealous husband.

The lasting importance of the *Decameron* is similar to that of Petrarch's *Canzoniere*. The tales were used and reused. With a hundred stories to choose from, this is a one-stop shop for plagiarists. Tales were stolen by Shakespeare, Keats, Chaucer, Spenser, and ten thousand small fry. By the seventeenth century, one of Ben Jonson's characters refers to a snake oil seller beguiling crowds with "some moldy tales out of Boccaccio."

	Importance	Accessibility	Fun
The *Decameron*	10	10	7

ABOVE THE LAW

Boccaccio and Petrarch (who were friends) both studied law, and both managed to make a living by writing instead of practicing as lawyers. Petrarch said sniffily: "I couldn't face making a merchandise of my mind."

Being a writer wasn't "making a merchandise" because there were no buyers yet, only patrons. Therefore Petrarch could hold his head up high, while holding out his palm.

THE AUTOBIOGRAPHY OF
BENVENUTO CELLINI (1500–1571)

Cellini was one of the most successful sculptors of Renaissance Europe. Michelangelo was his friend; his clients were popes, kings, and despots. His reputation as an artist has declined somewhat, but his fame as a swaggering, gleeful sociopath has never dulled. There literally are no people like Cellini anymore, because we put them in prison as teenagers. That tends to take the wind out of their sails.

He dictated his autobiography while working to a fourteen-year-old boy.

Perhaps the fourteen-year-old audience influenced the tone. The book is jampacked with visions, superhuman feats, and daring crimes. Cellini reports impossibilities, like seeing a salamander—the kind that lives in fire. He tells of performing feats of amazing prowess in war—feats that witnesses didn't remember. In all, he confesses to murdering five people, for reasons ranging from blood revenge to bad mood. There are love affairs with both girls and boys; there are wars and fires and intrigues.

"In a work like this there will always be some natural bragging," Cellini says. But his bragging is more divine than natural; if he were any less extreme, he would be unbearable. As it is, his boasts are pure joy.

	Importance	Accessibility	Fun
Autobiography	5	8	9

FRANÇOIS VILLON (1431–AFTER 1463)

In the long history of disreputable writers, Villon stands head and shoulders below. When he was not sponging off of his patrons, he was robbing them with a gang. He is thought to have been a member of the Coquille, an underground guild of thieves, and some of his verses are written in thieves' cant. His poems often begin with a reference to the prison where they were written; they often end with a plea for cash. He is the pauper prince of literary bad boys.

His poetry expresses the abject misery of the poor, but with the surly glamour of a genius who can't help also showing contempt for his audience. There are begging poems; there is a rhyming epitaph for himself, written as he's waiting to be hanged. His major work is his *Testament*, a mock will. Here Villon tells his picaresque life story and details his bequests. These are mostly insulting joke bequests made to people he disliked. But the *Testaments* also include songs, one with the famous refrain "Where are the snows of yesteryear?" Another, "The Ballad of Fat Margot," has the refrain "In this whorehouse where we are enthroned," and includes one of the earliest hand jobs in literature.

	Importance	Accessibility	Fun
Villon, poems	6	5	10

FRANÇOIS RABELAIS (1494–1553)

If you are squeamish, read no further. Rabelais is the most disgusting writer who ever lived. While sex and gore occur in Rabelais, they are overshadowed by the thing humans find most difficult to love. Rabelais really cannot let one of his characters go to the bathroom alone. He uses startling ingenuity in shoehorning scatological material into law court scenes, sex scenes, animal fables, birth, death.

His second greatest preoccupation is booze; he typically addresses the readership as "You drinkers." His characters can go for hundreds of pages without once sobering up. Finally, his characters are gluttons, and even here Rabelais gives his trademark ew to the activities—every menu in the Pantagruel household features tripe. Soon anything seems squeaky clean by comparison—*South Park*, gonzo porn, actual feces.

Rabelais was—as the worldly reader will have guessed—a monk. He entered a Franciscan monastery as a boy. Despite various attempts to leave, and despite nearly being burned for heresy several times, he died as he lived, a monk. Rabelais had one illegitimate child, but committed no known rapes or murders—by Renaissance standards, a boy scout. There isn't even any evidence that he drank, ate, or defecated more than anyone else.

He did know more than anyone else, however. Interlarded with the boozing and pooing in *Gargantua and Pantagruel* is an informed satire of every field of learning: natural science, law, theology, classics—the result of Rabelais's life as a perpetual student.

The unique nature of his comedy is that Rabelais does every kind of humor at once: there is constant wordplay, slapstick, gross-out humor, and wild satire of philosophical concepts. *Gargantua and Pantagruel* is worth looking at as a study in silliness, even for those readers who will want to let it go to the bathroom alone.

Key scenes and characters:

Pantagruel—Pantagruel is the son of Prince Gargantua and his lady Gargamelle; all three are giants. Many episodes in the book depend on the comedy of big-little, as when the war-faring Gargantua drowns enemy forces by taking a leak. Many of these episodes come from an earlier Gargantua novel, a bestseller that gave Rabelais the idea for his book. Often Rabelais forgets his heroes' size and has them operate completely normally. Rabelais really doesn't care; he is as oblivious to consistency as he is to taste.

Friar John—Friar John is Rabelais's model friar—one unapologetically devoted to hunting, war, wine, fine dining, and love. He distinguishes himself in the cake-peddler's war in Book I, by killing 13,622 men with a staff of the cross. As a reward for his service in this war, Gargantua's father builds for him . . .

The Abbey of Theleme—This is a Rabelaisian Utopia. Theleme is set up on contrary principles to every other abbey. Equal numbers of men and women are admitted, and they are selected for their charm and good looks. Instead of taking vows of chastity, poverty, and obedience, they can marry, are all rich, and live in complete freedom. The rule of their order consists of four words: DO WHAT YOU WANT.

Panurge—Pantagruel's Falstaffian sidekick, a scholarly boozer and sneak. A typical passage with Panurge has him suggesting that the walls of Paris should be rebuilt from the genitalia of Parisiennes. Firstly, they are cheaper than stone. Second, there is no metal that can stand pounding better. And finally, the enemy would all die of syphilis. In the first edition of the book, this scene was so heavily censored that the ink-wet page fell off, leaving big black smears on both facing pages.

Rabelais's cameo—The author tells how, in one of Pantagruel's military campaigns, he himself hid from the pouring rain in Pantagruel's mouth. There he discovered an entire country with farms, forests, cities, and a resident population with no knowledge of the world outside. He lived in the mouth for several months in great prosperity, getting a job as a sleeper which was paid according to the volume of the snore.

	Importance	Accessibility	Fun
Gargantua and Pantagruel	10	5	10

MICHEL DE MONTAIGNE (1533–1592)

Montaigne is the father of the personal essay. He was even the first to use the word "essay" or *essai* ("attempt" in French) for a short nonfiction work in prose. If that does not impress you, I throw up my hands.

He was an early product of hyper-parenting. His father devised a unique scheme of education for baby Michel. The infant was nursed in a peasant family for his first three years, to bring him close to the People. When he was three, he was brought back home. Here no one was allowed to speak to him in any language but Latin. (Closeness to the people was now apparently no longer the goal.) Music was played to him from the moment he woke up; someone followed him around with a zither and would play whenever the boy got tired. You might imagine that this would end with Michel murdering his whole household with a meat cleaver. In fact, he grew up to be a cheerful adult who loved his father. He even followed his father (who had been the mayor of Bordeaux) into a career in municipal politics.

Then, on his thirty-eighth birthday, Montaigne "long weary of the servitude of the court and of public employments," retired. Finding that his new idleness made him depressed, he turned to writing. Although this was a time of political ferment, and religious wars raged in the countryside all around, he didn't write about religion or politics. He wrote: "The world always looks straight ahead; as for me, I turn my gaze inward. . . . I have no business but with myself; I continually observe myself."

The result is a series of wandering, quote-heavy ruminations on everything and nothing—Of thumbs, Of cannibals, Of sleep, Of Cato the Younger. Montaigne's self also turns out to be a treasure chest of the wonderful cock-and-bull stories sixteenth-century scholars took seriously. Turning to a page at random, you find trained elephants who practice their dance steps in their leisure time, or the idols of Themistitan, which are "cemented with the blood of little children," or the statement: "It is a fact that there are nations that accept a dog as their king."

The *Essais* were massively popular and became part of a slow revolution in thought which led to the Enlightenment. This spawned the New Science and ultimately the modern secular state. Yes, it is thanks to Montaigne that we have democracy, freedom of religion, and can evolve instead of being created in seven days. You may think this is an exaggeration, but without Montaigne, you wouldn't even be able to think that.

	Importance	Accessibility	Fun
Essays	10	8	10

DON QUIXOTE, BY MIGUEL DE CERVANTES SAAVEDRA
(1547–1616)

Considering that Cervantes is the most revered writer in the Spanish language, we don't know that much about him. However, what we know is colorful. Before settling down to become a professional writer, he fought the Turks at the Battle of Lepanto and lost the use of his left hand. He was in and out of jail, and was captured at sea and held as a slave for five years in Algiers.

He tried his (one) hand at poetry and playwriting but had no success until writing *Don Quixote*. To this day, almost nothing else is read of his work in English. The one exception is the *Exemplary Novels*, a smart and entertaining set of novellas much like the tales woven into the first volume of *Don Quixote*.

Many people say that Don Quixote is the greatest novel ever written. Some of the same scholars also call it the first novel. This would seem like amazing beginner's luck, if the first novel were also the best. Happily, as our readers will remember, novels had been written for more than a thousand years, and *Don Quixote* is only the first novel to be erroneously called the first novel. (We will meet many more in pages to come.)

The hero is an impoverished gentleman of a certain age; having read too many romances, he comes to believe he is a knight errant, persecuted by an evil magician. He sets out on his starved nag—which he believes to be the charger Rocinante—to right wrongs. A local peasant, Sancho Panza, is roped in with promises of an island kingdom as his portion of the knightly spoils.

In the first volume, Don Quixote's adventures follow a fairly set pattern. He believes something is something else—windmills are giants; flocks of sheep are armies; the peasant girl Aldonza is his imaginary beloved, the lady Dulcinea of Toboso. Sancho comments doubtfully and amusingly, but ultimately goes along, and the knight charges in. These attacks typically end with Quixote and Sancho, and sometimes their mounts, getting a drubbing. Much of the humor here makes the Three Stooges look sophisticated. Nobody will ever point to the scene where Quixote and Sancho throw up on each other as proof this was the Golden Age of Spanish literature.

But the book is as much about books and stories as it is about Don Quixote and his adventures. As he charges his enemies, he lectures Sancho on the traditions of chivalry and which books about knight-errantry are the best. The book is filled with opinions about books and writers (including the writer Cervantes). About a third of it consists of interpolated novellas about people Quixote encounters, much of it sending up then-popular styles like the pastoral and the picaresque.

Characters we meet in the second volume, published ten years after the original, recognize Don Quixote from having read the first book. (There was also a spurious second volume that appeared before Cervantes had a chance to publish his own. To add insult to copyright infringement, the unknown writer used his preface to berate the author of the original. It's easy to pick out the moment when Cervantes found out about the competing book. Starting in Chapter 59, Don Quixote and Sancho Panza object strenuously and often to the "false history" that has been published about them.)

Volume II is darker and more autumnal than volume one. This time, Quixote is more vulnerable, and his fantasy becomes unstable, exposing him to the cold wind of reality. In one episode, Sancho Panza tricks him into believing that a random peasant girl is his beloved Dulcinea. A sadistic duke and duchess pretend to treat Quixote as an honored guest, while they stage elaborate scenarios in order to watch him make a fool of himself. In the end he dies, cured of his delusion, but we by now believe that the world is a lesser place without the mournful knight and his fantasies.

	Importance	Accessibility	Fun
Exemplary Novels	3	7	7
Don Quixote	10	7	10

ON THAT FATEFUL DAY

Many find it striking that both Cervantes and Shakespeare died on April 23, 1616. This overlooks the fact that Spain and England were using different calendars at the time and had different April 23s. This confusion of dates was fatal to the Spanish Armada, which, by the English calendar, would have had perfect sailing weather.

Elizabethan England

English literature in the Renaissance is relatively decorous. There is no Villon, or Cellini, or Rabelais. Instead, there is Spenser, whose work could be used as a form of birth control. The bawdy elements are already markedly more prissy than Chaucer. Why? It may be because, for much of this time, England was ruled by a queen who had to pretend to be a virgin—or, still worse, really be a virgin. (No one is quite sure which.) This could embitter a person and, through trickle-down psychology, embitter all the people who worked for her, and the people who worked for them. This creeping misery, however, would later be eclipsed by the fun Britons weren't supposed to have under Victoria.

Note: almost all really important Elizabethan literature is drama. What that means is you don't even have to read it. You can watch it at the theater, or just order it on Netflix. It's the next best thing to literature in pill form.

A BRIEF HISTORY OF THE ENGLISH STAGE

Before there was a professional theater in England, drama took the form of mystery plays. These consisted of scenes from the Bible, liberally embroidered by the amateurs involved. They were usually produced by guild members and staged on religious holidays. Typically clumsily written, mystery plays are interesting for their anarchic energy. They often include bawdy humor and slapstick alongside a bloodthirsty religiosity. In short, they are much like Greek drama, if Greek drama had been written by stupid people. In addition to mystery plays, there are miracle plays and morality plays. Students of early English drama can tell these three genres apart.

CHRISTOPHER MARLOWE (1564–1593)

Marlowe is an early example of an artist with an exaggerated mystique because he died young. But unlike the namby-pamby twentieth-century version, who dies of an overdose in a puddle of groupies, Marlowe was stabbed.

No one knows why he was murdered. It may have had to do with his career as a spy, if he really was a spy. It may have had to do with his crimes, if he really committed them. It may even have had to do with his homosexuality, if he was gay, or his atheism, if he didn't believe in God. Almost nothing is known about Marlowe, but he has been accused of all these things and more, by adoring fans.

We will take a stand on one thing. Although we are skeptical of the fad for identifying long-dead authors as gay, Marlowe was probably gay. The grounds? He regularly wrote about gay characters; he never married or had a known girlfriend; and someone who knew him well said he was gay. If you compare this to other writers of the period, they score 0, and Marlowe scores 100. The final proof? Unlike these other writers, Marlowe is gay.

Marlowe's Plays

Marlowe's first play was *Dido, Queen of Carthage*, a dramedy version of the classical love story (see page 21), with all-new, extra love stories. Here Anna loves Iarbas, who loves Dido, who loves Aeneas. When Aeneas takes off, not only does Dido kill herself, but Iarbas kills himself and Anna kills herself—all on the final page, so the curtain comes down on a still-twitching death pile. The play was probably coauthored by Thomas Nashe, which would explain the part where a man has sex with a woman.

Tamburlaine the Great (Parts I and II) consists essentially of three scenes, which repeat. In one scene, a king, a sultan, or an emperor rants that his unstoppable war machine will pwn the lowly Tamburlaine. In the second, Tamburlaine rants that he will pwn this so-called "war machine," then keep the machine. In the third, Tamburlaine strides on, wearing the king's/sultan's/emperor's crown and towing its previous owner in a cage, while ranting about how totally he pwned the war machine and now has that much more machine to pwn with. Ten acts of this.

In *The Jew of Malta*, Marlowe again demonstrates that his wingéd genius soars above the drudgery of plotting. The action begins when the Maltese government dispossesses the main character, Barabas. Although he manages to preserve plenty of money, Barabas goes on a sanguinary rampage against all Christians, motivated by the fact that Marlowe didn't like Jews. Marlowe's plot requires disbelief to be suspended, and stay suspended with its eyes shut. Example: Barabas cunningly murders three people by wearing a hat with a poisoned flower in it. Just as he had known they would, the people ask for the flower, and all three sniff it in turn. Murderers, don't try this at home.

Doctor Faustus is about a man who craves power, wealth, and sex. He sells his soul to the devil and hey presto! According to the contract, Faustus has twenty-four years to enjoy his perfect life. Bonus: as long as he truly repents, he won't have to go to hell. From time to time, a "good angel" and an "evil angel" appear on either side of Faustus to give advice. (Yes, the origin of that old chestnut.) The good angel says "Repent," the bad angel says, "Who are you kidding? You're no good, you'll never repent." Finally, Faustus is hauled off to hell, screaming. Bad angel was right.

In *Edward II*, Marlowe really hits his stride. Newly crowned Edward II is in love with Gaveston, a nasty, low-class reptile. Edward doesn't even care about the crown, he just wants to be left alone to frolic with his minion Gaveston. Is that too much to ask? Yes. The nobility of England goes into revolt, blood pours in rivers, Gaveston is beheaded. Rats! Finally, Edward himself is imprisoned in a castle sewage system, while a man next door plays a drum day and night so he can't sleep. It's uncannily like living in a New York apartment. Except, in a New York apartment, assassins don't come in and murder you with a red hot poker. Oh, well, it's better to have loved and lost.

And *The Massacre at Paris*, Marlowe's last play, well. It's about a Catholic massacre of Protestants and has the usual Marloviana—ranting, dozens slain, poisoned gloves, poisoned knife—really just another play that makes you think, "Wow, Shakespeare is great." Our advice: stop at *Edward II*.

	Importance	Accessibility	Fun
Dido, Queen of Carthage	2	4	5
Tamberlaine the Great	2	4	6
The Jew of Malta	8	5	6
Doctor Faustus	9	6	7
Edward II	7	5	6
The Massacre at Paris	2	4	4

The Passionate Shepherd to His Meal Ticket: Courtier Poets

As well as playing the theatrical John the Baptist to Shakespeare's Jesus, Marlowe wrote one of the most famous poems in the English language, "The Passionate Shepherd to His Love." This is basically a plea for sex, which begins:

> Come live with me and be my Love,
> And we will all the pleasures prove . . .

The shepherd/narrator promises his lover nice clothes, like slippers with gold buckles, and hours of fun watching sheep. (We assume this is "watching sheep" in the biblical sense.)

Marlowe's friend Sir Walter Raleigh wrote a sonnet in response, "The Nymph's Reply to the Shepherd." This says: You're all talk, shepherd, you have no money for gold buckles; I'm not getting any younger and I need to marry. Raleigh poses here as the worldly cynic. Of course he is missing the point that Marlowe's Passionate Shepherd (who does not specify gender) is probably writing not to a "nymph" but to a Dispassionate Shepherd, or simply a Bi-Curious Shepherd.

This sort of poetic conversation was part of the environment of the royal court. It was also common for courtiers to write a letter in the form of a poem—to congratulate someone, or argue a point, or to thank someone for their hospitality. Then there are the love poems. Many of these were formal exercises, intended as meaningless flattery. Some, however, were heartfelt expressions of the wish to sleep with someone else's wife because she was very good-looking. The beloved is always beautiful but "cruel," meaning that she won't put out. (NB: In real life, she usually put out.)

For a courtier, a successful writing career meant gifts from the monarch, which could include castles, commercial rights to provinces, and high-born wives. Failure meant poverty, prison, or beheading. Typically a writer seesawed back and forth between success and failure until he drew the beheading card.

Here are a few of the most famous:

Sir Thomas Wyatt (1503–1542): known for being a lover of Anne Boleyn, and for the quirky, lumpy, rhythms in his poetry. (Instead of rumpy tumpy tiddly tum, it goes rumpy tumpy missed a step in the dark tiddly tum.) Wyatt was imprisoned in the Tower twice and also served as a diplomat in various countries. As a boy, the story goes, he fought off a pet lion that had turned on him. Tower or no Tower, an era can't be all bad if children get to have pet lions.

Sir Philip Sidney (1554–1586): wrote a great sonnet sequence, *Astrophel and Stella* (translated: Star-lover and Star) which is the usual "cruel lady" stuff, but even more elegant. He also wrote a picaresque novel called *Arcadia*. "Arcadia," of course, is the land of poetificating shepherds. But Sidney isn't writing the usual pastoral dullness, but channeling the trashy novels of late Rome. On every page there's some over-the-top plot twist: shipwrecks, pirate abductions, slave revolts. Sidney was also the author of the first important English work of literary criticism, *The Defence of Poesy*, which explains why poets are better than everyone else.

And then you have Sir Walter Raleigh (1552–1618), a pleasantly grumpy poet who has the distinction of probably having done it with Queen Elizabeth. But the story about him spreading his cloak in the puddle for her to walk on? Not true. Also, he did not bring back tobacco, or discover the potato, or invent the raccoon, or whatever stories you've heard about Raleigh and America.

THE FAERIE QUEENE BY EDMUND SPENSER (1552–1599)

The Faerie Queene is an epic written in glorification of Elizabeth I, and in the hope that Elizabeth I would give its author money. It is renowned as a very long book that you have to read to get a PhD in English, and that you have to have a PhD in English to read.

There are six books, and sketches toward a seventh. Spenser had intended to write twenty-four but was interrupted by the Grim Critic. Each book is about a virtue: holiness, temperance, chastity, etc. (Yes, in those days, there were twenty-four virtues, not just the seven or eight we recognize today. These included the completely lost virtues of spasmosium and quat. We no longer know what these were, but descriptions of quat suggest that it may explain the wearing of ruffs, which caught the juices.)

The main thing to know about *The Faerie Queene* is that it is an allegory. Sometimes the characters are named Envy or Temperance to make this crystal clear. But they all represent ideas. Una is the one true faith (the Church of England). Duessa is false faith (the Catholic Church). Florimell and Britomart are different types of chastity. To complicate matters, the characters often simultaneously represent real people, as in a roman à clef. Duessa is usually identified with Mary Queen of Scots, for instance. Once you get a few characters into play, this becomes a semantic Grand Central Station. Readers should not worry their pretty heads about decoding the allegory. If you enjoy decoding, by all means decode. If you don't, just remember that it boils down to:

We're good. They're bad. There's a fight. We win.

One saving grace of *The Faerie Queene* is that it's in orgasmically bad taste. An example: in Book III, a giantess appears (out of nowhere, like everything else in The Faerie Queene), riding through the countryside, grabbing knights by the nape of the neck, slinging them over her saddle, and carrying them off to be her sex slaves. She will make do with animals if there are no knights to hand. She and her brother Ollyphant, being twins, were already doing it in the womb; in fact, they were born fucking.

Most champions of Spenser would say his claim to greatness is the Musyck of his Poesie. But even the pretty style was/is considered tasteless by some.

Spenser used a lot of words that were archaic even in the seventeenth century, and twisted his syntax up into bizarre curliques. In short, even in Elizabethan times, it read like Tolkien writing for an elf.

A tip: try starting with Book III, the one on the virtue of chastity. As a general rule, writers are at their best when they talk about sex. Also, it was the sweet spot for the writing of *The Faerie Queene*, when Spenser had ripened in his craft, but before he realized that Queen Elizabeth was never going to give him real money for writing it.

	Importance	Accessibility	Fun
The Faerie Queene	6	5	6

WILLIAM SHAKESPEARE (1564–1616)

Some readers may question my decision to leave William Shakespeare out of this book. I, however, feel so strongly about the gross inflation of this second-rate dramatist's reputation, I decided to take a stand. For me, the question is not, who wrote Shakespeare's works? It is rather, who needs Shakespeare's works?

Now it can be said: the Bard has no clothes!

Okay, actually, I'm giving Shakespeare his own chapter. See, nothing has changed, the status continues quo. Sorry, but Shakespeare is actually great.

BEN JONSON (1572–1637)

Like many Elizabethan playwrights, Jonson was an actor before he tried his hand at writing. He lost his first acting gig spectacularly, though, by killing a fellow actor in a duel. For this crime, he was branded on his thumb and narrowly escaped the gallows. Unabashed, Jonson boasted about the duel for the rest of his life, claiming that his adversary's sword was ten inches longer than his.

That was what he was like. When he wasn't boasting, he was putting other people down, attacking them, and refusing to see that he was in the wrong. In his comedies, he brutally satirized the government, his bosses, his protégés, his collaborators, and his audience, while fulsomely praising himself. For years, he was widely hated, but eventually he became a beloved curmudgeon, the sort of person whose venom is met with a laugh and an affectionate "That's so you!"

Jonson was renowned for being learned. His erudition gave him entrée to aristocrats' homes and also allowed him to steal his best lines from a slew of classical authors. As well as plays, he wrote lyric poetry ("Drink to me only with thine eyes," etc.), which was mysteriously overrated, right up until it was unmysteriously forgotten. For a hundred years, no one thought of imitating Shakespeare, while imitators of Jonson were everywhere. The Cavalier poets (see page 86) were even called "The Tribe of Ben" for their emulation of Jonson's writing. His poetry is really extremely well crafted, and very nice for what it is. Yeah, it's boring.

	Importance	*Accessibility*	*Fun*
Volpone	7	8	7
The Alchemist	7	7	8
Bartholemew Fair	5	6	7

JONSON'S TOP THREE

As a playwright, Jonson's hallmark was the "Comedy of Humors." This may sound weirdly redundant, like "Tragedy of Dramas" or "Cuisine of Cookeries." But in Elizabethan lit crit, humor meant a single trait that entirely defined a character. One character is belligerent, and that is his only quality. His sister is compliant, and all she does is comply. Characters are not three-dimensional people, but adjectives. The compliant sister is named Pliant. The frank man is named Downright, while the suitor is named Winwife. Sound a little forced? Well, the thing about Jonson is, Shakespeare was great.

Jonson's comedies are often funny, however, and include strikingly beautiful passages and clever ideas (even if not all of those were Jonson's). Here are his greatest hits.

In *Volpone*, the eponymous main character is a man who accumulates untold wealth by pretending to be at the point of death, and ready to revise his will at all times. In *The Alchemist*, the faux alchemist Subtle bleeds money from a variety of marks, from the dreamer Mammon to the hypocritical Puritan Ananias. Last of Jonson's major plays is *Bartholomew Fair*, set in a real fair of the time—complete with puppets, masks, pimps, and another low-minded Puritan, here seen in a holy war against gingerbread men. (Jonson, like most of his colleagues, detested Puritans; the Puritans hated the theater right back, and abolished it as soon as they took power, along with Christmas, bright clothes, and the female orgasm.)

CHAPTER 5

William "Look At Me, I Get My Own Chapter" Shakespeare

No matter what you say, Shakespeare is the greatest writer who ever lived. There's no point fighting it. Centuries of reading, argument, and discussion have gone into this conclusion. Today, if you deny Shakespeare's genius, yours is a tiny flea voice struggling to be heard over a shouting throng of people who don't care.

We know very little about Shakespeare's life. Here are the facts: He was from Stratford-on-Avon, where his father was a glover. He married an older woman, Anne Hathaway, when he was eighteen and she was already pregnant. He went to London, where he became an actor. With Richard Burbage, he ran the Lord Chamberlain's Men (later the King's Men), the most successful company of actors in London. Shakespeare drank at the Mermaid Tavern with Ben Jonson, Robert Herrick, and other assorted great poets. In his day, he was considered brilliant but undisciplined. By the end of his life, he had made a considerable fortune by his various endeavors. He had three children: Susanna, Hamnet, and Judith. Shakespeare is definitely dead.

He also wrote some plays; or so most people believe. There is, however, a faction that refuses to accept this. These people, known as anti-Stratfordians, say that Shakespeare didn't have enough education or experience to have written the plays. Therefore, his plays must have been written by Francis Bacon, the Countess of Pembroke, the Earl of Oxford, Christopher Marlowe (who faked his own death in order to ghostwrite Shakespeare), or any of seventy-odd other candidates. There have also been theories proposing that a cabal of writers worked together, or that the plays were written by the Jesuits or the Rosicrucians. The anti-Stratfordians have found evidence everywhere, from Shakespeare's ill-attended funeral to the varied spellings of his name.

This debate is complex, but happily we can simplify it for you. William

Shakespeare wrote William Shakespeare's plays. His authorship was never questioned by any of his contemporaries—including the actors in his company and the many other poets who were his personal friends. In fact, no one doubted his authorship until the nineteenth century. Since then, this issue has entered the colorful world inhabited by people who insist Obama was born in Kenya, that the moon landings were faked, or that 9/11 was the work of an unholy cabal including Republicans, Mossad, and Godzilla. Also, these anti-Stratfordians are really just a stalking horse for the Freemasons. Those bastards have their fingers in everything.

THE TRAGEDIES

On one level, appreciating Shakespeare's tragedies is easy. The poetry is glorious: line after line is a miracle of beauty and profundity. His characterizations are subtle and insightful; his stories have a universal resonance.

However, standards for plotting were very different in the sixteenth century. Crucially, there was no requirement that stories should be plausible. There was, though, an iron-clad rule that the stage be covered with corpses when the curtain fell. Elizabethan audiences also had an insatiable appetite for mad scenes, in which the plot stops dead while someone dances around the stage in a nightie, singing nonsense rhymes. Shakespeare, who wrote for a living, generously accommodated these tastes.

Finally, the tragedies are long. In many ways, a five-act tragedy functions more like a novel than like a modern play. This is not a problem for the reader, but attending a performance of *King Lear* means three hours of ringing declamations, grisly murders, and mad scenes. Sometimes, the experience is mind-alteringly wonderful. Sometimes, you would be willing to gnaw off your leg to escape. Amateur productions should be approached with great caution, and with a plan for successfully concealing your phone while you play Angry Birds on it for three hours.

Hamlet, Prince of Denmark

The most striking thing about seeing *Hamlet* for the first time is that it seems like a tissue of clichés. "To thine own self be true." "The play's the thing." "To be or not to be." Basically, so many lines from *Hamlet* have become part of the language that the only fresh material is in lines like "He's coming!" and "Ha ha!" There's nothing to be done about this, just as we can't change the fact that some symphonies now evoke ads for insurance products.

Hamlet has powerful political themes. When Marcellus says "Something is rotten in the state of Denmark," he is expressing the universal disgust of the young for the corrupt status quo. But Shakespeare also ingeniously represents Hamlet's rebellion as a father issue. Hamlet has two father figures. One is his actual father, who is dead but comes back as a ghost to demand that Hamlet avenge his murder. Hamlet's uncle Claudius seems like a better deal, except that, first, he's having sex with Hamlet's mother, which no one likes to think about, and second, he killed Father #1.

Hamlet learns about this murder in Act I. At this point, he could easily march into Claudius's bedroom and stab him. Finished. Instead, he decides to pretend he's gone crazy. He does not kill Claudius; he does not confront him; he does not tell his mother about the crime. No, he wanders around cackling and blathering about hawks and handsaws.

The baffled audience immediately notices this makes no sense. Hamlet seems to think acting crazy is a brilliant ploy, but it only draws attention to himself, so it would be ten times harder to kill his uncle, should he ever get around to it. It's possible that Shakespeare wants us to wonder whether Hamlet is, in fact, insane. After all, he is hearing voices that tell him to kill his family—often a warning sign.

In Act II, the second phase of Hamlet's plan kicks in. He will stage a play in front of Claudius, in which his father's murder is acted out. Hamlet can then see whether Claudius seems guilty. When Claudius does seem guilty, though, Hamlet just carries on acting crazy. This gives Shakespeare a bumper crop of mad scenes, but it makes no sense at all.

Scholars over the ages have looked at this and decided Hamlet's tragic flaw is indecisiveness. He is a dreamer, who likes having a grievance more than he likes actual justice. What's key here is that, while Hamlet's behavior makes no sense, rather than seeming like something the playwright is doing for his own convenience—say, in order to generate fun mad scenes—it feels like the ineffectual way people behave in real life. Watching Hamlet try to avenge his father is uncannily like watching your teenaged son try to get a job.

The play also features Polonius, an old windbag played for laughs. His daughter Ophelia—Hamlet's girlfriend—goes insane and drowns herself after the old windbag is killed, tossing the audience an extra mad scene on the way. Polonius's son Laertes then springs into action, avenging his father and sister while Hamlet is still getting his shoes on. Laertes' revenge ends in the death of all the main characters, who drop like flies in about two minutes. (Laertes here is basically your best friend's son, who's interning with a political consultancy before he goes to Princeton in the fall.)

A BARREL OF MONKEYS

It is often said that, if you put an infinite number of monkeys in front of an infinite number of typewriters, they would eventually produce *Hamlet*. They would also eventually perform *Hamlet*, update *Hamlet* to the First World War, and conclude that *Hamlet* was written by the Countess of Pembroke.

	Importance	*Accessibility*	*Fun*
Hamlet	*10*	*3*	*9*

King Lear

King Lear is *Hamlet*'s main competition for best play ever. People are less familiar with it, though, because it is incredibly confusing. At one point, Shakespeare has a mad person talking to someone who is pretending to be mad, while a fool comments in riddles. The plot is pretty simple, though, if you can find out what it is.

King Lear is getting old. Therefore, he is going to turn over his kingdom to his three daughters. The biggest part will go to the one who loves him most, etc. How does he determine who loves him most? He asks them. It's as brilliant a bit of statecraft as dividing his kingdom based on which daughter can name more of the capital cities of Europe, or based on how they complete the sentence, "Skippy's peanut butter is my flavorite because . . ."

The two evil daughters, Regan and Goneril, predictably deliver speeches about how madly they love Lear. But nice-girl Cordelia, disgusted by this farce, says she loves Lear exactly as a daughter should, and *basta*. This enrages Lear, who throws her out with nothing. The king of France, however, still wants to marry her, so Cordelia goes off to be queen in Paris. She totally lands on her feet here.

Lear moves in with Goneril and her husband, but soon there are ructions. Really, do not have your aged parents living with you if you can help it. Goneril tells Lear his entourage is too large and rowdy; Lear smacks one of Goneril's men "for chiding of his fool." And presumably, though Shakespeare doesn't mention this, there are turf wars over the bathroom. Anyway, now that Lear has given away his lands, he has turned overnight into King Albatross.

Lear stomps off in a huff to Regan, but she doesn't want his entourage, either. Driven mad by this ingratitude, Lear goes out into a howling rainstorm. His fool goes with him for some fool reason that is never explained. Maybe he is actually stupid. Soon, Lear, his fool, and Edgar, a character who is pretending to be mad, are all raving at one another amid storm sound effects.

Shakespeare uses the rest of the play to get to the point where he can kill off every major character. As this is something at which Shakespeare excels, the play now goes from strength to strength to climactic deathpile. Six characters die in Act V, making it difficult for the survivors to move around the stage without hopping. This death toll, however, is nothing compared to the gore-fest in Macbeth.

	Importance	Accessibility	Fun
King Lear	*10*	*2*	*8*

HAMLET BLOGGS, CPA

Hamlet and Lear, like all of Shakespeare's heroes, are not especially likeable. Partly for this reason, despite Shakespeare's hallowed status, parents almost never name their sons after his heroes. No one wants to raise a little Othello or Macbeth; much less a Hamlet, ready to go on a killing spree if they remarry.

Middle-class British parents, however, feel no shame about calling their daughters Portia or Cordelia. Presumably this is due to a subconscious hope that their girls will be so uncool they won't get laid until they're well into their thirties.

Macbeth

Almost all the scenes in this play end with everyone on stage covered in blood. It's noisy, unrelenting, grand guignol: a perfect choice for that Hallowe'en outing, or to firm up your resolve when you've just embraced vegetarianism.

The play begins with two Scottish generals, Macbeth and Banquo, returning from battle. On the way, they meet three witches. The witches predict that Macbeth will be made Thane of Cawdor, and "king hereafter." (Thane of Cawdor is not, as you might imagine, a Scottish cabbage dish, but a title.) Moments later, a messenger comes to tell Macbeth that King Duncan has made him Thane of Cawdor.

With his ambition roused, Macbeth goes home plotting to murder Duncan, so he can be king. This reveals a massive gap in his understanding of how prophecies work. If you had to make the prophecy come true yourself, what would be the point of the prophecy? I can give you prophecies like that all day long!

Furthermore, when he talks to his wife, she is even more gung ho, expressing herself in terms like "fill me, from the crown to the toe, top-full / Of direst cruelty!" Well, be careful what you wish for. During Duncan's murder, Lady Macbeth acts like a demon-possessed freak and goads Macbeth viciously whenever he gets chicken. He gets chicken a lot, wailing about how scary the murder was, and how he will never sleep again, blah blah—a surprising sensitivity in a guy who just got back from war.

Anyway, now he's king. All's well that ends well. King Macbeth can improve the school system, fund some needed infrastructure, and put people back to work again after Duncan's wasteful wars.

No. Instead, he opts to kill anyone who looks at him funny, including his old friend Banquo. But Banquo's ghost returns, totally ruining a fancy dinner party. (This scene is the source of the phrase "ghost at the feast," usually used for an ex who shows up when you're getting off with someone at a party.) Meanwhile, Lady Macbeth sleepwalks every night and washes imaginary blood from her hands. They have everything they dreamed of, but they are still not happy.

Macbeth goes back to the witches for another prophecy, because the first one did him so much good. They prophesy that he cannot be killed by any man "of woman born." Due to his tragic inability to understand how prophecies work, Macbeth goes off whistling and carefree. The audience, of course, is only wondering who this guy "not of woman born" is going to be. Funnily enough, it turns out Macbeth's worst enemy was cut from his mother's belly after her death. He duly kills our hero, amid much caterwauling, decapitation, and stage blood.

CANDYMAN, CANDYMAN, CANDYMAN

After several actors playing Macbeth died during the show's run, a tradition developed in the theater that you must never call the play by name, because it carries a curse. Instead, actors call it *The Scottish Play*. Doing this around theater people shows you are down with theater history, although it may also make you feel silly. We suggest you go ahead and say *The Scottish Play*, but with heavy irony. This tells people you know all about it, while also giving you the air of a daredevil who would make wisecracks while opening a mummy's tomb.

	Importance	Accessibility	Fun
Macbeth	10	3	9

Othello

Desdemona, the daughter of a Venetian bigwig, has secretly married Othello, a Moorish general. Her father is outraged and insists Othello must have drugged the girl—why else would she marry a black dude? Desdemona, however, explains that she was won over by his thrilling war stories. This is the only known example where talking about yourself all night has actually gotten someone laid.

Meanwhile, one of Othello's men, Iago, is plotting the general's downfall. Iago hates Othello, because he passed Iago over for promotion and because Iago suspects him of having slept with his wife. Because he is eaten up with this double jealousy, the most natural revenge Iago can think of is to make Othello jealous. This is a very cool idea, and Iago is a clever boots for having thought of it.

His plan goes like clockwork. People are simply putty in his hands. Every few lines someone admiringly calls him "Honest Iago," they are so totally taken in. As soon as he tells Othello his wife is cheating, the general is ready to kill her. Iago dummies up some proof pointing to Cassio, the guy who got his promotion, as Desdemona's lover. Obviously, Cassio too must be killed. Revenge is a breeze!

At the end, Othello strangles Desdemona in her bed, overwhelmed by "the green-eyed monster" of jealousy. Once he realizes she was innocent, he's overwhelmed by the red-eyed monster of weeping, then by the X-eyed monster of stabbing oneself to death. Iago stabs two extra people, because he may be sneaky but at least he does his share of the work. He is then taken off to be tortured and executed. While his plan up to this point was ingenious, he totally blanked the part where he got away with it.

	Importance	Difficulty	Fun
Othello	*10*	*4*	*9*

THE IDIOT PLOT

Othello is an example of what science fiction writers call an idiot plot, where the story only works because all the characters are idiots. Othello never suspects Iago might be lying. Cassio never suspects his rival Iago is not looking out for his best interests. Iago's wife, Emilia, is duped into helping with the plot, even though she is completely aware Iago is a duplicitous bastard. Of course, for Elizabethan audiences, none of this was a problem, as long as there was a heap of corpses at the end of the play.

Julius Caesar

As this play opens, a soothsayer tells Julius Caesar to "Beware the Ides of March." There are signs and portents of upheaval in the state. His wife has a horrible premonition and warns him to stay home. Nonetheless, he goes off to the Senate and is stabbed to death by a bunch of rebellious senators. As the noble Brutus puts his knife in, Caesar says, "*Et tu, Brute?*"— reverting, in his death throes, to speaking in his native Latin.

Now Brutus makes a speech to the populace about how democracy can return, now that the dictator is dead. Everyone is very gung ho about this, until— uh-oh! Here comes Marc Antony. He delivers the "Friends, Romans, coun- trymen, lend me your ears . . ." speech. It is a first-class tearjerker. Antony presents himself as a simple man who can't argue with Brutus and all his book-learning. But shucks, it sure seems mean to kill Caesar, after all the nice things he's done.

The citizens completely fall for this, and turn on the conspirators. Mob vio- lence breaks out.

The rest of the play follows the painful demise of the democratic rebellion. Both Brutus and his sidekick Cassius die by suicide as their enterprise goes south. The empire is left in the control of a triumvirate, which includes— what a surprise—Marc Antony.

	Importance	Accessibility	Fun
Julius Caesar	9	4	7

Antony and Cleopatra

Antony is now living in Egypt, where he has fallen prey to the charms of Queen Cleopatra. "Age cannot wither her, nor custom stale her infinite variety," as the famous line goes. To be fair, age and custom don't get much of a chance.

Anthony and Cleopatra contains some of Shakespeare's most beautiful writing, and one of his most compelling heroines. Cleopatra is a brazen tramp. She is neurotic, hot-tempered, extravagant; "her infinite variety" actually seems like it would be exhausting to live with. She is also a terrible employer, who kills a messenger for bringing her bad news.

The story sets up a struggle for Antony's soul, between his duty to the empire and his love for Cleopatra. Just as he would in a contemporary drama, Antony turns his back on the empty trappings of power, realizing that true love is what really matters. In Shakespeare's world, this leads inevitably to mass slaughter and the suicide of both lovers. The moral is: love conquers all, leaving nothing but ashes and heaps of corpses. Better off sticking to your career.

	Importance	Accessibility	Fun
Antony and Cleopatra	9	3	9

Romeo and Juliet

After seeing *Romeo and Juliet*, Samuel Pepys famously wrote: "It is a play of itself the worst that I ever heard in my life." While it isn't quite that bad, it is an early play and very uneven compared to the other big name tragedies. However, it's also easier to follow, which accounts at least partly for its popularity. It's almost as if Shakespeare wrote this one specifically to be used in schools to introduce tweens to his work.

Everyone knows the story, but here is a refresher. Two wealthy families of Verona, the Montagues and the Capulets, have a long-running feud. Wearing a mask for disguise, Romeo Montague goes to a Capulet party, where he sees Juliet Capulet and falls instantly in love. He exchanges a few words with her, and she too falls instantly in love. They marry secretly, hoping it will all work out somehow. But—oops!—Romeo then kills Juliet's cousin in a spot of last-minute feuding.

Meanwhile, the Capulets want to marry Juliet to someone else. Rather than explain that she is already married, Juliet decides to feign suicide. A helpful friar gives her a mystery drug they had in the Renaissance that made you seem dead. You stopped breathing, your body became cold, and your heart stopped beating. Then a few hours later, you woke up full of beans. It was like a roofie for necrophiliacs. People used this drug in the Renaissance with all sorts of things in mind, but the result was invariably that you woke to find your lover had killed himself at your side.

So Juliet finds Romeo dead beside her, and kills herself too. Then the feuding families gather in the crypt and say, gee, we're sorry about that feuding, we thought it was all in fun.

	Importance	Accessibility	Fun
Romeo and Juliet	10	5	9

Cymbeline

This is a romance with a winningly ridiculous plot. The princess Imogen marries secretly, her husband is exiled, a trickster convinces the husband Imogen is unfaithful, and seventeen other things happen, in no particular order. At a high point in the follies, Imogen has faked her death and gone into the wilderness in men's clothing. There the first people she meets turn out to be her long-lost brothers. Some scholars have seriously suggested that Shakespeare was just bored and fooling around.

	Importance	Accessibility	Fun
Cymbeline	6	4	8

Coriolanus

This is a solid tragedy with strong writing and a clear plot arc. It's based on Plutarch's life of Coriolanus, the great Roman general who was banished for his disdain of the common people. It is seldom performed because:

1. A purely political play, it has none of the comic episodes, love scenes, and slaughterfests the public loves.
2. The character of Coriolanus lacks the complex internal life of most Shakespearean heroes.
3. It has "anus" in the title.

	Importance	Accessibility	Fun
Coriolanus	6	3	7

The History Plays

A feature of the developing Elizabethan stage were the history or chronicle plays, reflecting a growing sense of English nationhood. Nowadays, these plays are mainly notable for being hard to tell apart. *Henry IV Part Two; Henry VI Part One, Richard III Part Chihuahua; Henry I Give Up.* The only way it could be worse is if Shakespeare had also created for each one a unique password of at least eight characters, including a capital letter and a number.

Happily, we can simplify this. Only five of these plays are significant. First, there's the War of the Roses tetralogy: *Richard II, Henry IV Parts One* and *Two*, and *Henry V.* Then there's *Richard III.* You can pretty much forget the other history plays, which are mostly either early plays, written before Shakespeare got his groove on and/or co-written with some lesser being. Anyway, they will never turn up even in the most exacting trivia quiz.

Richard II (ruled 1367–1400)

This play chronicles the fall of Richard and the rise of Bolingbroke (later Henry IV), due to Richard's spinelessness, and Bolingbroke's greater aptitude and sneakiness. It is remarkable for its political poetry about the nature of kingship, and for its winningly feeble hero. When Richard is really up against the wall, he receives the news by wilting completely, saying: "For God's sake let us sit upon the ground / And tell sad stories of the death of kings . . ." Then he sends away his remaining followers and goes off to a castle to mope.

Monarchs have never enjoyed this play. A revival during the Restoration was actually shut down by the nervous Charles II.

King Henry IV Part One

This one is famous for the relationship between Crown Prince Hal and his disreputable sidekick, John Falstaff, a fat, drunken, criminal knight. It is notable for its endless series of Elizabethan fat jokes. Falstaff is called, among other things, a grease tallow-catch, a horseback-breaker, a huge hill of flesh, a swollen parcel of dropsies, a huge bombard of sack, a stuffed cloak-bag of guts. All these epithets come from our hero, Prince Hal; since he is the crown prince and Falstaff is a criminal nobody, all Falstaff can really say in response is, "But I love you so!"

As Part One begins, England is in a state of seemingly perpetual civil war. This is very frustrating for King Henry IV, who wants all this pointless bloodshed to end so he can send everyone on a Crusade and outsource war to the Middle East (still a popular piece of statecraft). The king is also upset about the crown prince, Hal, a spoiled good-for-nothing—so unlike his father, who worked his fingers to the bone to become king.

Next, we meet Hal drinking and planning a robbery with Falstaff and other lowlifes at a seedy inn. However, at the end of this first seedy inn scene, Prince Hal, left alone with the audience, tells us in confidence that he is only pretending to be a good-for-nothing. He is actually a stand-up guy, and at the right moment, he will tear off his mask. Then won't everyone be amazed! It will be way more impressive than if he had been good all along.

In the end, battle is joined with the rebels. Hal saves his father's life on the battlefield, thereby proving that he is, after all, a stand-up guy and a true warrior. Meanwhile Falstaff behaves like a sneaking coward, thereby winning the hearts of the entire audience. (Theatergoers aren't that warlike as a group.)

King Henry IV Part Two

This is everything you might expect from a half-baked sequel. The character growth in Part One is forgotten. Prince Hal becomes the same slacker he was at the beginning, as if nothing happened. King Henry has totally forgotten Hal saved his life. Everyone goes to war again, and Hal plays practical jokes on Falstaff again, while calling him various Elizabethan versions of "fatso." Why mess with a winning formula? Subconsciously feeling guilty about serving up this mess of warmed-up leftovers, Shakespeare has Falstaff keep harping on how old, tired, and worn-out he is.

At the end, having assumed the crown, Hal publicly rejects and humiliates Falstaff. Since everyone loves Falstaff, this scene outrages the whole pusillanimous, sneaky audience. If we had brought rotten tomatoes, Hal would be covered in them. Now, having sacked everyone's favorite character, Hal sets off to prove that he can carry one of these history plays without Falstaff's help.

King Henry V

Oh well, he's successful. This is one of the greatest representations of war ever written, taking us through Hal's great victory over the French at Agincourt. It's most famous for the St. Crispin's Day speech, the new king's pregame pep talk to the soldiers:

> And Crispin Crispian shall ne'er go by,
> From this day to the ending of the world,
> But we in it shall be remembered,
> We few, we happy few, we band of brothers.
> For he to-day that sheds his blood with me
> Shall be my brother

Obviously, we no longer even remember when St. Crispin's Day is, never mind recalling these nameless soldiers. This has not stopped patriotic types from quoting this speech ad infinitum, with joyous tears in their eyes. Probably even French patriots quote it. Patriots do not quote the many scenes in the play about the rank-and-file soldiers, who listen to this speech and then go off to extort money from any French soldiers they can disarm.

The Life and Death of King Richard III

While none of Shakespeare's heroes is exactly lovable, here the main character is an insidious, mustache-twirling, hunchbacked villain. Like Iago, Richard manipulates everyone effortlessly, even convincing Anne Neville, whose beloved husband he has just killed, to marry him. However, he runs out of idiots long before the end of the play, and ends up dying in battle.

This was an early play, and it's reminiscent of Marlowe in its premise (the villain rubbing his hands together as he plots the doom of innocents) and its messy plotting. Its fascination comes from Shakespeare's complex treatment of the evil genius figure, showing the life cycle of the envious worm who metamorphoses into a paranoid insect, and finally ends life as an ugly stain.

	Importance	Accessibility	Fun
Richard II	9	3	8
Henry IV Part One	10	3	9
Henry IV Part Two	7	3	6
Henry V	9	3	7
Richard III	9	3	8

The Comedies

In his comedies, Shakespeare starts with a ludicrous premise and fills it up with genius. Most of these are love stories and start from the assumption that love is bullshit. We fall in love for no reason—because our luck has run out—then experience this brain malfunction as a matter of life and death.

There is also a strong incidence of cross-dressing, twins, obscene puns, drunks, and fart jokes. Whatever your candidate for the lowest form of comedy is, you will find it here in abundance.

When performed well, the comedies are still exquisite and funny. Not everyone can honestly say that they enjoy *King Lear*, but if you don't enjoy *Twelfth Night*, shoot the director.

A Midsummer Night's Dream

Here Shakespeare engineers a perfect A loves B loves C loves D loves A formation, which ends in the lovers literally chasing one another in circles around the stage.

Malicious fairies enchant two pairs of lovers, causing them to switch affections violently. Having protested eternal love for Hermia one second, Lysander now chases Helena with the same ardor—while being harassed by boring Hermia, who unreasonably expects something from him, based on some crap he said in the past. Meanwhile, Demetrius is still in love with Hermia, while Helena is in love with him.

Titania, the queen of the fairies, is meanwhile enchanted into falling in love with a "rude mechanical" named Bottom, who is himself under a spell that gives him a pair of donkey ears. Here, Shakespeare somehow makes the proposition that love is a delusion feel life-affirming.

Much Ado About Nothing

This one is famous for the sparring between sworn enemies Benedick and Beatrice. Out of boredom, B and B's friends play a trick on them. Benedick's mates convince him Beatrice is in love with him; her friends do the same to her. By the time they discover the imposture, the joke has become a self-fulfilling prophecy.

Meanwhile, the nice lovers Hero and Claudio are also victims of trickery. You have to sit through these parts to get back to Beatrice and Benedick.

The Taming of the Shrew

The sweet, mild Bianca is surrounded by avid suitors. Her sister Katharina, however, is a shrew (Renaissance word for "female dog") who insults everyone she meets. Therefore the audience loves Katharina, but the other characters really, really don't.

The trouble is, the girls' father refuses to let Bianca marry until Katharina has a husband. All Bianca's suitors are in despair. Surely no one will ever marry Katharina!

Enter Petruchio. The first words out of his mouth are that he is looking for a rich wife—regardless of looks, age, or shrewing. In no time flat, he is telling Katharina: "I am he am born to tame you, Kate; / And bring you from a wild Kate to a Kate / Conformable, as other household Kates."

Unsurprisingly, she hates his guts. However, she is forced to marry Petruchio against her will. (This is where female audience members begin to feel a little fidgety.) He then torments her with mind games until she is a nervous wreck and agrees to anything he says. At the end of the play, he and two other recently married men have a competition to see whose wife is the most docile. Katharina wins—even over her goody-two-shoes sister. Then Katharina delivers the famous "I am ashamed women are so simple" speech, saying women should obey their husbands because men are the breadwinners, and big enough to beat the wives if they object.

Female audience members are now nauseated, not to mention incredulous. The only way to make sense of these events, in fact, is to assume that "taming" is a euphemism for sex. Mind games are all very well, but this play only works if the actor cast as Petruchio is smoking hot. It then becomes a respectable version of *The Story of O*. This rape fantasy subtext, combined with the controversial text text, explains the play's enduring popularity.

The Merchant of Venice

Antonio is a rich Christian merchant, Shylock is a rich Jewish merchant. These two just can't get along. Antonio spits on Shylock in the street for being a Jew. Also, whenever Shylock gives someone a loan, and is perfidiously, Jewishly hoping for a return on his money—Antonio dashes in and pays off the principal before Shylock gets any interest. Being spat on and losing business upsets the touchy Shylock, who, meanwhile, injures Antonio by existing while Jewish.

But then one day Antonio turns up on Shylock's doorstep—wanting a loan! All Antonio's money is tied up, see, but his dear, dear friend Bassanio needs cash.

Shylock agrees to lend the money, without interest—but if Antonio can't pay it back on time, he has to forfeit a pound of flesh. Antonio and Bassanio can't see anything wrong with this deal, and sign the contract happily. If the pound of flesh came out of Antonio's brain, he would never miss it.

Meanwhile, another virtuous Christian runs away with Shylock's daughter Jessica. Adding insult to injury, Jessica steals a heap of her father's money on her way out. Then everyone laughs at the anguished Jew's cries of "O my ducats! O my daughter!" It's so funny when your children rob you and abandon you! This mockery inspires Shylock to make the famous "If you prick us, do we not bleed?" speech, which moves no one, because they are all good Christians.

Of course, the news soon comes that Antonio's ships are lost at sea. He can't pay Shylock back! But surely Shylock will forgive the loan. No: to everyone's complete astonishment, Shylock wants his pound of flesh. (We still say someone "wants their pound of flesh" when they unreasonably want us to suffer because we have treated them like garbage for years.)

It's hard to escape the conclusion that Shakespeare meant this play as an attack on anti-Semitism. Nonetheless, theater companies from Elizabethan England to Nazi Germany have successfully escaped this conclusion and produced it as anti-Semitic agitprop.

The Tempest

Prospero, the rightful duke of Milan, had his throne usurped by his brother many years ago. Ever since, Prospero has lived in exile on an island with his daughter, Miranda, who has grown up into a beauty, as daughters in stories will. Couldn't she have grown up into a beady-eyed hog woman, just for a change? No, she could not.

Prospero found the island inhabited by the witch Sycorax and her son Caliban, a "deformed monster." He defeated Sycorax, although her magic was so strong she could "control the moon." What she did with the moon is not recorded. Anyway, Prospero won because he is an even greater magician, although he mysteriously didn't think of using his magic to keep the throne of Milan, or to get the throne back. Instead, he uses his awesome powers to command the local sprite Ariel and the monstrous Caliban to fetch and carry for him, which can't help striking the audience as petty and unfair.

Caliban is the focus of much contemporary interest in this play. He was based on early reports of Native Americans, and his name actually comes from an inversion of "cannibal." His character has none of the complexity of Othello or Shylock: he is more like an African in a Tarzan movie. He once tried to rape Miranda; and when the comedy underlings who set the play in motion appear, he worships them as gods. Throughout, he is stupid, servile, and envious. Still, contemporary audiences tend to root for Caliban, willing him to club Prospero on the head and free Ariel, after which Miranda will be free to confess her secret love for him. Alas, they root in vain.

The Comedy of Errors
Two pairs of identical twins are accidentally separated as infants. Now they're all in the same town! Is mistaken identity ever actually funny? Yes.

The Merry Wives of Windsor
Queen Elizabeth loved Falstaff so much, she asked Shakespeare to give him his own spin-off play. Shakespeare wrote the worst play he was capable of writing, perhaps to discourage any more suggestions from helpful monarchs. The rare Shakespearean comedy you should cross the street to avoid.

Love's Labour's Lost
Here four men swear off love. Then four women come to town. Four times the fun of a play in which one man swears off women. Say the title five times fast, and by the end, you will be speaking Polish.

Twelfth Night
Cross-dressing, twins, practical jokes, drunk scenes.

Best known for the character of Malvolio, pompous head steward of Lady Olivia. The other servants trick Malvolio into believing Olivia loves him and, from there, into wearing ridiculous clothes and making bizarre faces to signify that he returns her love. Amazingly, unprecedentedly, because Shakespeare is a total genius, this is funny.

As You Like It

Cross-dressing, shepherds, a near-total lack of plot. Yet it works. We're hoping Shakespeare won a bet by writing this, because he totally deserved to.

	Importance	Accessibility	Fun
A Midsummer Night's Dream	10	5	10
Much Ado About Nothing	8	5	10
The Comedy of Errors	8	5	8
Love's Labour's Lost	6	5	6
The Merry Wives of Windsor	6	5	5
Twelfth Night	8	4	9
As You Like It	8	5	9
The Taming of the Shrew	8	5	8
The Merchant of Venice	10	5	8
The Tempest	10	4	7

Shakespeare's Problem Children

Three works of Shakespeare are usually classed as "problem plays": *Measure for Measure*, *Troilus and Cressida*, and *All's Well That Ends Well*. These were first called problem plays by the critic F. S. Boas, who suggested that they should be regarded like the plays of Ibsen, which set forth a controversial question and dramatize possible solutions.

Measure for Measure really does consistently address an issue: the question of justice versus tolerance. The other "problem plays" are really more of a problem of classification, because they shift unpredictably from bawdy comedy to wailing tragedy. It's hard to find a center of balance in them. The tragedy is cheapened by the jokes, and many of the jokes fall flat because Shakespeare has worked successfully to put us in a somber mood.

This is not just a problem when one classifies these plays of Shakespeare's; it's also hard to know how to produce them successfully. Although they have excellent parts, they don't knit easily into a whole. Therefore, you could suggest, the real problem is coming up with an excuse for Shakespeare, instead of just admitting that he fucked up.

This problem becomes even worse with a group of plays we may call the "Special Needs Plays." With these, scholars have concentrated on proving they were partly written by someone else. Any patches of good writing can be attributed to Shakespeare, while the botched parts can be pinned on John Fletcher. These disputed-authorship plays are *Titus Andronicus*, *Timon of Athens*, *Pericles*, *Henry VI Parts One*, *Two,* and *Three*, *Henry VIII*, and *The Two Noble Kinsmen*. Some of these are perfectly fine, unless you compare them to Shakespeare.

No one, however, has managed to pin any part of *The Winter's Tale* on Fletcher. While this contains some lovely speeches, it also contains a lot of dross, including one unmissably stupid scene. Here Shakespeare has a dramatic task: he needs to have a character, Antigonus, abandon a child on a beach. Then he needs to get rid of Antigonus and his ship. Here's how he does it.

Antigonus sets down the baby and makes a speech about how sad it is. Then he sees that the weather is getting rough, so he heads off stage. A bear appears and follows him off.

A shepherd comes out and finds the baby and makes appropriate exclamations. Then another rustic runs on stage crying, "Oh my God! I just saw a guy get killed by a bear! And a ship go down!"

Here Shakespeare stops everything, and Time comes on stage and announces that sixteen years have passed.

Do not point the finger at John Fletcher. He has carried the can for Shakespeare long enough. John Fletcher is also not the immortal bard who conceived of the climactic scene in *The Two Gentlemen of Verona*.

Here Proteus, driven mad by unrequited love, is about to rape Silvia. Valentine, Silvia's fiancé—and Proteus's best friend—steps in to prevent him. Once prevented, Proteus realizes how wrong it is to rape people, especially if they are your best friend's fiancée. He begins to wail about how incredibly awful he feels.

"Oh, poor you," says Valentine, "If it makes you feel better, take Silvia, after all."

At this point Proteus's page (who has been standing there the whole time) faints. Everyone gathers round, and it is revealed that the page is really Proteus's old flame Julia, dressed in men's clothes. Now that he knows this, Proteus realizes he is in love with Julia and pledges eternal fidelity to her, forgetting all about raping Silvia.

So here is the essence of our problem. How could Shakespeare, the great thinker and subtle psychologist who wrote *Hamlet*, have created this bilge?

Reader, we are here to solve this problem. Shakespeare was a very great playwright and could never, ever, have made beginner mistakes like these. We have to assume that Shakespeare could have written terrific material here, instead of drivel. He could have, but we didn't deserve it. If we were a better audience, he would have written a great play every time. It is just the same as the time that Daddy didn't buy you Christmas presents but instead spent all his money at a bar, because you didn't deserve to be loved.

The Sonnets

Once you have sufficiently mastered Shakespeare's English, the sonnets are rewarding, fascinating, and all things cool. When all you can make of a line like "tender churl mak'st waste in niggarding" is that it sounds racist, the sonnets are just plain frustrating. Even with notes, reading them without a good grasp of Elizabethan English is like being stuck in stop-and-go traffic. Therefore, we suggest you save these for last (or nearly last: don't feel you have to read *Two Gentlemen of Verona* under any circumstances.).

The first 126 sonnets (out of 154) are to a young good-looking man of dissolute habits, who is reluctant to marry. This person is usually called the "Fair Youth." Many critics believe these sonnets are evidence that Shakespeare was in love with the Fair Youth. The others are ostriches with no gaydar. Consider sonnet 20:

> A woman's face with nature's own hand painted,
> Hast thou the master mistress of my passion,
> A woman's gentle heart but not acquainted
> With shifting change as is false women's fashion,
> An eye more bright than theirs, less false in rolling:
> Gilding the object whereupon it gazeth,
> A man in hue all hues in his controlling,
> Which steals men's eyes and women's souls amazeth.
> And for a woman wert thou first created,
> Till nature as she wrought thee fell a-doting,
> And by addition me of thee defeated,
> By adding one thing to my purpose nothing.
> But since she pricked thee out for women's pleasure,
> Mine be thy love and thy love's use their treasure.

Now think of it surrounded by 125 other sonnets, addressed to the same person, many of which are clearly love poetry. "Shall I compare thee to a summer's day," for instance, was written to this man. Shakespeare stays up nights, consumed by jealousy; Shakespeare harps on the youth's beauty again and again, swears fidelity, despairs when they are separated, is jealous when another man writes poems about him. If Shakespeare is not gay, Shakespeare was the last one to find out. Finally, pause to consider that William Shakespeare was an actor.

Some scholars have found Shakespeare's gay love affair so hard to accept that they've proposed the sonnets have no actual relationship to Shakespeare's life. When the completely straight Shakespeare sat down to write love poetry, he just decided to write the poems as if to a man. Because straight guys do that all the time, right? Just because you can't think of any examples doesn't mean it's never happened.

A further wrinkle appears when we get to the "Dark Lady" sonnets. After 126 poems to a guy, suddenly out of nowhere, a woman appears. These sonnets are again surprising in their content. In poem after poem, he points out that the Dark Lady isn't conventionally pretty. Everyone else insists she's ugly, in fact, but he sees the beauty in her anyway. Perhaps, he suggests, he is blinded by love. (A tip to men: do not try this on your girlfriend.)

A further twist comes in sonnet 133, where it turns out that the Fair Youth is also in love with the Dark Lady. In sonnet 135, the Fair Youth is called by name for the first time; it turns out that he too is called Will. When Shakespeare is not making catty remarks about the Dark Lady's complexion, he is urging her to accept both Wills as her lovers.

Make of it what you will. Probably there is nothing autobiographical in this. Shakespeare just invented a fictional bisexual love triangle, although it is not like anything in his plays, in other Renaissance writings, or in anything else ever written by a heterosexual man.

Finally, some desperate people have argued that Shakespeare didn't write the sonnets. It wasn't uncommon for publishers to use famous names to sell products by nameless hacks. However, we would be impressed by the suicidal daring of a publisher who bought a pack of homosexual poems and attributed them to a heterosexual public figure.

Although the book was published in Shakespeare's lifetime, the dedication was written (or at least signed) by the publisher. This reads:

TO.THE.ONLIE.BEGETTER.OF.THESE.INSUING.SONNETS. MR.W.H.

ALL.HAPPINESSE.AND.THAT.ETERNITIE.PROMISED.BY.OUR.

EVER-LIVING.POET.WISHETH.THE.WELL-WISHING.ADVENTURER.

IN.SETTING.FORTH.

It's generally agreed that "W.H." is the Fair Youth; in many sonnets, Shakespeare promises him that these verses will make him immortal. Although many theories have been put forward identifying both the Fair Youth and the Dark Lady, none are conclusive, and these two characters now enjoy the limited immortality of the anonymous.

Venus and Adonis, The Rape of Lucrece, The Passionate Pilgrim

These are extra poems for you to read when you've just finished the sonnets, and you're thinking, "Damn, I want more beautiful, immortal poetry." Start reading Venus and Adonis and you'll get over it in record time.

	Importance	Accessibility	Fun
Sonnets	10	4	10
Other poems	6	5	5

CHAPTER 6

Here Come the Puritans:
Parade, Meet Rain

Having spent centuries perfecting their franchise until they could literally charge people money to get into heaven, in the 1500s the Catholic Church was threatened by two new foes. The first was translation. Across Europe, people began translating the Bible into languages that ordinary people understood. The second innovation was the printing press, which spread these translations far and wide.

Suddenly able to understand what Jesus had said, Europeans were stunned to learn that Christianity was difficult. Previously, everyone just prayed to a casket of St. Peter's toenails and slipped the priest a twenty on the way out. But God's actual instructions turned out to involve giving up all your favorite things. Some, fearing hell as never before, rushed to join the more austere Protestant faith. Others were willing to fight to preserve the pay-for-hire God of their forefathers. The result was a bloody era of religious wars in mainland Europe. Regions were depopulated: soldiers pillaged and ravaged and carnaged and roughaged, and famine cleaned up any leftover people. At least those people who were bound for heaven got there a whole lot quicker.

Meanwhile, in England, Parliament tried to take power away from King Charles I, claiming that he was too Catholic-friendly, too bossy, and too expensive. This led to the English Civil War. The Parliamentarians, or "Roundheads," formed the New Model Army, whose troops were largely Puritans inspired by religious conviction. The Royalists, or "Cavaliers," formed an army with no cool nickname and inspired by first-class attire. Needless to say, the Cavaliers were creamed, wiped out, squashed like a bug, toast. Oliver Cromwell became the lord protector, and a new age dawned in which people tried like hell to be Christians and succeeded in becoming curmudgeons.

The Renaissance begins with lusty wenches laughing at dirty jokes and ends with a gouty old pastor whining that women aren't chaste. In fact, John Donne, all by himself, begins and ends that way. By the time of Cromwell's death, the only pleasure left is schadenfreude, and young people grow up wanting to write like Milton. So we present the seventeenth century, a historical period that comes with the consolation that you didn't have to live then. It really, really wasn't better.

THE CAVALIER APPROACH

You can define the Cavalier poets in two ways. Either they were poets who remained sympathetic to the cause of Charles I, or they were poets influenced by the style of Ben Jonson—the "Tribe of Ben." The big names here are Robert Herrick (1591–1674), Richard Lovelace (1618–1657), Sir John Suckling (1609–1642), and Thomas Carew (1595–1640). The archetypal Cavalier poet was a courtier who fought alongside Charles I, shared Charles II's exile, and lost everything, but always looked fantastic.

Their poems are often smutty and almost never serious. Here's a typical short-short lyric from Herrick: "I fain would kiss my Julia's dainty leg, / Which is as white and hairless as an egg." Or here's Suckling's reaction to the complex political tumult of the Civil War: "I am a man of war and might, / And know thus much, that I can fight." These were not deep thinkers, and they didn't innovate at all, and they don't matter. Obviously, it's time for a revival.

Herrick is also the author of the famous "Gather ye rosebuds while ye may," which warns girls that they should sleep with him, because they're getting old, and soon no one will want them. We suggest our male readers try this line for themselves and have a confederate film the results.

	Importance	Accessibility	Fun
Robert Herrick	5	8	7
Richard Lovelace	4	8	6
John Suckling	4	8	5
Thomas Carew	4	7	5

JOHN DONNE, AND ON AND ON:
THE METAPHYSICAL POETS

The term "metaphysical poet" generally indicates a poet who expresses himself through the use of weird and complex images. Instead of singing that his love's like a red, red rose, he explains that: "Our eye-beams twisted, and did thread / Our eyes, upon one double string . . ." For a metaphysical, love talk might begin with the movements of the spheres, pass through the guts of a flea, and end in Christ's eyeball. These far-fetched images are called conceits.

The metaphysicals were heavy-duty Christians, and they expend much of their hysterical weirdness on Christ's passion. If Christ is not bleeding on these poets, Mary Magdalen is weeping on them, or the Virgin is dispensing milk. Anyway, they are wet. None of this dampness is expressed in plain English. In a famous example, Crashaw talks of Christ "opening the purple wardrobe in [his] side." This means that, after being speared, Christ was robed in his purple blood. Reading too much of this morbid stuff can make you think about opening the purple wardrobe in your wrists, but for short stretches, it's intriguingly strange.

The metaphysicals fell out of favor in the next generation, which disliked and dismissed them both for this weirdness and for making people feel stupid. Most of the other poetry we've discussed would have been clear to anyone living at the time. But Donne leaves readers feeling like they have the intellect of a rabbit, and always has.

There is no agreed-upon method for deciding who is a metaphysical poet. Some scholars demand to see conceits, unwholesome religious mania, three academic referees, and hairy palms. Others happily toss in anyone who lived around then. You can trust my classifications, though, because I'm only discussing the handful of poets everyone agrees about. This is not at all because I'm lazy; I just happen also to be lazy. It's a total coincidence.

John Donne (pronounced "dun") (1572–1631)

While Cavalier poetry comes from Jonson, metaphysical poetry comes from John Donne. Since the metaphysicals also influenced early twentieth-century poetry, you could say that contemporary poetry comes from Donne. Then again, you could say that Donne invented the steam engine, whatever, talk is cheap.

Donne seems to have been a likeable character. As a young man, studying law in London, he blew much of his small inheritance on women, drink, and travel. He then scuppered his job prospects for the sake of true love. After his elopement with Anne More, her powerful uncle persecuted Donne relentlessly, until the couple were sunk in long-term poverty. They lived on charity for years. Still, Donne continued to dote on his wife. He never remarried after Anne's death, even though she left him ten children to raise alone.

Always morbid, as a widower Donne became obsessed with death and the hereafter. At one point, he posed for his portrait in the winding-sheet in which he would be buried. He then hung the portrait by his bed, to remind himself every day of the transience of life. He at last turned his gloominess to good advantage by making a career in the Church. As dean of St. Paul's, Donne was reknowned for the brilliance of his sermons, and for that creepy portrait beside his bed.

Unlike most metaphysicals, Donne wrote a huge number of love poems, which mingle sauciness with his school's trademark lunacy. When the love becomes serious, the two lovers' souls leave their bodies and intermingle in the air, while they admire each other's body not in person, but in the reflection given by a tear's surface. Donne's later works employ similar means to express religious devotion. He never had his works printed; they enjoyed a great popularity, however, in manuscript form, and he had begun to spawn other metaphysical poets long before his much-anticipated death.

	Importance	Accessibility	Fun
Donne's poetry	10	3	9

INFORMATION WANTS TO BE WRONG

So why wouldn't Donne have published his works, considering their popularity and his poverty? Well, while the printing press had been invented at this time, copyright hadn't. As a result, it was difficult for authors to make money from their works, even when they were massively popular. This is the reason less affluent writers tended to work for the stage, where they could be sure of being paid.

Writers also had no control over their works or the use of their names. Rabelais took immense pains to expurgate his controversial writings, only to find that someone had published an uncensored version without consulting (or paying) him. Sir Thomas Browne's diaristic musings on his personal feelings about God, *Religio Medici*, fell into the hands of a publisher without his knowledge and became a bestseller behind his back.

It was a golden age of fan fiction, when someone could read *Don Quixote* and fall in love with it, then copy it out, adding a sex scene between Quixote and Sancho, and make more money than Cervantes did from the original. As Lope de Vega wrote in his play *Fuente Ovejuna*: "Many a famous man has been mortified by having fools issue books in his name. Others have written arrant nonsense and attributed it to their enemies out of spite." These are just a few lost joys of the Creative Commons.

OTHER METAPHYSICALS

George Herbert (1593–1633): Herbert's life was alarmingly chaste: the only woman he ever wrote a poem for was his mother. When he writes "Thou art my loveliness, my life, my light, / Beauty alone to me," he's talking to God. In fact, all his poems are about God. Not a single line about a dewdrop or a nightingale, his best friend or the girl next door. God.

When he was on his deathbed, so the story goes, Herbert said his only poetry collection, *The Temple*, should not be published unless it "might turn to the advantage of any dejected poor soul." Otherwise, the poems should be burned. Notice how low a bar Herbert is setting here. He specifies one (1) soul. Nor does he address the possibility that lines like: "Sweet rose . . . Thy root is ever in its grave, / And thou must die" might deject a poor soul who felt just fine before picking up *The Temple*.

Henry Vaughan (1622–1695): Vaughan was inspired by Donne and Herbert. He is known for his depictions of nature, regarded as a source of divine revelation. Yes, more God. "The rising winds, / And falling springs, / Birds, beasts, all things / Adore him in their kinds." Sigh. Oh well, it beats Herbert, whose love of nature was confined to graveworms.

Abraham Cowley (1618–1667): In his lifetime, Cowley was considered an epoch-making genius. His first volume of poetry was printed when he was thirteen and included one long poem written at ten. Late bloomers will be happy to hear that Cowley's reputation has now fizzled out. He is chiefly remembered for being viciously mocked by Samuel Johnson in his *Life of Cowley*: "a degree of meanness that surpasses expectation . . . continued until it is tedious . . . puny poetry . . ." page after page. A literary historian after our own hearts.

Richard Crashaw (1612–1649): Herbert is the sort of person you might expect to stumble upon in a graveyard with suspicious-looking dirt on his hands. Crashaw is creepier. He combines Herbertian religious imagery with signs of sexual arousal. Many of Crashaw's poems are written to holy women, in a spirit of weirdo rapture that is almost sticky.

This is the purple wardrobe man, who also describes the Virgin Mary's breasts as "Two sister-seas of Virgin milk," and Mary Magdalen's tearful eyes as "Two walking baths; two weeping motions; / Portable and compendious oceans." His poems were collected and published under the title *Steps to the Temple*, in tribute to Herbert. With Crashaw, we feel strongly that this temple has odd stains on the floor, and strange cries come from its windows late at night.

Andrew Marvell (1621–1678): Marvell is best known for "To His Coy Mistress," a "please can I put it in?" poem of the sub-type "gather ye rosebuds." The lover here offers the charming argument that if she doesn't have sex with him, when his mistress dies, "worms shall try / That long preserved virginity." Well, if that doesn't get you into the mood.

	Importance	Accessibility	Fun
George Herbert	6	5	5
Henry Vaughan	5	5	4
Abraham Cowley	5	5	3
Richard Crashaw	5	5	6
Andrew Marvell	6	6	6

JOHN BUNYAN (1628–1688)

Bunyan is the voice of Puritan fanaticism, and his self-loathing, raptures, and earnest goofiness have echoes in today's evangelical Christianity. His autobiography, the sweetly named *Grace Abounding to the Chief of Sinners*, is the first of his works that is still read. It's basically a redemption story: bad boy sees the light. This genre remains popular to this day, though the emphasis has shifted. Now we tend to dwell on the badness for most of the book, gloating over the crack-smoking, violence, and degraded sex, until the boy sees the light in the last chapter. In Bunyan's day, the "bad" was hinted at in Chapter 1, while the varieties of light the hero saw were the stuff of fascination.

Bunyan's parents were illiterate, and he himself had only a few years of education. When he married, he and his wife were very poor, "not having so much as a Dish or Spoon betwixt us both." Therefore, his confessions are yeoman confessions: the insights raw, the honesty bald, the naïveté naked, this mental picture getting a little frightening. Okay, so Bunyan's style is only wearing a hat and a loincloth. You get the idea.

While his sincerity is plain and Baptist, his psychology is more troubled teen. At one point, he decides to test his faith by attempting to dry up puddles with the force of prayer. At the last minute, though, he chickens out and doesn't pray, because—what if he fails? That will mean he is going to hell! At another point he panics, realizing there are exemplary Christians who live nearby: maybe after God saved those people, he'd filled his quota for that part of the country. If only Bunyan had been saved a few years sooner, beating those people out! In fact, if only he'd been born as a fish. Fish don't go to hell! At last he relaxes into his faith, and begins to preach this mix of navel-gazing and hysteria to other hapless people. *Grace Abounding* ends at the point where Bunyan is imprisoned for preaching without a license. He would remain in prison for twelve years. By the end of this time, he was preaching to the other prisoners, for which apparently no licence was required. He was also writing *Pilgrim's Progress*.

In *Pilgrim's Progress*, Bunyan's neurosis is rendered as a geography. A man named Christian has become unaccountably nervous about living in a city named Destruction. So he heads off through the Slough of Despond, the Valley of Humiliation, Doubting-Castle, and Vanity Fair, arriving at last at the Land that Flows Milk and Honey. People with names like Vain Confidence, Ignorance, and Money-love try to lead him astray, but he escapes by the staunch help of his friends Faithful and Hopeful. These worthies pass the time by discussing theological questions. There are glimpses of hell and heaven, described with the gusto of a really dedicated dungeon master. Because Bunyan spent much of his life examining his own motives and reactions, the psychology is as acute as the imagery is naïve. It is Augustine's *Confessions* filtered through *The Faerie Queene* by a member of the honest toiling classes.

Pilgrim's Progress was a runaway bestseller. It was such a hit that Bunyan wrote a second part, almost identical to the first, about Christian's wife and sons navigating the same psycho-terrain.

A note: In Bunyan's heaven, the streets are paved with gold, the buildings are coated in jewels, there's great food and even wine—it's a feast of materialism. Except, no sex. This, of course, is the familiar deal one gets wherever Baptism is sold.

Pop Quiz

Bunyan's very first work is a story called "The Life and Death of Mr. Badman." If you've been paying attention, you can answer the following questions without reading a word of the book! Good luck!

a. Did Mr. Badman have a lot of good qualities?
b. The story is told by Mr. Wiseman to Mr. Attentive. Does Attentive listen?
c. What happened to Mr. Badman after he died?

Answers:

a. No.
b. Yes.
c. He went to Mr. Hell.

	Importance	Accessibility	Fun
Grace Abounding	4	7	5
Pilgrim's Progress	9	6	7

JOHN MILTON (1608–1674)

John Milton inaugurates a new tradition of poets whose lives aren't interesting. He worked hard at school, became a schoolmaster, wrote tracts against the tyranny of Archbishop Laud. He began to lose his eyesight, which prevented him from doing anything interesting in the English Civil War. Under Cromwell, he was a secretary, with the thrilling job of writing letters in Latin to other European governments. Milton's first wife left him for two years, apparently because life with her husband was so insufferably tedious. For his political writings, he was briefly imprisoned after the Restoration, but he was soon released back to his life of imponderable boredom. By then, he was totally blind. He was not missing much.

Milton had no sense of humor, wasn't good with women, and had Puritan attitudes toward drinking, theater, sex, and fun in general. So few things in Milton's life are interesting that you could count them on the fingers of one hand and still have enough fingers free to do ten things that are more fun than Milton ever had. However, he did write some of literature's most intellectually ambitious poetry, including the game-changing *Paradise Lost*. This is all the more impressive since, being blind, Milton had to hold the pen in his teeth.

Paradise Lost

Okay, this was actually composed by dictation, and written down by other people, notably Milton's daughters. So far, critics have heroically abstained from theorizing that Milton's daughters are the real authors of *Paradise Lost*.

The poem opens in hell, with all the just-fallen angels sprawled on its burning floor. "Ow," say the ex-angels, "we hate this, make it stop." Satan, though, is undaunted. "Better to reign in hell than serve in heaven," says Satan/Pollyanna. While they can't beat God, he says, they can still bother Him. Since bothering Him directly is too dangerous, Satan sets out to attack the freshly created Earth, thus becoming the first terrorist in history.

The rebellion originally began when God introduced the angels to Jesus, the new kid in town. "This is my son," said God—though since there was no woman in sight, the angels must have been scratching their heads as to what "son" meant. Clearly God just created Jesus the same as anyone—but the angels all bit their tongues and clapped loudly. Now they were expected to obey and venerate this Johnny-come-lately. And for the rest of the book, God and Jesus act as a little mutual admiration society.

It seems very understandable, then, that Satan could rally a force of rebellious angels overnight. Roughly a third of the angels join the rebellion.

Milton's epic poem is a masterpiece of fantastic writing, somewhat marred by a ridiculous premise. Here, all-powerful God creates Adam and Eve, who are beloved by Him above all things. He gives them one rule: do not eat the fruit of a particular tree. He puts the tree near their house, so it's handy. God knows ahead of time that Adam and Eve will be tricked by Satan into eating the apple. In fact, He spends a lot of time talking about exactly what's going to happen and how well it suits His plans.

Once they have eaten the fruit, God punishes Adam and Eve, and Satan, and the snake who was possessed by Satan, and all the other animals, and the plants. There is endless punishment from this one apple, the apple is like a clown car of punishment.

Milton claimed that he wrote all this "to justify the ways of God to man." If so, he did a lousy job. William Blake proposed that Milton was "of the Devil's party without knowing it." This is a polite way of saying Milton's God is a humorless asshole, and his Jesus an insufferable brownnosing prig.

A true Puritan, Milton has Adam and Eve doing a full day's work in Eden; they comment that it would be terrible if they didn't feel they had earned their keep. They also have sex in Eden—in fact, it comes up so often that the reader begins to feel Milton was touching himself when he wrote these parts. In the angels' rebellion, Satan invents artillery, which almost defeats the celestial forces, until they come up with the tactic of tearing up mountains by their roots and dumping them on Satan and the other bad angels. Boom! Baff! Pow! In short, through the gorgeous wordsmithery and the seventeenth-century pedantry, readers will glimpse the fuzzy outline of a really, really, immature guy.

BOREDOM ADVISORY

For modern readers, Milton's masterpiece might more aptly be named *Consciousness Lost*. Whenever the narrative pace seems about to pick up, Milton flies into action, writing a long-winded metaphor which references one obscure Greek myth, two Scythian rivers, and three theological concepts. No foregone conclusion can be arrived at without several pages of argument. Happily an abridged version of *Consciousness Lost* is available to us in the first few pages of Genesis.

MILTON ON WOMEN

At Cambridge, for his long hair and dainty manner, Milton was called the "Lady of Christ's College." Wherever we find a young male writer being called effeminate, we know there's misogyny a-brewing. Milton is no exception.

As long as a person had male genitalia, Milton believed in that person's liberty; he was an uncompromising republican, for people with male genitals. Girls were different. In *Paradise Lost*, Eve tells Adam: "My Author and Disposer, what thou bidd'st / Unargu'd I obey; so God ordains / God is thy Law, thou mine: to know no more / is Woman's happiest knowledge . . ." If this is the good girl, Sin—Satan's wife/daughter—is the bad girl. She is represented as half-woman, half-snake. Sin is surrounded by a brood of hounds which, from time to time, dive back into her womb. There they feed on her guts.

If you are wondering how all this was received by the women in his life, his eldest daughter's reaction to the news of Milton's third marriage offers a clue. "That is no news, to hear of his wedding," she said. "If I could hear of his death, that would be something."

But Milton isn't dead yet.

He has time to write two more long poems: *Paradise Regained* and *Samson Agonistes*.

Paradise Regained disappointingly does not pick up with Adam and Eve, but switches to the temptation of Jesus Christ by Satan in the desert. Since Jesus doesn't feel tempted, nothing happens at all. The plot is basically Satan saying to Jesus, Please let something happen in this book, please, please. Jesus crosses his arms with a superior smile and replies, I see through all your tricks.

Samson Agonistes is much better. It offers us Samson in the days of his servitude, blinded and lamenting in front of his Gaza prison. No matter how much you may have grown to dislike Milton, the autobiographical element here is sad.

> Light the prime work of God to me is extinct
> And all her various objects of delight
> Anull'd . . . In power of others, never in my own . . .
> The sun to me is dark / And silent as the Moon . . .
> Myself my Sepulcher, a moving Grave.

Happily the comic relief is close behind. Delilah comes to beg forgiveness from Samson, explaining that she betrayed him not only for the money, but to serve her God and her people, many of whom Samson had, after all, killed. "Out, out, hyena," Samson replies. He then launches into Milton's favorite material: "God's universal Law / Gave to the man despotic power / Over his female . . ." A chorus of Hebrews nods approvingly, while Delilah walks out, rolling her eyes and swinging her bag of money. Samson then goes and does his grand finale with the pillars, squashing himself along with the Philistine nobles, and freeing Delilah to remarry.

There are also a great many shorter poems, dating from all periods of Milton's life. The most beloved is his sonnet on his blindness, which begins "When I consider how my light is spent . . ." and concludes with the axiom "They also serve who only stand and wait." (We imagine his daughters making faces at each other as they copied this one.) Then there's the sonnet in which he dreams of seeing his late wife—"my late espoused saint," as he calls her. This has long puzzled scholars because the poem is convincingly mawkish, but it's anyone's guess which wife is meant.

	Importance	Accessibility	Fun
Paradise Lost	10	4	4
Paradise Regained	5	4	3
Samson Agonistes	6	5	5
Other poems	6	5	5

EXTRA CREDIT: THREE ODDITIES

Every educated person should know who John Donne and John Milton are. No one, however, really needs to know who Samuel Butler, Sir Robert Burton, and Izaak Walton are. While they have dropped out of the Western canon, they are still great for dropping into conversations. Neurotic people should already be intrigued, and rarin' to know this superfluous crap. Neurotics, you are among friends here.

Samuel Butler's *Hudibras* (1663–1678) was a runaway bestseller in its day. It's a mock-epic poem about the Roundheads, featuring a Quixote-like hero (Hudibras) with a Sancho-like sidekick (Ralph). But while Cervantes loved his ridiculous knight and peasant sidekick, Butler hates everyone. Throughout the three books of *Hudibras*, Butler heaps derision and hatred upon his heroes and upon every other character. Even the horse comes off badly. The book is also written in an ear-shattering doggerel style. A typical rhyme is: "Pulpit, Drum Ecclesiastic, / Was beat with fist, instead of a stick." In case you aren't getting the drift; now that that you know what *Hudibras* is, you can avoid it.

Infinitely more lovable is Sir Robert Burton's encyclopedia of lunacy, *The Anatomy of Melancholy* (1621). At one-thousand-odd pages, this book is not designed to be read, but to be sampled. People have been sampling it and marveling for centuries. Burton begins with the ultimate cause of all human unhappiness ("the sin of our first parent Adam," what else?) and proceeds through every proximate cause that years of work and his fertile mind could discover. He is a cornucopia of great insights, anecdotes, and facts, gleaned from previous writers and repackaged in his slow, straying prose. It feels like a gourmet meal with a bewildering number of courses. Here, he advises the reader to go to sleep lying on the right side; there, he tells the story of how Caracalla accidentally saw his mother-in-law's breasts, fell in love, and married her. And more of the same for another 999 pages. The book itself is as heavy as a four-year-old child, and useless for reading on the subway, in bed, on the toilet, or sitting in a chair. If it falls on you, good night. Frail people may need the help of the fire department to read this book.

Our third oddity is Izaak Walton's *The Compleat Angler* (1653–1676), a whimsical—and once fantastically popular—fishing primer. It's presented as a dialogue between a keen fisherman (Piscator) and a reformed hunter (Venator) who becomes the fisherman's apprentice. They wander through the idyllic English countryside, stopping at inns where their catch is cooked and the beds are made with lavender-scented sheets. Piscator waxes eloquent about the glory of angling, citing the fact that Christ chose three fishermen to be his disciples and reciting fishing poetry from memory. Walton was a friend of Donne, Herbert, and other metaphysical poets and shares their finicky morals, but not their psychic clamminess. *The Compleat Angler* is therefore good, clean fun. You get the sense that all pleasures but fishing are snares of the Prince of Lies. It is also piercingly, almost antiseptically, English.

	Importance	Accessibility	Fun
Hudibras	2	4	2
The Anatomy of Melancholy	4	5	8
The Compleat Angler	2	6	4

CHAPTER 7

France and England in the Seventeenth Century: The Shallows

Charles II was restored to the throne in 1660, amid great rejoicing from his people, who were good and sick of civil war, Puritans, and a Jesus with standards. The reign of Charles II is commonly known as the Restoration period because of the totally obvious reason. His court was reknowned for its debauchery. The king himself had flocks of illegitimate children by his flocks of mistresses—who were not just openly acknowledged but celebrities. An extreme but not atypical courtier was John Wilmot, Earl of Rochester, who actually briefly posed as a gynecologist. These people put the ew into ooh la la.

This is the golden age of frivolity. Cattiness is raised to a high art; in both England and France, masterpieces of gossip are written. Farce flourishes, and smut thrives. Smut really thrives. This smut only wants a video camera to make it porn.

Reading the works of this period may not make you a better person. However, it will make you feel like a better person by comparison.

THE DIARIES OF SAMUEL PEPYS (1633–1703)

Pepys was an official in Charles II's Navy Board, who lived on the pleasant periphery of the Restoration court. His diaries include eyewitness accounts of the return of Charles II, the plague, and the Great Fire of London—but also the mundane routines and thoughts of 1660s Britain. When escorting the new king home after twenty years' exile, Pepys notes that the king's dog "[dirtied] the boat, which made us laugh, and methink that a King and all that belong to him are but just as others are." Or he tells of spending a night in conversation with a charming widow who "seems to love her niece very well, and was so glad (which was pretty odd) that since she came hither her breasts began to swell, she being afeard before that she would have none."

The great preoccupations of Mr. Pepys are chasing girls, amassing his fortune, music, and chasing girls. He accepts bribes—a barrel of sturgeon, a set of flagons, or just cash money—with a winning embarrassment. Here is Pepys receiving a letter from an office-seeker: "I did not open it till I came to my office; and there I broke it open, not looking into it till all the money was out, that I might say I saw no money in the paper if I should ever be questioned." Like his greed, his vanity seems oddly innocent: he writes with pride how, when his household is singing in the garden, the neighbors open their windows to listen.

Above all, the diaries are the record of a happy life. When Pepys records going to bed while his wife and servants stay up to make pies for Christmas, a potent contentment rises from the book. For a moment, you bask in the sense of being there, in Pepys's cozy house in jolly Restoration England. Then he refers to his chamber pot, and the glamour fades.

	Importance	Accessibility	Fun
Diaries	5	9	9

JOHN DRYDEN (1631–1700)

Dryden started his career with a eulogy of Cromwell. When the king returned, without missing a beat he burst into song about the awesomeness of Charles II. His works for the stage include prim tut-tutting about the immorality of contemporary comedies, and immoral comedies. When he isn't flattering the ruler, he is pandering to popular taste. Yet we never get the feeling that Dryden is laughing behind his hand. He seems to have been no simple hack, but a full-blown hypocrite.

In Restoration England, he was considered the genius to beat. The period is sometimes even called the Age of Dryden. Since then, his reputation has lost ground with every generation. This is partly due to the topical nature of his best works. Once we lost interest in the Popish Plot, British naval wars with the Netherlands, and the Whig thing with the Tory other thing . . . well, we lost interest. No matter how great Dryden's treatment of these subjects, our indifference to them is greater. One thing you can say about us, boy, when we lose interest, it stays lost.

Another problem Dryden has for contemporary audiences is that most of his work is written in heroic couplets. For reference:

Heroic couplets are the kind of verse
In which the second line rhymes with the first
The third and fourth will also rhyme, of course,
And sooner or later, some rhyme will be forced.

It's hard for us to take heroic couplets seriously now. It's like poetry read by William Shatner or a cartoon duck. To give Dryden his due, it's also incredibly hard to write heroic couplets well, especially in a long poem. Most products of the style—Butler's *Hudibras*, for instance—are both stilted and flat-footed. Dryden's verse seems magically natural, as if the rhymes were falling into place by chance, in a monkeys-with-typewriters-producing-*Hamlet* fluke. His style is miraculously nimble, if dated; it's like watching Fred Astaire dance.

Unfortunately, Dryden also lacks all passion. He sounds like a priggish schoolboy writing a composition on "Why We Should Obey the Laws," or "The Hazards of Gateway Drugs." The closest he comes to genuine feeling is when he attacks other poets, which he does at every opportunity. Dryden is the main reason anyone remembers the poet Thomas Shadwell, for instance. Thanks to Dryden, what they mostly remember is that Shadwell was very fat.

There is no compelling reason to read Dryden. The bottom line is, he wasn't writing for us. Giving his books to twenty-first-century readers is like feeding cat food to a Chevy, or putting unleaded into your cat.

	Importance	*Accessibility*	*Fun*
Poems	8	5	3
Plays	4	7	3

RESTORATION DRAMA

With the Puritans out of the way, London's theaters reopened. At first, the companies staged old plays—Shakespeare and Jonson were favorites. But before long, people lost all self-control and began to write plays of their own.

Restoration drama is Elizabethan drama, minus. There is really nothing wrong with Restoration drama, unless someone wants you to read it. The craft and intelligence is all there, but the genius somehow isn't. With the exception of a few standout comedies, these plays feel like they were written to be background noise. Given the rowdy nature of Restoration playhouses, this was probably wise.

There were some important innovations in the theatrical practice of the time. In Elizabethan times, it was considered immoral for women to appear on stage. In the Restoration period, they dispensed with the stupid idea that immorality was bad. Actresses appeared, and were relentlessly presented as sex objects. Also, while Elizabethan stages were bare, Restoration stages employed complex machines and moving scenery. Actors would fly over the stage and leap from trapdoors, while turning into crocodiles and singing arias. In the background, ships sailed and the city of Carthage appeared on the horizon, in flames.

Another change was the loss of the groundlings, those low-class members of the audience who had paid only a penny to stand at the Globe. The cheap seats were now priced at a shilling, making them unaffordable for the poor. The new audience was mainly gentry, and the only members of the toiling classes present were the prostitutes who worked the audience. They wore full-face masks—a common accessory for Restoration women when they were up to no good.

Restoration comedy was written with the morals of the court in mind, so it's common for every human weakness to be crowded into one play. A typical premise, in Wycherley's *The Country Wife* (1675), for example, has a London rake putting about the story that he has been castrated, so that he can cuckold husbands without arousing suspicion. One scene is notorious for its repeated use of a double entendre on "getting into her the back way." While the pace is frantic, there's an enervating cynicism and shallowness in these plays. This sentiment from the heroine of Congreve's *The Way of the World* (1700) sums up the outlook: "One's cruelty is one's power, and when one parts with one's cruelty, one parts with one's power, and when one has parted with that, I fancy one's old and ugly."

The tragedies, by contrast, are stridently moral. A favorite trick was to revise one of Shakespeare's plots so that good was rewarded and evil punished. An example is Dryden's *All for Love* (1678), which is basically Shakespeare's *Antony and Cleopatra* if it was boring. Then there is Nahum Tate's *King Lear* (1681), which is *King Lear* if it was boring. Of course, many Restoration dramas are boring without Shakespeare's help.

One interesting exception both to the morality and the dullness is Thomas Otway's *Venice Preserved* (1682). In this bloody, bloody drama, a revolution is planned against a corrupt and repressive Venetian Senate. The revolutionaries and the senators are variously flawed, and neither cause is presented as just. Every single character does the wrong thing; the sympathetic characters die like flies. It also includes what is possibly the first humiliation-fetish scene in stage history: an aged senator gets his mistress to whip him, barks like a dog while fawning on the ground, and then falls to worshipping her feet.

	Importance	Accessibility	Fun
The Country Wife	5	8	8
The Way of the World	6	8	8
All for Love	5	7	5
King Lear	3	6	3
Venice Preserved	6	6	8

APHRA BEHN (1640–1689)

Another first in Restoration drama is the appearance of female playwrights. The most eminent of these was Aphra Behn. In *A Room of One's Own*, Virginia Woolf says that all women should "let flowers fall upon the tomb of Aphra Behn, for it was she who earned them the right to speak their minds." This is hyperbole, unless Behn's activism was very slow-acting; it took another 250 years for women to get the vote. However, if the flowers are already falling, let them.

We know very little about Behn's life. We do know she went to South America as a teenager. We know she spied for the British government in Antwerp and that she turned to writing because the government was slow in paying her wages for her services. Her pen name, Astraea, was originally her secret spy name. In short, the only thing we know for certain is that Aphra was way cooler than Dryden. She is also widely considered to have been bisexual, based on the fact that we know nothing about her sex life.

Her reputation has had its ups and downs. She was greatly respected in her lifetime, but Victorian critics hated her: "She was a mere harlot . . . a wanton hussy." Contemporary feminist critics find "homosocial" and "gender deconstructing" themes in her work, which is their way of saying they like something. On the other hand, Harold Bloom has called Behn a "fourth-rate playwright." This is very unfair: Aphra Behn is a second-rate playwright. Also way cooler than Harold Bloom.

She was the author of at least seventeen plays. They are rollicking, filthy, witty romps, full of rakes, courtesans, lusty maidens, and bon mots. *The Rover*, about Cavaliers in exile, is the best, and the best known. It features a depiction of Behn's friend, the noted ne'er-do-well Lord Rochester (see below). In typical Restoration fashion, the women are always dressing in men's clothes, the better to chase boys (and to let the audience see their legs in tights). Meanwhile, the heroes are always on the point of raping the women, when they aren't two-timing them with a prostitute. Ha ha ha! Sex can be so funny!

Behn also wrote a short novel, *Oroonoko*, which is one of the first critical works about slavery. In it, a perfectly honorable, brilliant, and also beautiful African prince is betrayed into slavery by his rival. He, and his beautiful girlfriend Imoinda, are taken to South America—still looking beautiful, we might add (and Behn does add, in every place where an adjective fits). In South America, they look fantastic, and are duly admired by the whole colony. However, promises to free them are not kept, so Oroonoko foments a slave rebellion. Offered an amnesty, he surrenders. Naïve fool! He is dismembered alive by the lousy lying colonists. He dies without a peep, noble to the last, and his several pieces looking simply goddamned beautiful.

While this book is generally read as a criticism of slavery, it should be noted that Behn was a passionate royalist, and apparently thought nothing of the rank-and-file Africans being kept in slavery. What bothers her is when the prince—whether a noble African like Oroonoko or a sleazy Englishman like Charles II—gets no respect.

Oroonoko has also been called the first novel, making it the first novel written by a woman that has been called the first novel—but not the last.

	Importance	Accessibility	Fun
The Rover	4	8	7
Oroonoko	5	8	7

JOHN WILMOT, EARL OF ROCHESTER (1647–1680)

You may imagine that when we mentioned Rochester's time posing as a gynecologist, we told the best part of this story. In fact, the imposture was more complex. It began when he disgraced himself at court and had to lie low. His way of lying low was to pose as an Italian astrologer and snake oil salesman called Alexander Bendo. As part of his cover, he invented a wife, who treated women for barrenness. Mrs. Bendo (Rochester in women's clothes) apparently succeeded in impregnating more than one of her patients.

Rochester is also notable for having kidnapped a girl named Elizabeth Malet—which he might have gotten away with, except that she was of his own class. For this, he spent some time in the Tower. Elizabeth, though, forgave him, and they later married. Rochester had this effect on women—and seemingly on Charles II, who repeatedly forgave him for his many offences. Rochester once fled from court after mistakenly giving the king a scurrilous poem about the king himself, instead of another Charles had asked for. Anyone who has ever sent an e-mail to the wrong person will appreciate poor Rochester's panic when he realized he had sent the king this:

> Poor prince! thy prick, like thy buffoons at Court,
> Will govern thee because it makes thee sport.
> 'Tis sure the sauciest prick that e'er did swive,
> The proudest, peremptoriest prick alive.
> Though safety, law, religion, life lay on 't,
> 'Twould break through all to make its way to cunt.
> Restless he rolls about from whore to whore,
> A merry monarch, scandalous and poor.

and so on, until he ends with the utterly damning:

> . . . had I but time to tell ye,
> The pains it costs to poor, laborious Nelly,
> Whilst she employs hands, fingers, mouth, and thighs,
> Ere she can raise the member she enjoys.
> All monarchs I hate, and the thrones they sit on,
> From the hector of France to the cully of Britain.

From Rochester's poetry one discovers how very little profanity has changed in the intervening 350 years. The c-word, the f-bomb—all censorship's old friends are here. (Great job, censorship! Another two hundred years or so, and babies will be born swearing.) His poetry is so potently filthy that even the Restoration wits deplored him—while reading him. He died at thirty-three, of alcoholism, syphilis, God striking him down, that kind of thing. On his deathbed, he supposedly renounced his atheism. His penitent speech was published and became a popular tract, although contemporary scholars believe it was no more authentic than Mrs. Bendo.

	Importance	Accessibility	Fun
Poems	3	7	8

THE COURT OF THE SUN KING

In France, the reign of Louis XIV began and quickly stretched on endlessly. For his belief that everything revolved around him, Louis was called the Sun King. The Sun King disappointingly did not live in a ziggurat, nor did he preside over primitive rites involving gold masks, the hearts of virgins, and a live volcano. Instead, he built Versailles, which is fine, if you like that kind of thing, but it's no ziggurat. Likewise, a rebellion against him, called the Fronde, did not involve giant tendrils of alien vegetation creeping into his bed to throttle him. This is just one of the reasons we find French history disappointing.

So we're at Versailles. The flowers in the beds are changed every day for variety; there are a zillion fountains. Men wear puffy satin bloomers with tights and high-heeled shoes. They gesture gracefully using slender canes with ribbons entwined around them. It is, in a word, gay.

This period of French history is called the Grand Siècle. No, we cannot tell you why. Why is a dog called a "dog"? Why does that dog say "woof"? These are questions for scientists.

THE PRINCESSE DE CLEVES
by Madame de la Fayette (1634–1693)

The Princesse de Cleves is the only one of the many novels written in the era of Louis XIV, often by members of the higher nobility, that is still widely read. Partly this is because it is the only one that can be read. The then-popular novels of Madeleine de Scudéry came in ten fat volumes: the much-beloved *L'Astree of Honoré d'Urfé* was about shepherds. By contrast, *The Princesse de Cleves* is a compact and neatly plotted love story. Also, while it poses as a historical novel, it's really a deft portrait of intrigues at the court of the Sun King, written by a jaded insider.

This is a novel of the movement called *préciosité* (see page 106). While the setting is the ultra-cynical world of the court, the main characters are strenuously, almost extraterrestrially, noble. Two out of three of them literally die of love. While they are suffering major organ failure from their love, they remain extraordinarily polite, expressing their passion in terms like "If I dared, I should even say that it is within your power to make it your duty, one day, to preserve the feelings you have for me." To which the only answer can be: "My duty forbids me ever to think of anyone, and less of you than of anyone else in the world, for reasons which you do not know." Well then!

Meanwhile, the story is alive with filthy subplots. While the heroine agonizes over how to remain perfectly faithful, every other person she knows is blithely cheating. The heroine and her *amants* are like the only prudish members of a troop of bonobos.

At last, the eponymous heroine rejects her beloved, the Duc de Nemours, for the reason that her late husband (dead of you-know-what) was "the only man in the world able to preserve something of love within marriage." That is, the *duc* is bound to get tired of her and cheat, so why bother consummating their relationship? Much better to go to a convent and die of love.

But, we hear you asking, is it the first novel? Well, it is the first French novel, according to no less an authority than Stendhal. This might have surprised Madame de Lafayette, since it was her third.

	Importance	Accessibility	Fun
The Princesse de Cleves	6	8	8

THE SALONS AND LES PRECIEUSES

It was in this period that France developed the tradition of literary salons—homes at which the intelligentsia and high society would meet, once a week, to practice the art of conversation. These were mainly presided over by women. Madame de la Fayette had one of the most successful; among her guests were Molière, la Fontaine, Corneille, and Mme. de Sévigné.

The salons of this period were also the breeding ground for the cult of the *precieuses*. The *precieuses* prided themselves on being hothouse flowers. They were pathologically refined and particularly concerned to both sanitize and adorn the French language. Plain words were considered tasteless, and replaced by bizarre circumlocutions. A hat was called the defier of the weather, tears the pearls of Iris, teeth the furniture of the mouth. Antoine de Somaize wrote a dictionary of these expressions, so that a neophyte wanting to ask for a glass of water would know to call it an interior bath. In *precieuses* salons like Mlle. de Scudery's, the guests used aestheticized nicknames like Bradamire, Barsinian, Hamilcar, and Sappho. The *precieuses* prided themselves on the fact that common people could not understand them, or stand them. Many of their linguistic innovations persist in modern-day French, which explains a lot.

They are mainly remembered for the satire of their manners written by Molière, *Les Precieuses Ridicules*. The play is really about a pair of provincial girls clumsily aping their Parisian betters. Still, it scored a few points against the more ludicrous aspects of the salons, like the idea of women thinking. Later critics gave up the subtleties of Molière and simply accused the *precieuses* of being ugly, frigid spinsters. Here we have arrived at the common phenomenon of goons jeering at ninnies. Nowadays, we call this phenomenon "class struggle." In France, it would lead, by various winding paths, to that most trenchant critic of upper-class affectations, the guillotine.

MOLIÈRE (1622–1673)

Molière was the stage name of Jean-Baptiste Poquelin. The son of an upholsterer, Jean-Baptiste spent his youth as a ragged actor playing the provinces with his ragged troupe. His works show the effects of being written by an actor and impresario: they are always both character-based and box office–based. Molière always played the lead in his own plays; he actually died from a pulmonary hemorrhage suffered while he was playing the hypochondriac in *The Imaginary Invalid*.

His company's acting was renowned for its naturalness. In an era when actors howled their lines while flailing their arms, Molière's players spoke and walked around. This was considered tasteless when the company performed tragedy, in the same way saying "teeth" instead of "the furniture of the mouth" was tasteless. With a comedy, however, the audience could not help noticing that they were laughing.

Molière's plays all center on a main character with a striking flaw. Other, normal characters are duped, bullied, and annoyed by the aberrant person. Finally, he is punished, and happiness is restored. So in *Tartuffe*, a religious hypocrite tries to fleece a pious man; in *The Misanthrope*, a curmudgeon tries to marry a light-minded flirt; in *The Bourgeois Gentleman*, a middle-class man tries to marry his daughter to an aristocrat. Then they fail. Molière loves a simple premise with a pat ending.

The execution is likewise simple. The characters spend most of the first act explaining to one another who they are. "I am only a servant girl," the servant girl tells her mistress, "while you are wealthy, since the death of your husband who ruled you with an iron fist. Since he died, I'll say you are a happier lady! You are all smiles, especially for the handsome Valere, the son of that miser, the one who expects to marry you because he thinks his money will appeal to you despite his decrepit looks, for he is over fifty."

When he is not making fun of the miser for being miserly, Molière likes to have his characters comically beat one another with sticks, or trade leering innuendos. All this is in rhyming couplets. So:

> The dirty fellow thinks he'll give my wife a pat,
> But all he will feel is the wood of my bat.

At this point, you may be shivering at the thought of Molière. The trouble is, he really is funny. He is not just something the French are trying to do to us because they relish human suffering. You may be above this sort of material. You may be the sort of person who frowns in concern when you see a man dressed as a lady fall into a barrel of eggs. Still it will go on being funny, over your dead body eventually.

	Importance	Accessibility	Fun
The Miser	8	8	8
Tartuffe	10	8	8
The Misanthrope	8	7	7

CORNEILLE (1606–1684) AND RACINE (1639–1699)

Unlike Molière, these writers are something the French are trying to do to us because they relish human suffering. The French are failing, as the rest of the world has mostly ignored these playwrights. Refusing to admit defeat, the French continue valiantly pretending to think they're as good as Shakespeare. They even go to see productions of Racine and Corneille. This is a measure of how much French people hate us for being taller than they are.

Corneille is the author of *Le Cid*, *Cinna*, and *Polyeucte*; Racine is the author of *Andromaque*, *Phèdre*, and *Athalie*. Tell these plays apart. Just try it. The difference between Corneille and Racine is that Corneille came first and Racine is also a town in Wisconsin. Any other things that seem like differences are just some schmutz that got on your reading glasses.

One of the first things you will notice about Corneille/Racine is that there are no jokes. There are no witticisms, there is no lighthearted fun. Mixing tragedy and comedy was then considered in poor taste. No reason was given. It just was, in the same way wearing a wig that looked like a full-grown sheep was in good taste.

Corneille/Racine do not attempt to make characters or situations seem real. They are instead "noble." Also, no one in a Corneille/Racine play ever says just one sentence. All language comes in monologues. Finally, in Corneille/Racine, everyone has grand, suicidal emotions. No one in these plays just loves someone a normal amount. To deal with this hysteria, the thoughtful playwright provides each main character with a confidant, a sort of live-in therapist, to whom he can tell all his feelings. The playwright has apparently forgotten the audience is also in the room—if the audience is still in the room.

If you were really determined to enjoy this, you could concentrate on the loftiness of the sentiments and force a thin smile onto your face. Don't. That will only encourage the French. From kindness, we want to gently steer them away from things like tragedy and back to things at which they excel—like French accents and making smoking look cool.

	Importance	Accessibility	Fun
Corneille	7	5	1
Racine	7	5	1

EXTRA CREDIT IN FRENCH

One of the absolute foundation stones of French literature and culture is La Fontaine (1621–1695), whose *Fables* in verse are so well known in France that a Frenchman can say simply "It is like the lion and the rat," or "She is the vixen who married the hound," or "It is a case of the frogs, the priest, and the enema," and everyone knows exactly what is meant. Ha ha ha! they laugh, in French. Meanwhile, we stare past them, silently congratulating ourselves on how much taller we are.

On the whole, La Fontaine's fables are pretty entertaining, they're good fables and all. However, think carefully before you buy a copy: do you really want to understand what the French are talking about?

Another much-beloved and much-French writer is Mme. de Sévigné (1626–1696), whose *Letters* contain all the gossip fit to print about the French nobility. The letters are almost all to her daughter, who was the love of Mme. de Sévigné's life. This personal affection lends warmth to the icy cynicism of the time. At one point, Sévigné reports how Vatel, the maître d'hotel to the prince, stabbed himself to death for shame, because a shipment of fish didn't arrive in time for a party. She comments chillingly: "It is an annoying thing to happen to a fete costing fifty thousand francs." Later, we have: "The Duchesse de Bouillon went to ask the Voisin for a little poison to kill off an old husband who was killing her with boredom, and for some scheme for marrying a young man. . . . It was a real laugh." But there is a bracing frankness in "M. de Morangis is dead, and the Barillons are very afflicted and very rich. That silences the natural feelings."

	Importance	Accessibility	Fun
Fables, La Fontaine	3	8	5
Letters, Madame de Sévigné	4	8	6

CHAPTER 8

The Age of Reason or:
When People Wised Up and
Started Believing What We Believe

As the seventeenth century came to a close, a new age of revolutionary thinking began. People began to question orthodox theology more boldly—and then to question the brutal punishment of people who questioned orthodox theology. Soon they had invented something called Liberalism, which continues to cause trouble to this day. In its then form, it overturned cherished beliefs about the hereditary rights of kings and eventually spawned the French Revolution. In its current form, it is why mothers no longer care for their children, but instead gad about having "careers," leaving the children to be raised by a deadly cocktail of Facebook, cocktails, and gateway drugs that disappointingly lead to Lipitor. It is why we can be put in jail for celebrating Christmas, and why men no longer wear hats, except when they're ironic jazz hats and the men don't realize what they look like. It is why men aren't men, women aren't women, and tautologies aren't tautologies. In short, it is the best thing ever, and we should be eternally grateful to these people for inventing it.

While Restoration literature is the voice of the nobility, eighteenth-century literature is by, for, and about the middle class. Literature becomes professionalized, and even serious authors begin to write "Five Things No Girl Should Wear" pieces for journals. While poetry continues to be read, the novel now takes center stage, presumably because it's better value for the money.

A note: the eighteenth-century novel is subtly different from our conventional novels. It tends to break the fourth wall, reminding the reader again and again that this is a novel and that the author can, if he wishes, turn the hero into a rabbit at any moment. It also tends to go off on tangents, suddenly breaking into a parody of a completely different literary form. In short, it is what we now call postmodern.

Every innovation of twentieth-century postmodernist fiction arose, was imitated, became a genre, and grew stale in the eighteenth century. In fact, the conventional realist novel should be called post-postmodernism, which would make modernism post-post-postmodernism. In any case, this is more evidence that those who forget history are doomed to repeat it, with the happy proviso that sometimes what they forgot was really cool.

ALEXANDER POPE (1688–1744)

Alexander Pope was the acknowledged Great Poet of the Augustan Age. Famous and beloved, he nonetheless managed to have a miserable life. Unlike most writers whose acquaintance you have made in these pages, Pope was not to blame for his own misery. The poor little guy had rotten luck.

First off, he had tuberculosis. It wasn't the simple cough type, either; Pope had it in his bones. This gave him a hunchback, as well as breathing problems, chronic pain, and fever. Due to the degeneration of his bones, he was only four feet six inches tall. Pope was also Catholic, in a time when Catholics were persecuted. They couldn't teach school, vote, attend university, or go to heaven. It is not known whether Pope shat in the woods, but it would have been just his luck.

While successful men can usually get some groupies, regardless of their looks, women drew the line at Mr. Pope. He did supposedly have one affair, with his lifelong friend, Martha Blount; some even speculate that they were secretly married. However, there is no solid evidence that they ever "did it." Worse, according to Samuel Johnson, during Pope's last illness, Blount met a messenger from his sickbed with the cry, "What! Not dead yet!" Married or unmarried, she was waiting on an inheritance worth a few thousand pounds.

If his health and love life were dismal, his career was the polar opposite. By the time he was twenty-two, he was a celebrated poet, hobnobbing not only with great writers such as Swift, Addison, and Steele, but with the crème de la crème of society. To give you an idea, here's one of Pope's best-known epigrams:

EPIGRAM ENGRAVED ON THE COLLAR OF A DOG

WHICH I GAVE TO HIS ROYAL HIGHNESS

"I AM HIS HIGHNESS' DOG AT KEW;

PRAY TELL ME, SIR, WHOSE DOG ARE YOU?"

The take-away message is that he knew the prince well enough to give him a dog as a present. So, while it may not have been all roses for Pope, at least he was a big celebrity. If he felt like it, he could snub all the healthy, attractive, pain-free people in the street who were going to heaven. In fact, those beautiful people were likely to have a portrait of Pope hanging in their houses (in which you couldn't tell, incidentally, that he was a four-foot-six hunchback).

Most of Pope's major works are essays written in heroic couplets. The first was his "Essay on Criticism." This is what the name says: a rhyming essay on literary criticism. It has the feather-light wit and elegance that made Pope famous; it has brilliant put-downs of critics. It has deathless lines, like "Fools rush in where angels fear to tread." But ultimately, none of this changes the fact that it's a work of eighteenth-century literary criticism. If you really grit your teeth and pretend you're in the eighteenth century, you can still read it with pleasure. As soon as you relax your vigilance, though, it's like listening to a lecture on Hispano-Christian motifs in the weavings of the Huguenots.

His later essays—the "Essay on Man" and his Epistles—are worth a try, even if rhymes and essays leave you cold. The arguments are genuinely interesting, and the poetry is so cunningly crafted and lucid, it has the ingenious quality of a Bible inscribed on a grain of rice. Pope's poetry is so perfect that some people dislike it for that reason alone. It's too perfect, they say; it's sterile, or cold, or just better than their poetry. This is an okay reason to dislike Pope, but it's probably cooler to go the route of the Romantics, who felt that Pope's poetry was no poetry at all. It lacked Imagination and Beauty. It was all a lot of syllogisms and paradoxes like "His Principle of action once explore, / That instant 't is his Principle no more."

This is less of a problem in Pope's major non-essay work, "The Rape of the Lock," a jeu d'esprit about a rejected suitor cutting off one of the tresses of a celebrated beauty. It is based on a true story, but Pope riffs on it to a startling degree. He adds sylphs, gnomes, and a pagan goddess, and ends the story with the lock of hair being immortalized in the stars as a new constellation. Because of the flippant abandon of his riffing, it's surprisingly fun to read; a deliriously girly piece of tomfoolery, and possibly the only classic work about grooming. A perfect gift for that homophobic friend you don't like.

Three moons of Uranus were named after characters in "The Rape of the Lock": Belinda, Ariel, and Umbriel. Belinda is the heroine, Ariel a sylph, and Umbriel an evil gnome. Uranus's twenty-four other satellites are all named after characters from Shakespeare. An ice giant planet, Uranus is composed primarily of hydrogen and helium. It has the coldest surface atmosphere in our solar system. Alexander Pope probably couldn't have survived there, even if he'd lived long enough to lay claim to his moons. I'm also not sure if he technically owned these moons (I am not a scientist), though it seems fair. Doesn't it seem like he would get the moons?

	Importance	Accessibility	Fun
"Essay on Criticism"	6	7	4
"Essay on Man," etc.	7	6	5
"The Rape of the Lock"	5	5	6

GRUB STREET

Grub Street was an actual street in London, which was populated by struggling, down-at-heel writers. It was a byword for the poverty of its inhabitants and for their dirty, disreputable lifestyle. In this Grub Street ghetto, a startling percentage of children were born out of wedlock, and many of these children followed their parents into a life of scribbling. (Of course, writers are now allowed to live wherever they want, and even to marry non-writers, thanks to the heroic desegregation efforts of our parents' generation.)

Over time, the phrase came to denote the whole world of the eighteenth-century hack and the periodicals that provided them with bread and butter, if not much else. Many of these were party political organs, like the *Tory Examiner*, edited for a time by Jonathan Swift. But the ones we now remember—partly because new magazines keep stealing their names—are the chatty cultural periodicals, like *The Spectator* and *Tatler* of Joseph Addison (1672–1719) and Richard Steele (1672–1729).

Each issue of a journal typically included only one essay, or "letter." It was therefore possible for every issue of a journal to be written by one person, and some were, like Samuel Johnson's *The Rambler*. That person's name, however, didn't appear in the magazine. *The Rambler*'s letters were signed by The Rambler, *The Spectator*'s by The Spectator. Sometimes the magazine's persona would be given a proper name, as with *Tatler*, which appeared under the pseudonym of Isaac Bickerstaffe. These fictional personas had fictional friends, who had fictional adventures.

A typical letter consisted of an anecdote told to demonstrate a moral lesson. The anecdotes are feel-good humor. The morality is that of the Eternal Bourgeois. Common sense can resolve all difficulties; everyone should marry and have children; handsome is as handsome does; hard work will be rewarded.

While the circulation of these papers may sound unimpressive—*The Spectator* at its height sold three thousand copies—the actual readership was many times higher. Coffeehouses subscribed to all the popular journals, and people gathered there to read and discuss them. Coffeehouses were also meeting places for clubs like the Kit-Kat Club, which operated much like Parisian salons, but without the cynicism, affectations, and women.

This brings us to an interesting French version of the journal. In addition to regular periodicals, the French also had clandestine ones. These were written in Paris, but copied over the French border, beyond the reach of the censors. The most famous was Baron von Grimm's *Correspondance Litteraire*, written by Grimm and a small group of radicals, including Denis Diderot and Mme. d'Epinay, beginning in 1753. It only had fifteen-odd subscribers, but these were all European royals, including Catherine the Great of Russia. *Correspondance* is mainly remembered now for the original literature it published. Many of Diderot's best known works, including the filthy, scabrous "Jacques the Fatalist," (see page 129) were published only in its pages.

DANIEL DEFOE (1660–1731)

Daniel Defoe is often called the father of the English novel, in a scenario where its mother was journalism. He typically presented his novels as factual accounts of amazing experiences and used verisimilitude in details to make that imposture more convincing. Realist fiction, in short, started its life as a bald-faced lie.

Defoe didn't write his first novel, *Robinson Crusoe*, until we was almost sixty and already well known for his political writings, of which there were no end. In hundreds of books and pamphlets, he took positions on everything from union with Scotland to the Spanish Succession. In the calmly titled "Conjugal Lewdness; or Matrimonial Whoredom," for instance, he determined that using contraception with your husband made you no better than a prostitute. In 1704, Defoe founded a political periodical, *The Review*, and cranked out three issues a week for almost ten years.

The literary crowd didn't think much of Defoe. In their eyes he was a Grub Street hack, with the low instincts of a tradesman. But with *The Life and Strange Surprising Adventures of Robinson Crusoe*, Defoe had both a commercial and critical hit. The story of a castaway Englishman who spends twenty-seven years on a desert island, *Robinson Crusoe* was presented as, and widely taken for, a true account by Crusoe himself. Even without that fake-memoir frisson, the book remains entertaining three hundred years later. It is hard not to enjoy Crusoe's steady mastery of his island, the satisfied clerkish toting up of his accumulated wealth, the cozy appeal of his tidy homestead, shared with his animal friends and his devoted cannibal companion, Friday.

The only impediment to the contemporary reader is Defoe's attempts at moral instruction. He regularly pauses the story to have Crusoe beat himself up for the horrible sin that led to his horrible fate. That sin was not listening to his father, who advised him not to abandon his God-given, middle-class station in life to seek excitement. The disasters that befall him, enslavement and shipwreck among them, all follow from this. It is like an anti-Disney children's story the moral of which is "Whatever you do, don't follow your dreams." His fate, anyway, is ultimately pretty sweet. Crusoe has grand adventures, defeating cannibals and rescuing a ship from mutineers, and is ultimately rewarded with happiness, wealth, and dominion over an island empire.

Defoe's other widely read book is *The Fortunes and Misfortunes of the Famous Moll Flanders*. Moll Flanders is best known for being a whore, and the book for being an honest and sympathetic portrait of a prostitute. Really, though, if you fall into the broad middle demographic for sexual behavior—slept around a bit in college, been through a few relationships—you're more of a whore than she was. She does, shockingly, admit to enjoying sex, but who hasn't let that slip from time to time? Some readers probably even use contraception in the marriage bed.

Instead of an exotic island, Moll's story take us into England's lower classes. Born to a woman bound for the gallows, Moll is eventually taken in by a proper family. She is seduced and abandoned by one brother and, heartbroken, marries the other. When that husband dies, the attractive young widow goes through a few more, leaving a trail of abandoned children. After various misadventures, Moll becomes a master thief, a legend of the underworld. Eventually, though, she lands in Newgate, where she is reunited with her favorite husband, a highwayman. Together they are transported to America, where they make their fortunes and live happily ever after, humble sinners smiled upon by Providence. So, as in *Robinson Crusoe*, the sinner here is ultimately rewarded, for little more than whining that she's a sinner, over and over.

Of his many, many other books, the best is considered *Roxana: The Fortunate Mistress*. The story is similar to *Moll Flanders*, but here the heroine attempts to find a place in life among the upper classes, rather than the middle and the gutter. Finally, *A Journal of the Plague Year* is a fictional account of the plague that swept

London in 1665, told in the form of a shopkeeper's journals. Based on careful research, it can make even modern readers temporarily forget that Defoe wasn't really there, this shopkeeper never existed, and fiction is a bald-faced lie.

	Importance	Accessibility	Fun
Robinson Crusoe	8	6	8
Moll Flanders	8	5	9
Roxana	6	5	6
A Journal of the Plague Year	4	6	4

SAMUEL RICHARDSON (1689–1761)

Richardson was the opposite of a man's man. All his life, he preferred the company of women and the manners of women; he sincerely believed they were morally superior to men. Women loved Richardson back, both in person and via his books. This love was platonic, but Richardson didn't mind—he was that rare freak of nature, a Puritan who wasn't a hypocrite.

He has now been ridiculed by other men for this effeminacy for 250 years. Manly critics jeer at his fear of mice and belief in chastity for men, and treat the absence of drunken brawls from Richardson's life as an intersex perversion. Even the use of mundane details in his writings was considered womanish until it became Realism. In our postfeminist world, these distinctions have blurred, however, and now readers of both genders are likely to find Richardson prissy.

Like all of Richardson's novels, his first, *Pamela, or Virtue Rewarded*, is an epistolary, meaning it is composed entirely of letters. It was written when he was already fifty and a successful printer with his own thriving shop. Pamela has been called the first novel so many times, it makes you want to smack someone with a copy of *Don Quixote*. What it really is, is the first novel of everyday life. Even Defoe wrote tall tales of robbers and castaways, while *Pamela* is about a servant girl in an ordinary British house. It was the beginning of fiction that immersed the reader in the world the reader was already in.

In the course of the book's six hundred pages, only one thing happens. The master of the house, young Mr. B., tries to seduce Pamela, while she defends her chastity. This happens again and again. He tries everything; it's basically the plot of *Green Eggs and Ham*, except with sexual intercourse instead of green eggs and ham:

"Will you do it with a fox? Will you do it in a box?"

"I will not do it with a fox! I will not do it in a box! I do not like sexual intercourse! I do not like it, Mr. B.!"

At last she does it with a ring, but the ending is not as thrilling as the Dr. Seuss version because she doesn't go back and orgiastically do it on a boat, with a goat, etc.

Pamela was written in three months, making it one of those rare books that will typically take longer to read than it did to write. It was a massive bestseller with all classes of people. At Slough, for a time, the whole town gathered every evening at the village forge while the blacksmith read it aloud. When Pamela got married, they all cheered and ran to ring the church bells in ecstasy. The book's popularity and prudishness helped inaugurate a mania for feminine delicacy. Soon a woman who said the word "leg" was considered little better than a prostitute.

To contemporary readers, Pamela may seem slow. It gallops along, though, compared to Richardson's later novels, *Clarissa* and *Sir Charles Grandison*. *Clarissa* is another seduction novel, with the difference that its chaste heroine is finally drugged and raped by the rake character, Lovelace. It only takes him a thousand pages of letters to get the job done. He then wants to marry Clarissa, but she prefers to die of a broken heart, presumably because it takes longer. After her death, the surviving characters write another three hundred pages to one another about how nice she was.

To read *Clarissa* requires the patience God gave a sea sponge; to read *Sir Charles Grandison* takes the attention span of furniture. If you are looking for a birthday present for a beloved sofa, look no farther. This book offers Richardson's ideal gentleman caught in a love triangle with two perfect ladies, for so many weary pages that it dwarfs *Clarissa*, the Bible, and some government archives. Like Pamela and Clarissa, Sir Charles won't have sex before wedlock. The sofa will especially appreciate this part; humans, however, may find it hard to take.

	Importance	Accessibility	Fun
Pamela	8	5	5
Clarissa	6	3	3
Sir Charles Grandison	2	ugh	0

HENRY FIELDING (1707–1754)

Fielding's novelistic career began with a burning itch to ridicule *Pamela*. He wrote not one, but two books before this itch was scratched.

Fielding's first anti-*Pamela* book was *An Apology for the Life of Mrs. Shamela Andrews*. This rewrote the letters of Pamela, with the difference that she was a mercenary slut, deliberately coercing her master into marriage. It's basically a one-joke book, and in the natural course of things, it and its author would have been forgotten. That all changed with the brilliant follow-up spoof, *Joseph Andrews*. Joseph is the equally chaste brother of Pamela, who nobly resists the illicit advances of Mr. B.'s sister, Lady Booby. Here, Fielding dropped the epistolary form, and gave up the *Green Eggs and Ham* plot in favor of one where more than one thing happens. He based his work on Cervantes and called it a comic epic. Whatever he called it, it's a work of genius. Then he improved on it in his magnum opus, *Tom Jones*, which is a version of *Joseph Andrews* in which the hero doesn't say no to sex.

These novels are like Dickens without the sentimentality. There are jokes everywhere, like firecrackers going off left and right. The style, at once ornate and deadpan, is a joke in itself. Meanwhile plotlines branch out in all directions. Any compromising letter will fall into the wrong hands; any chance meeting will have far-reaching consequences. Just before the curtain falls, a birthmark identifies the impecunious hero as a rich person's long-lost son. This frees him to marry his true love, and all loose ends are tied up in a neat bow—which is itself a big joke.

Fielding wrote two other novels, collectively known as "those other novels." The first is *Jonathan Wild*, which uses a story about a notorious gangster to satirize Robert Walpole, the prime minister everyone loved to hate. It's a shameless rip-off of Gay's *The Beggar's Opera*. Gay's operetta has been updated by Brecht as *The Threepenny Opera*, and this is the form in which *Jonathan Wild* is best appreciated.

The other "other" novel is Amelia, a fictionalized account of the miserable time Fielding gave his late wife, Charlotte. In it, Charlotte appears as a perfect model of womanly goodness: beautiful, patient, kind, doomed. His second, very much alive, wife's opinion of this book is not recorded. Perhaps she didn't mind: she had been his first wife's maid, and sympathetic commentators suggest Fielding married her because the two bonded over their grief for Charlotte. Unsympathetic commentators suggest he married her because she was six months pregnant.

	Importance	Accessibility	Fun
Joseph Andrews	6	8	10
Tom Jones	9	8	10

SAMUEL JOHNSON (1709–1784) AND
JAMES BOSWELL (1740–1795)

Most periods of literature are dominated by one commanding figure, a star who symbolizes his age and is courted by both the mighty and the mediocre. Often he rules by force of personality more than by outstanding works, and therefore blends into the crowd after death. With time, Ben Jonson is eclipsed by Shakespeare; Byron slips onto the B list; the once-worshipped Algernon Swinburne is now just a silly name. From their writings, we struggle to see what the big deal was. We know, however, how the eighteenth century became the Age of Johnson, thanks to Boswell's remarkable biography.

Boswell is often ridiculed for the exhaustiveness of his *Life of Johnson*. Even in an abridged version, it gives the impression of Boswell trotting behind Johnson like a besotted poodle, notebook in hand. The unabridged version, which runs to fifteen hundred pages, is a testament to the obsessive-compulsive disorders of both its writer and its subject. Johnson himself once complained, "Sir, you have but two topicks, yourself and me. I am sick of both." (We now know, from Boswell's own diaries, that he had at least two other topicks, prostitutes and binge drinking, but neither of those was likely to be popular with his staid idol.)

Afraid to be alone, due to a tendency to depression, Johnson spent much of his life chatting brilliantly to a group of adoring friends. *The Life of Sanuel Johnson* is a faithful record of this scene. You can open it at random and understand in one minute flat why everybody loved this man.

Johnson was legendary not only for his wit, but for his bizarre mannerisms. One of his many tics was entering a room with a fixed number of steps; if he crossed the doorway on the wrong foot, he would go back and start again. He also chewed compulsively, gestured restlessly with his hands, and twisted in his chair. In Boswell's words: "When he walked, it was like the struggling gait of one in fetters; when he rode he had no command or direction of his horse, but was carried as if in a balloon."

SO WAS THIS GUY JUST TALK?

Johnson is mainly remembered for his *Dictionary of the English Language*. This was an astonishing solo feat of scholarship, then. Now it's an obsolete dictionary. He also created two periodicals, *The Idler* and *The Rambler*, which may be the best of their kind, and some poetry, which certainly isn't. His best known poems are "London" and "The Vanity of Human Wishes." No matter how many times you read these, all you will remember are their names.

Finally, Johnson wrote a book of critical biographies, *The Lives of the English Poets*. Here, Johnson has a good word for everyone, then three bad words. His most famous put-down is of Milton: "*Paradise Lost* is one of the books which the reader admires and puts down, and forgets to take up again. None ever wished it longer than it is."

	Importance	*Accessibility*	*Fun*
The Life of Samuel Johnson	7	7	9
The Rambler/The Idler	4	6	6
Johnson's poetry	3	4	3
The Lives of the English Poets	4	4	6

KITTY LIT BOX

Boswell on Johnson's love of his cat:

"I never shall forget the indulgence with which he treated Hodge, his cat: for whom he himself used to go out and buy oysters, lest the servants having that trouble should take a dislike to the poor creature. . . . I recollect him one day scrambling up Dr. Johnson's breast, apparently with much satisfaction, while my friend smiling and half-whistling, rubbed down his back, and pulled him by the tail; and when I observed he was a fine cat, saying, 'Why yes, Sir, but I have had cats whom I liked better than this;' and then as if perceiving Hodge to be out of countenance, adding, 'but he is a very fine cat, a very fine cat indeed.'"

JONATHAN SWIFT (1667–1745)

Swift was born in Dublin, the son of English immigrants. After spending his childhood in Ireland, and attending Trinity College, he fled to England during one of those spells when the Irish tried to kill all the English. Nonetheless, Swift is generally called an Irish writer. Even in his lifetime, the Irish considered him their own and celebrated his birthday with fireworks. Of course, at the time, they had no full-blooded Irish writers who were internationally acknowledged. Really this adoption of Swift should be rescinded, now that the Irish have Yeats, Joyce, Beckett, and an economy.

Like many writers of the time, Swift started his authorial career as a political pamphleteer. These pamphlets tended to satire, and the satire was the angry kind. Now that we no longer hate (or remember) their targets, most are unreadable. "A Tale of a Tub" is impressive for its postmodernist furbelows—Swift begins his preface with a satire on prefaces and moves on to satirize satires—but its concern with obsolete disputes ultimately makes it heavy going.

The exception is "A Modest Proposal" (full title: "A Modest Proposal for Preventing the Children of Poor People in Ireland from Being a Burden to Their Parents or Country, and for Making Them Beneficial to the Public"). Here Swift suggests that the poor children of Ireland should be sold for their meat, providing tender steaks for the well-to-do and a steady income for their parents. As long as there are poor people, and rich people who figuratively feed off them, this essay will remain funny. It also has a morbid glee that makes it one of those rare literary works high schoolers like.

But his most famous work, of course, is *Gulliver's Travels*, which presents itself as the real memoir of a ship captain who strayed into uncharted lands. It is divided into four books:

A Voyage to Lilliput

This is the best known section, in which the shipwrecked Gulliver is taken prisoner by a race of people who are just five inches high. Tiny people are adorable, and much of this part involves them scampering over Gulliver's hanky, or scrambling into his snuff box and having ever so big a sneeze. Lilliputian politics are likewise toy-sized. Wars are waged to decide which end of a hard-boiled egg to crack before eating it. Ministries are allocated according to the candidates' skill at ropedancing. These episodes are meant to satirize contemporary affairs: the egg wars, for instance, represent the English wars of religion. But the satire is forced; it's like someone minutely describing a pratfall, with the idea that readers will compare it to the fall of Communism and laugh uproariously. Best to imagine the little dudes dancing on a string and leave it at that.

A Voyage to Brobdingnag

Now the shoe is on the other foot. Gulliver finds himself among giants, seventy-two feet high. The magnified humans are disgusting; you can see every pore and freckle. Even breasts are gross. Gulliver is now the adorable one; he is treated as a darling pet and given a little house in a suitcase. However, the king of Brobdingnag finds him less cute after Gulliver describes his people's pastime of artillery warfare. Moral: Europeans are disgusting at any size.

A Voyage to Laputa, Balnibarbi, Luggnagg, Glubbdubbdrib, and Japan

Here Swift fires satire in every direction, mostly hitting the shrubbery. There's a floating island that blocks the sunlight from the land below (England's treatment of Ireland) and a send-up of unworldly scholars and scientists (the Royal Society). The latter falls especially flat now that science has turned out to be right about everything.

The most memorable section concerns a race of people who live forever. The catch is that they continue aging and soon degenerate into eternal, grotesque senility—a dig at people who want to live forever. Here, you can't help feeling that Swift is running out of targets and is resorting to just being mean. Like, okay, we'll die, then. Look at us dying. Happy?

A Voyage to the Country of the Houyhnhmns

People are gross, and don't deserve to live. We've learned this. Horses, however, are furry and nice. In the country of the Houyhnhmns, a race of degenerate humans called Yahoos live in trees, throw ordure at one another, and rut. Meanwhile, a civilized race of horses lives a noble, ascetic life. Gulliver finds true happiness among the horses but is finally cast out for being a Yahoo, despite all his book-learning.

He goes home, where he spends his days with his own horses, seemingly unconcerned that instead of talking and having a higher civilization, they just stand there. At least they are not doing any dumb science.

	Importance	Accessibility	Fun
"A Tale of a Tub"	3	3	6
"A Modest Proposal"	6	7	7
Gulliver's Travels	10	8	7

LAURENCE STERNE (1713–1768)

The Life and Opinions of Tristram Shandy, Gentleman presents itself as an autobiography. It begins with the narrator's conception, and the domestic misadventures of the day of his birth occupy two hundred pages. Interpolated are digressions of every kind—long descriptions of two people going down a flight of stairs, remarks on how long it takes to describe two people going down a flight of stairs, discourses on noses, silly parodies, shaggy dog stories nested within shaggy dog stories. The main characters are the narrator's father and uncle. The father, Walter, is an acerbic rationalist with pet theories about the importance of Christian names and of well-formed noses. Uncle Toby is a kindhearted, shy creature, with the hobby of reliving his military adventures by building fortifications on his bowling green.

Tristram Shandy is famous for its use of typographical oddities—a black page to express mourning, or a series of squiggly lines representing the haphazard course taken by the plot. It's also still funny to a remarkable degree. Page for page, it's possibly the funniest novel ever.

However, before it can be funny, you have to get the jokes. The book is flamboyantly difficult, and while some jokes depend on a familiarity with the literature that came before, it also really helps to be very smart. (This often gives people a head start in understanding things.) However, if you don't understand this book, it doesn't necessarily mean you're not smart. It means you might not be smart. That's one of many possible reasons. If you're smart, you'll be able to think of some others.

At the time he wrote *Tristram Shandy*, Sterne's life was abysmally sad. His mother and uncle both died, and his wife had a nervous breakdown. Both he and his wife were rapidly dying of tuberculosis. Yet no ray of gloom even obliquely enters the book. Even when the tuberculosis gets a mention in Volume VII, Sterne turns it into a jeu d'esprit: Death knocks at the door while Shandy is in the middle of telling a dirty story. Annoyed at the interruption, Shandy tells

Death to come back later, in such a careless tone that Death doubts himself and leaves. A long digression follows, in which Shandy goes on the lam in France, with Death at his heels. This section was written when Sterne himself was traveling through France, ill and weakening, with roughly a year to live.

Sterne's next book, *A Sentimental Journey Through France and Italy*, was written on that same trip. It's far more straightforward: Sterne was gravely ill, and presumably didn't have the energy to make you feel stupid. *Sentimental Journey* is kindasorta travel writing, but mainly consists of riffs and digressions. It hardly ever matters which part of France or Italy we're in. The book is all about inns and girls, the servant the hero hires, and the daydreams he has on the road. One of the most celebrated sections is about a caged starling which addresses every passerby with the same phrase: "I can't get out." This sparks a sentimental digression about all the people held in miserable capitivity; and the reflection that, although the starling had had many admirers, none of them had ever let him out. Here the circlings and circuitings and circumambulations have a dreamy serendipity to them, like a day that gets hijacked by a series of unexpected adventures.

	Importance	*Accessibility*	*Fun*
Tristram Shandy	*10*	*5*	*10*
A Sentimental Journey	*6*	*7*	*9*

Imagine . . .

In Sterne's lifetime, his sermons outsold his novels. Imagine how boring people were in England then! Hard to imagine.

No, imagine this. . . .

After Sterne's burial, grave robbers sold his body to anatomists. A friend of his recognized the body, and it was reburied. Imagine being that friend, scalpel in hand, when he recognized his buddy Sterne on the dissecting table. . . .

RISE OF THE NOVEL TIMELINE

1719: With *Robinson Crusoe,* Defoe introduces realism, showing that concrete details and interior monologue enhance a reader's experience of a story.

1740: With *Pamela*, Richardson shows that realism works even when the story is mundane. He also creates the modern plot arc with a simple "Will she, won't she?" plot.

1742: With *Joseph Andrews*, Fielding introduces the subplot, demonstrating that a book that alternates between a few ongoing stories is even more effective.

1759: With *Tristram Shandy*, Sterne deconstructs the novel, writing a book that invokes all the new rules of fiction, then breaks and subverts them—a book as revolutionary and metafictional as *Infinite Jest*.

1759 to the present day: People write derivative novels.

THE SUPPORTING CAST

Thomas Gray (1716–1771) was an important poet during his lifetime, and he wrote one poem that has become an enduring classic: "Elegy Written in a Country Churchyard," where he pontificates about the poor people who are buried there. Apparently we shouldn't look down on them, because we will be dead too, pretty soon. Also, maybe they were really great people, who just didn't have our opportunities. Finally, death is sad. It should be called "The Five Most Obvious Thoughts to Have in a Country Churchyard."

Frances Burney (1752–1840) was once mainly known for her diaries, which she kept for more than seventy years. They include her time spent at the court of George III (yes, the American Revolution tyrant guy who lost his marbles), plus a first-person account of Waterloo. Of her novels, the best is *Evelina*, about a girl trying to make it in London society. It's full of the kind of wit that makes you smile at the thought that you're smart enough to understand it. Jane Austen was a fan and even imitator of her work; if you love Jane Austen, you can read this and note that it's not quite as good. But it will be really similar.

For more in the vein of not-quite-Austen, there's Oliver Goldsmith (1730–1774) and *The Vicar of Wakefield*. Here a good-hearted vicar loses everything in a Job-like trail of calamities. Finally he's in debtor's prison, sick and maybe dying; outside the prison walls, his unprotected family are dying like flies. Still, the vicar, unshaken in his faith, uses this golden opportunity to preach to the other prisoners, despite the jeering and abuse they shower upon him. Gee, you think his faith will be rewarded? What do you think, will there be a happy ending? (This is why we need the French; a Parisian novelist would have killed that vicar stone dead.)

	Importance	Accessibility	Fun
"Elegy Written in a Country Churchyard"	7	7	3
Fanny Burney, journals	1	6	8
Evelina	2	9	7
The Vicar of Wakefield	5	9	7

Meanwhile, in France . . .

On the one hundredth anniversary of Voltaire's death, Victor Hugo said of him and his cohort: "Those powerful writers disappeared, but they left us their soul, the Revolution. . . . We see behind Danton—Diderot; behind Robespierre, Rousseau."

Here are the writers who put the light in the Enlightenment; the geniuses who first invented thinking. With this new tool, men like Voltaire made wisecracks that would change the world forever, by making it funnier. With his encyclopedia, Diderot opened the world of knowledge to ordinary people and inaugurated the tradition of seeding knowledge with liberal propaganda. Rousseau gave us the "noble savage," thanks to which, even today, undergraduates believe in the moral superiority of undergraduates. Taken together, these writers helped to turn Earth into the political Utopia it is today.

I also include a couple of authors who didn't do anything that important. Still, their books are pretty good, or else there was some other reason. Honest, I wouldn't include an author for no reason, since it takes work.

VOLTAIRE (FRANÇOIS MARIE AROUET) (1694–1778)

Voltaire has become the flagship writer of the French Enlightenment, although he is not the best writer, or the most radical writer, or the most read writer. It might just be because he has the best pen name. (Take note, Detroit: Is Voltaire not the perfect name for a compact electric car?)

Voltaire was the most-exiled writer of his time, although his beliefs were far from being the most extreme. He found Catholicism silly, but he wasn't even an atheist like his contemporary Baron d'Holbach. Instead, he expressed a wishy-washy deism—the belief that God exists in everything, but you can't talk to him and it doesn't matter. Voltaire wasn't a democrat either, but an advocate for a more liberal monarchy. Like other philosophes, Voltaire believed that reason, rather than faith, held the key to the world's problems. Even for a nation that had just invented thinking, this was not shocking.

His downfall was that he was a born gadfly. He could make "the" sound sarcastic. He could make scratching sound sarcastic. If he wrote a scene in which a priest had sex with a woman, it somehow implied that priests were all sex creeps. Meanwhile, even Voltaire didn't believe this literally. He just couldn't help himself when a gadfly thought came into his head. He was once told, "No matter what you write, you will never succeed in destroying the Christian religion." He replied, "We'll see about that."

However, Voltaire was also a phenomenally successful and prolific writer. For him, being exiled meant going to live at the court of Frederick II (one of his fans) or renting a palatial mansion in the countryside. He was laughing all the way to the border.

His first exile came in 1726, when he was thirty-two. He'd already had some success as a poet, and a few early scrapes with the law. Then a duel gone wrong landed him with a lettre de cachet. This was a French legal device which allowed people to ask the king to incarcerate someone indefinitely, often after slipping the king a twenty. The king also used these to satisfy his own grudges; it was a nice thing to have up your sleeve, in case some guy you hated annoyingly hadn't broken any law.

Voltaire managed to negotiate his lettre de cachet down to an exile and made tracks for England. He spent three years there, and on his return, he wrote his *Letters on England* (aka *Philosophical Letters*), which are musings on how terrific England is compared to France. English religion is so much more open-minded! Sir Isaac Newton—so much smarter than Descartes! Voltaire's Anglophilia is such that he doesn't even mention the weather or the food. Along the way, he gives a smart, readable account of Enlightenment ideas and English society.

His most famous work, *Candide*, is a novel ridiculing Leibniz's optimism—the doctrine that God, being so big and good and all, must have made this the best of all possible worlds. That means everything here is perfect, according to His design. Voltaire's way of attacking this is to heap atrocities on his characters. They are raped, mutilated, enslaved, eaten up by syphilis, cheated, impoverished—and again. The horrors are described with a brisk indifference and pass at a rate of three to a page. Wherever they go, the characters never meet a happy person. The poor are crushed by the rich; the rich are bored and despairing. Meanwhile, at every fresh horror, either starry-eyed Candide or his companion, the philosopher Pangloss, comments that "Everything is for the best in the best of all possible worlds."

	Importance	Accessibility	Fun
Philosophical Letters	4	8	7
Candide	10	9	8

DENIS DIDEROT (1713–1784)

Diderot was Mr. Enlightenment. In his lifetime, he was best known as the main editor of the *Encyclopedia*. This had originated as a translation of the much smaller *Chamber's Encyclopedia*, but soon spun out into a landmark work which gathered everything that was known about everything. The project employed hundreds of people and stretched to twenty-eight volumes. It also incorporated a bias toward Enlightenment values. (These are basically the values we now call "liberal," only without gay rights.) Due to this bias, the *Encyclopedia* was officially banned, but the government allowed it to carry on being published regardless. This was partly because it had friends in high places and partly because it employed so many people—an early version of "Too Big to Fail."

Both of the works of Diderot that are now most widely read went unpublished during his lifetime. They were eventually dug up as single manuscripts, in the attic of Catherine the Great, at the bottom of a box of old Legos and gnawed mittens.

The first, *Rameau's Nephew*, is a dialogue between Diderot and a professional toady, who happens to be the nephew of the great composer (and noted shit-heel) Rameau. *Rameau Neveu* blithely explains the sycophant's art and sketches the hollow amorality of his rich patrons. This is Madame de Sévigné & co. seen from below, and the angle is not flattering.

Jacques the Fatalist is a hyper-cerebral, hyper-carnal ado about nothing. It's essentially a long dialogue between a servant and his master, in which the servant tries to tell the story of his loves. He is interrupted at every turn by endless mishaps; also by the Reader (who objects, criticizes Diderot's writing, and asks impertinent questions) and by the author (who defends his writing and refuses to answer the Reader's dumb questions).

The story of Jacques's loves is taken from *Tristram Shandy*. The narrative logic, or illogic, of the piece is also an extended tribute to Sterne, and if you'd like to appreciate Sterne but can't get past his knotty style, Diderot is your man. Not only is the language simpler, but it's translated, so for you, it's all twentieth century. In fact, this is probably the easiest entry point to postmodernism, in either its eighteenth- or twentieth-century form.

	Importance	Accessibility	Fun
Rameau's Nephew	3	9	10
Jacques the Fatalist	5	8	10

CHODERLOS DE LACLOS (1741–1803): LES LIAISONS DANGEREUSES

Les Liaisons Dangereuses is possibly the greatest epistolary novel ever written. Its core is a correspondence between the dissolute Marquise de Merteuil and her ex-lover, the dissolute Vicomte de Valmont. The game begins when she writes to say she will only sleep with him again if he succeeds in seducing the prudish Madame de Tourvel. He takes the wager and approaches Tourvel posing as a repentant sinner—while conducting other intrigues and seductions right and left. At one point, he amuses himself by writing letters to Tourvel using a prostitute's buttock as a desk.

Of course, he falls in love with the prude. Men of this period find frigidity the only really lovable quality in a woman. Still, almost to the last, he poses to Madame de Mertreuil as the debauched cynic—and to us, because his letters to her are the only ones in which he is honest. Or are they? The whole novel is an extended exercise in reading between the lines.

Choderlos de Laclos was a military man; having achieved his stated aim of writing a book "which would remain on earth after his death," he never wrote another novel. He did, however, join Napoleon's army and invent the modern artillery shell, which also remained on earth after his death, eliminating many of his potential readers.

	Importance	Accessibility	Fun
Les Liaisons Dangereuses	7	8	10

JEAN-JACQUES ROUSSEAU (1712–1778): CONFESSIONS

Rousseau may be the most pivotal figure in European history. He was the father of Romanticism and of the French Revolution. He was also the uncle, or at least older man living next door, of the American Revolution. He is best known for his great political work *The Social Contract*, a founding document of Western democracy. His novel/manifesto *Emile* was a founding document of liberal education. His romantic novel *Julie, or the New Heloise*, refreshingly created no social movement, but was the biggest bestseller of the century. As well as giving us the idea of the social contract, he gave us the idea of the Noble Savage—the idea that humanity is innately good and is spoiled by civilization. This has seeped into our culture so indelibly that every schoolchild now grows up assuming Polynesian head-hunters are more ethical than we are.

The popularity of *Julie* in the eighteenth century is likely to remain as mysterious to the modern reader as the fad for head-collecting in Polynesia. Julie is an eight-hundred-page novel in letters, letters about the characters' feelings as they attempt—usually unsuccessfully—to get it on with one another. Almost every feeling they report rings false, because Rousseau was many things, but he was not an acute psychologist. This is also the fatal flaw of *Emile*, which might be useful to an educator who wanted to raise children who were completely unlike children, after breeding these in a laboratory.

Rousseau's *Confessions* is another kettle of fish. Just as groundbreaking as everything else Rousseau did, it's also still relevant and fascinating. It's unique as an honest autobiography from an important historical figure; an effort at self-revelation which essentially invented the modern memoir. In fact, it's so honest, it borders on Too Much Information; it really makes you think twice about democracy, liberal education, and anything else associated with Rousseau.

Within the first thirty pages, Rousseau is telling us about his spanking fetish. He writes about exposing himself to women in alleyways and describes his participation in a ménage à trois that ended in the suicide of the other man. In his early years, Rousseau comes across as a pathetic figure, a hypochondriac who got tongue-tied under pressure, could not concentrate enough to study, and quit every job he wasn't fired from. In a pinch, he would not just lie, but fabricate an entire persona. For a period, he earned a living teaching music, about which he then knew almost nothing. The gig fell through when he boldly arranged a performance of an original composition which resulted in total cacophony. But he later studied music in depth, composed well-received operas, and wrote articles on music for the *Encyclopedia*. This is the triumph of the underdog, deluxe, and for the first half of the memoir, the reader tends to feel inspired. If this lying, neurotic bag of symptoms could become a superstar, there's hope for all of us.

However, more chilling incidents gradually begin to accumulate. Rousseau steals and blames it on a maid, who is fired. Rousseau deserts an elderly friend when the man has a seizure, purely because Rousseau doesn't want to get stuck with him, and this is a good moment to make his get-away. Finally, he forces his mistress to abandon all five of their children as infants, on the steps of the Foundling Hospital. Since the survival rate of infants left there was low, this was a pretty cold thing to do. Rousseau claims he can't tell us his reason for abandoning his children, because it's such a good reason that it might encourage other people to abandon their children. He also claims that he wishes he had been left at the Foundling Hospital himself, so he could have been trained to be an honest workman. (Rousseau is one of those artistes who rapturously extols the ennobling effect of manual labor, which he has never done, and is not offering to do.)

Rousseau begins as a self-absorbed, irresponsible, dishonest kid and grows up to be more immature. By the time he is forty, he is an obnoxious brat, and he ends his life behaving like a two-year-old. There was never a worse representative for the idea that humanity is innately good. Diderot described him as: "false, vain as Satan, ungrateful, cruel, hypocritical, and wicked. . . . He sucked ideas from me, used them himself, and then affected to despise me." True on all counts, but this is what makes Rousseau's *Confessions* an enthralling read.

	Importance	Accessibility	Fun
Confessions	10	8	9

MARQUIS DE SADE (1740–1814)

We only include the Marquis de Sade because the last thing we need is to annoy a lot of sadists. Non-sadists won't get much from him, though, unless they are actually masochists.

Sade writes like the Ayn Rand of sexual violence. His style is flat-footed; he is baldly didactic, and the only lesson he has to teach is "Fuck thy neighbor." If he had written *Pamela*, in the first scene, Mr. B. would have raped her anally, flogged her until she ran with blood, then shared her with three friends. After another five pages of this, with restraints, dildoes, and several footmen, Mr B. would have explained to Pamela that there is no such thing as compassion and that weak people are just flesh to be used by the powerful. At the end, she would have been tortured to death, and the killers would have gone on to torture some other girl without skipping a beat, because that's the world, and there is no afterlife.

Some of Sade's horrible nature is understandable. When he wrote his books, he had been imprisoned for years under a lettre de cachet obtained by his own mother-in-law. (Of course, she had her reasons.) He spent most of his adult life in prison—a total of thirty years—and the rest of it on the run, destitute, and in fear for his life. He died in an insane asylum, where he was feigning lunacy to avoid execution. The king hated him; after the Revolution, the republicans hated him. Then Napoleon hated him. They hated him because he was a horrible sociopath, but still, it was hard for the poor Marquis. Really, we cannot judge him until we have walked a mile in his shoes on the naked chests of fourteen-year-old girls who are strapped on beds of nails on which they will die, bloodily, screaming, as we complete our unholy pleasure.

His most popular work is *Justine*, which starts with a virtuous twelve-year-old maiden, takes away all her money, and then shows her being raped and abused by every man she meets. Occasionally she meets women, who immediately pass her on to rapists. She behaves nobly regardless, exactly like the typical Richardson heroine, but instead of being impressed by her virtue and marrying her, they rape and torture her. At last she is struck by lightning and killed.

Justine was written when Sade was still just barely passing for sane. By the time he wrote his most notorious work, *The 120 Days of Sodom*, there was nothing left in his head but sadistic sex, and a few moths and candy wrappers. The story: a remote castle, four libertines, four months, a few dozen teenagers of both sexes (including the daughters of the four libertines, whom they have been molesting from infancy), a few old ladies thrown in for contrast, and four madams telling the stories of their lives to inspire the goings-on. Then unbridled goings-on until the horribly mutilated bodies of the teens are ready to be interred. This book makes a good present for anyone who doesn't believe in prison. It might even make readers long for the halcyon days of lettres de cachet.

	Importance	Accessibility	Fun
Justine	7	6	4
The 120 Days of Sodom	4	5	4

(Note: I am giving Fun ratings here for the average member of the population. Clearly, people with certain sexual preferences, or those who are in a really stinking awful mood, will get considerably more fun from these books.)

CHAPTER 9

The Romantics:
The Author as (the Author's) Hero

Romantic poets were above mundane concerns like making money. This was lucky, since no one bought their poetry. Some were trust fund kids, some parasites. The fact that they were later recognized as geniuses has been an unhealthy example to slackers for more than a hundred years. (Warning: If you are now leading the life of a Romantic poet, know that you will never be recognized as a genius. Instead, you will end up going back to school for social work in your mid-thirties.)

The Romantic movement in England began with the Lake Poets, Wordsworth, Coleridge, and Southey; writers associated with the Lake District in Northern England. Much of their poetic philosophy came from German idealist philosophy, which conceived of the world as a projection of Mind. This inspired the Lake Poets to elaborate a new theory of imagination, in which imagination was like a magic hat that made their writing better than other people's. They also revolutionized poetry by dropping the classical references and giving up the use of an artificial "poetic" language. Instead, they used the same ordinary English that was current in conversation.

The contemporary reader may be surprised to learn that their language was ordinary, but it was. In fact, readers at first considered these poems prosey and stupid. But it's impossible for a modern person to see it the way they did. It's like when someone has one of those 3-D pictures where you're supposed to unfocus your eyes and see a unicorn, except you never see the unicorn, and people keep giving you pointers on how to unfocus your eyes and see the unicorn, until you pretend to see it just to get them to leave you alone.

Incidentally, "romantic" in our sense has no relation to the sense of Romantic used here. Romantic poets were, if anything, less interested in love than other poets.

Their Romantic was about waterfalls, the creative process, and the French Revolution, not about Betty. When a Romantic mentions Love, he usually means the elemental force that fuels Art, not the elemental force that fuels teen pregnancies.

Finally, Wordsworth, in the preface to the *Lyrical Ballads*, uses the word "experimental" to describe his poetry. This is the first mention of "experiment" in literature, and it creates a colossal can, from which worms have been crawling ever since. Latter-day Romantics still seek to rejuvenate the novel, the poem, the short-subject animated film, through bold experiments in form. While this is not, strictly speaking, Wordsworth's doing, it's something to think about the next time someone takes you to a Tarkovsky film. And there's nothing more precious, when you're watching a Tarkovsky film, than something to think about.

ROBERT BURNS (1759–1796)

Although Burns was a great inspiration to many Romantic poets, he wasn't properly speaking a Romantic. Burns wasn't influenced by German philosophy; did not exalt the Imagination; was not a sighing milksop. Nor did he live off inherited money, even other people's. Burns came from down-and-dirty, hard-drinking, rural poverty. He was known as the Ploughman Poet, for good reason: the heavy farm labor he did in his youth left him with a permanent stoop. He was no Shelleyish vegetarian whose downfall was his love of sailing. He worked like an animal until he became a famous poet, then promptly drank himself to death.

While most English poets of this period are mistily euphemistic about sex, Burns had the foul mouth of his beloved Scottish country pubs. He wrote poems in celebration of illegitimate children, in vindication of sluts ("Comin' Through the Rye" is one), and worked his love of filth into even his political poems. Here he is commenting on how Catherine the Great brought Poland to heel by bullying King Stanislaus (her former lover). The poem is entitled "Why Shouldna Poor Folk Mowe?" where mowe means "fuck":

> Auld Kate laid her claws on poor Stanislaus,
>   And Poland has bent like a bow:
> May the deil in her ass ram a huge prick o brass!
>   And damn her in hell with a mowe!

Burns was an inspiration to the Romantic movement, then, not because his interests chimed with theirs, but because he happened to write at the right time, because his poetry celebrates the rural, and because it is mowing great. Even the crabbiest Romantics turn into besotted schoolchildren when they discuss Robbie Burns.

Contemporary readers will find his nineteenth-century Scottish dialect an obstacle. One line like "gie her doup a clink within his yett" will derail most people. Try to guess at the mystery words and blunder on. There is great joy in Burns's blunt and boozy lyricism. With many of his poems, he suggests the traditional tunes they can be sung to—and the tearful whiskey-voiced singing is there in the words. Take the middle verses of "A Red, Red Rose":

> As fair art thou, my bonie lass,
>   So deep in luve am I,
> And I will luve thee still, my dear,
>   Till a' the seas gang dry.
>
> Till a' the seas gang dry, my dear,
>   And the rocks melt wi the sun!
> I will luve thee still, my dear,
>   While the sands o life shall run.

No poet could put across a drunken sentiment better, never mind if it's strictly true. (Burns was not the most constant of lovers.)

Something to keep in mind: "A Red, Red Rose," like many of Burns's lyrics, originated as a real folk song. He collected these, and although he prettied them up, it's not clear how much he changed them. They are now published, mixed in with his original work, as "by Robert Burns." As a consumer, this needn't affect you personally. Still, it's more correct to regard the above poem as by "the Scottish people as a whole." Just don't expect them not to cheat on you.

	Importance	Accessibility	Fun
Burns, poems	9	5	10

WILLIAM BLAKE (1757–1827)

If Wordsworth was the Paul McCartney of the Romantics, and Shelley the John Lennon, Blake would be the homeless guy on the corner screaming nonsense about lizard people. From early childhood, he had hallucinations, which he called "prophecies." He saw trees full of angels; he heard the voice of his dead brother. His poems were dictated to him by these spirit voices, which explains the lack of editing. The catch is, he's actually a genius—as never, ever happens with your local Ranting Lizard Guy. This combination of madness and genius made him a hero to literary boomers. His championing of free love, his radical politics, his bonkers mysticism—Blake has everything to thrill the antiestablishment establishment.

Blake was a professional engraver, trained at the Royal Academy, and, despite his eccentricities, continued to get artistic commissions to the end of his life. He produced many of his first books himself, engraving them on copper plates and printing them at home. These books included illustrations that he and his legendarily docile wife colored by hand. Blake called the pictures "illuminations." They emphasize weirdly muscular men in contorted positions, colored in hellish reds.

His most accessible works are the early poems in *Poetical Sketches*, *Songs of Innocence*, and *Songs of Experience*. These are collections of simple rhyming lyrics which range from the saccharine ("Little lamb, who made thee?") to the scabrous (". . . the youthful harlot's curse / Blasts the new-born infant's tear / And blights with plagues the Marriage hearse").

The scabrous poems are the best, along with certain sweetly haunting works, like the chimney sweep poems, and those about the Little Girl Lost. These are achingly weird and lachrymose, lingering in the mind like a subtle, unsettling feeling that you left something at the restaurant. The saccharine poems, though, are downright ick; we defy anyone to read "The Laughing Song" without making a gross-out face. Try for yourself—here it is, in its entirety:

> When the green woods laugh with the voice of joy,
> And the dimpling stream runs laughing by;
> When the air does laugh with our merry wit,
> And the green hill laughs with the noise of it;
>
> When the meadows laugh with lively green,
> And the grasshopper laughs in the merry scene,
> When Mary and Susan and Emily
> With their sweet round mouths sing "Ha, ha he!"

This poem could only work if it were illustrated by Henry Darger.

Blake really hits his stride with *The Marriage of Heaven and Hell*. This consists of pure unstoppable fun, like the "Proverbs of Hell." Some examples: "The lust of the goat is the bounty of God" and "Prudence is a rich, ugly old maid courted by Incapacity." There is also a scene in which Blake visits a printing house in hell, and a fantasia in which he seizes an angel and shows him his "eternal lot," which involves a deep pit full of chained monkeys and baboons, busily tearing off one another's arms. No way, bullshit, says the Angel. Blake retorts, Yeah, talking to squares like you is a waste of time. Basically, if you just, e.g., slept with your brother-in-law, and you feel like scum, you can read this and feel instantly better. (Sending it to your sister when she finds out, though, doesn't help. Wow, did that not help.)

In *The Marriage of Heaven and Hell*, the devil is not the principle of evil, but of energy, while the angels are prating milksops. It's funny, beautiful, and incidentally wildly pro-sex. In fact, it's so dogmatically pro-sex, it makes you feel guilty for not being more promiscuous. Before you know it, you're back in the hot tub with your brother-in-law and a bottle of Tanqueray. In fact, if you see your spouse reading it, call a lawyer.

It has also been called the first free verse poem in English. However, readers who have been paying attention will know that saying something was "first" is the academic's equivalent of liking something on Facebook.

All of Blake's later works—usually known as the "Prophetic Books"—are based on a personal theology involving the Four Zoas. In Blakean thought, the four Zoas existed in the eternal time before our fallen age. They were: Urizen (reason), Tharmas (the body), Luvah (love), and Urthonah (the soul). Each of them also had an "emanation," i.e., a lady friend.

These characters were thoroughly elaborated in Blake's mind: Urizen drove the horses of instruction, which pulled the sun; Tharmas had a vagina instead of a penis, but was otherwise masculine, while his emanation, Enion, was built like a she-male. There were also sub-zoas and sub-sub-zoas, including Ozoth, who had eight million and eight children.

The world went wrong, in Blake's cosmogony, when Urizen (reason) began to write laws and proclaim himself the One God. He invaded the land of Urthonah (the soul), and all hell broke loose. The Zoas were separated from their emanations, and Man fell from a state of Innocence into a state of Experience. Man was then shut up in the Mundane Egg (the world), separated from the objects of desire.

Man's rent went up, and a decent T-shirt now ran Man twenty bucks. When Man looked in the mirror, he now had a noticeable double chin. Girls stopped looking at Man in the street, though Man could not stop looking at girls. It was impossible to find a good egg salad sandwich in Man's neighborhood anymore. Damned Urizen!

Even if you are determined to see the Zoas as an allegory for states of mind, once Blake starts on Urizen, Rintrah, Palamabron, and the gang, he sounds like a raving escapee from an H. P. Lovecraft novel. Worse, he writes as if his readers all learned about the Zoas and the Mundane Egg in primary school. In short, it's gobbledygook. Even with pages and pages of notes, it can be like banging your head against a Mundane Egg, while dread Cthulhu goes in and out of focus in your mind's eye.

	Importance	Accessibility	Fun
Songs of Innocence/			
Songs of Experience	10	9	8
The Marriage of Heaven			
and Hell	10	6	10
The Prophetic Books,			
Milton, etc.	2	1	2

WILLIAM WORDSWORTH (1770–1850)

De Quincey described Wordsworth's first book, *Lyrical Ballads*, as a "revelation of untrodden worlds." They are untrodden both because of the untrammeled nature of the poet's visioning and because the poet is living in the middle of nowhere. In fact, if nature leaves you cold, these poems will leave you asleep. However, if your heart has ever swelled with emotion at the sight of a whiskered catkin 'pon the wintry air, or a nice patio, this is the hard stuff. No one can beat Wordsworth for the way a cloud casts a shadow on a grassy slope, while a cow wanders out of the shadow, and its russet hide brightens in the sunlight, its muddied fetlock bends—oh! And the poet has a pure emotion, usually of rapture.

Basically all of Wordsworth's poetry is about this cow rapture. He may hang it on a portrait of a beggar, or a theory of immortality, or his friend Lucy's death, but basically he's saying, Damn, the Lake District rocks. The scenery is front and center, while the actors and the action are tiny, tiny elements somewhere in a dusty corner of the poem. Sometimes the predominance of scenery makes the poetry like a meal consisting of hundreds of plates.

thirst, Death himself sails by in a ghost ship, the sea is infested with tangles of snakes. At last our hero reflects:

> The many men, so beautiful!
> And they all dead did lie:
> And a thousand thousand slimy things
> Lived on; and so did I.

(Readers over forty will totally identify with this sentiment.)

This poem is the origin of the phrase "an albatross around my neck," meaning an unwanted encumbrance that haunts you and ruins your life. For instance, if Coleridge came to stay with you, you might say, "He is like an albatross around our necks," or simply "Coleridge? That stinking albatross!"

His other well-known poem is the haunting lyric "Kubla Khan," which describes a paradise kingdom: "In Xanadu did Kubla Khan / A stately pleasure dome decree," etc. This came to him in a dream, the transcription of which was interrupted by a hapless visitor described by Coleridge only as "a person from Porlock." This person has gone down in history as a stupid wrecker, although the poet Stevie Smith wrote a dissenting poem opining that these people from Porlock are a damn sight better than having to work.

	Importance	Accessibility	Fun
Poems	8	6	8

AND SOUTHEY?

Robert Southey (1774–1843) lost the game of musical chairs that is literary posterity. Tireless work by generations of scholars has determined that Southey is dreary. However, you should still mention him when you bring up the Lake Poets. Be sure to mention that he was a far nicer guy than Wordsworth or Coleridge. Then count silently in your head. By the time you reach ten, someone will sagely opine that geniuses are often really horrible people.

Some of his poems are simple, engaging lyrics like the Lucy poems ("She lived alone / and none could know / when Lucy ceased to be / but she is in her grave, and oh! / the difference to me!"). Some are dense, ambitious accounts of interior experience, like "Intimations of Immortality," an important vector for the idea that children are purer and wiser than adults. For Wordsworth, we come into this world "trailing clouds of glory." (This would be a very different poem if Wordsworth had ever changed a diaper.)

His magnum opus is *The Prelude*. (Not necessarily his best opus, but definitely the biggest.) This is an autobiographical account of his coming of age as a poet and a person who walks around looking at wildflowers. Despite its undramatic subject material, it's still surprisingly readable, as is Wordsworth's poetry in general. This quality eventually won him a wide audience, and toward the end of his life, Wordsworth was made Poet Laureate. This seems to have impressed him very little, and in his new position, he continued to walk around thinking about what cows looked like in the rain.

	Importance	Accessibility	Fun
Poems	10	5	7

SAMUEL TAYLOR COLERIDGE (1772–1834)

Coleridge was an opium addict, as every poetry lover and educated drug addict knows. When he really sat down and wrote a poem properly, it was ravishing. Mostly, though, he just got high. At last, he gave up all useful activity and became a pure waster, living in people's spare rooms on the strength of his acknowledged genius. He was the kind of houseguest who wakes at noon and staggers blindly down the hallway, looking like he's going to throw up.

Despite his wasterism, Coleridge not only created a theoretical framework for British Romanticism in his *Biographia Literaria*, he wrote several of the most beautiful poems of the century. Among his best known is "The Rime of the Ancient Mariner." This is about a sailor whose ship has a friendly mascot—an albatross. For no reason at all, the sailor shoots the albatross. Immediately, things turn ugly. The ship sails of its own volition to a desolate part of the ocean, where it will not budge. The sailor's shipmates string the rotting albatross around his neck to punish him, hoping to appease the vengeful ocean spirit. Not a chance. A Gothic nightmare ensues. Everybody begins to die of of pure unstoppable fun, like the "Proverbs of Hell." Some examples: "The lust of the goat is the bounty of God" and "Prudence is a rich, ugly old maid courted by Incapacity." There is also a scene in which Blake visits a printing house in hell, and a fantasia in which he seizes an angel and shows him his "eternal lot," which involves a deep pit full of chained monkeys and baboons, busily tearing off one another's arms. No way, bullshit, says the Angel. Blake retorts, Yeah, talking to squares like you is a waste of time. Basically, if you just, e.g., slept with your brother-in-law, and you feel like scum, you can read this and feel instantly better. (Sending it to your sister when she finds out, though, doesn't help. Wow, did that not help.)

In *The Marriage of Heaven and Hell*, the devil is not the principle of evil, but of energy, while the angels are prating milksops. It's funny, beautiful, and incidentally wildly pro-sex. In fact, it's so dogmatically pro-sex, it makes you feel guilty for not being more promiscuous. Before you know it, you're back in the hot tub with your brother-in-law and a bottle of Tanqueray. In fact, if you see your spouse reading it, call a lawyer.

It has also been called the first free verse poem in English. However, readers who have been paying attention will know that saying something was "first" is the academic's equivalent of liking something on Facebook.

All of Blake's later works—usually known as the "Prophetic Books"—are based on a personal theology involving the Four Zoas. In Blakean thought, the four Zoas existed in the eternal time before our fallen age. They were: Urizen (reason), Tharmas (the body), Luvah (love), and Urthonah (the soul). Each of them also had an "emanation," i.e., a lady friend.

These characters were thoroughly elaborated in Blake's mind: Urizen drove the horses of instruction, which pulled the sun; Tharmas had a vagina instead of a penis, but was otherwise masculine, while his emanation, Enion, was built like a she-male. There were also sub-zoas and sub-sub-zoas, including Ozoth, who had eight million and eight children.

The world went wrong, in Blake's cosmogony, when Urizen (reason) began to write laws and proclaim himself the One God. He invaded the land of Urthonah (the soul), and all hell broke loose. The Zoas were separated from their emanations, and Man fell from a state of Innocence into a state of Experience. Man was then shut up in the Mundane Egg (the world), separated from the objects of desire.

Man's rent went up, and a decent T-shirt now ran Man twenty bucks. When Man looked in the mirror, he now had a noticeable double chin. Girls stopped looking at Man in the street, though Man could not stop looking at girls. It was impossible to find a good egg salad sandwich in Man's neighborhood anymore. Damned Urizen!

Even if you are determined to see the Zoas as an allegory for states of mind, once Blake starts on Urizen, Rintrah, Palamabron, and the gang, he sounds like a raving escapee from an H. P. Lovecraft novel. Worse, he writes as if his readers all learned about the Zoas and the Mundane Egg in primary school. In short, it's gobbledygook. Even with pages and pages of notes, it can be like banging your head against a Mundane Egg, while dread Cthulhu goes in and out of focus in your mind's eye.

	Importance	Accessibility	Fun
Songs of Innocence/			
Songs of Experience	10	9	8
The Marriage of Heaven			
and Hell	10	6	10
The Prophetic Books,			
Milton, etc.	2	1	2

WILLIAM WORDSWORTH (1770–1850)

De Quincey described Wordsworth's first book, *Lyrical Ballads*, as a "revelation of untrodden worlds." They are untrodden both because of the untrammeled nature of the poet's visioning and because the poet is living in the middle of nowhere. In fact, if nature leaves you cold, these poems will leave you asleep. However, if your heart has ever swelled with emotion at the sight of a whiskered catkin 'pon the wintry air, or a nice patio, this is the hard stuff. No one can beat Wordsworth for the way a cloud casts a shadow on a grassy slope, while a cow wanders out of the shadow, and its russet hide brightens in the sunlight, its muddied fetlock bends—oh! And the poet has a pure emotion, usually of rapture.

Basically all of Wordsworth's poetry is about this cow rapture. He may hang it on a portrait of a beggar, or a theory of immortality, or his friend Lucy's death, but basically he's saying, Damn, the Lake District rocks. The scenery is front and center, while the actors and the action are tiny, tiny elements somewhere in a dusty corner of the poem. Sometimes the predominance of scenery makes the poetry like a meal consisting of hundreds of plates.

LORD BYRON (1788–1824)

Byron's reputation as bad boy has lasted better than his reputation as poet. The words of the hysterical ex who called him "mad, bad, and dangerous to know" are more often quoted than anything he ever wrote. Even when he was a best-selling poet (yes, they had those then), he was famous for his perverted morals and his sex appeal. He received anonymous letters with lines like "I cannot longer exist without acknowledging the tumultuous and agonizing delight with which my soul burns at the glowing beauties of yours." Ladies disguised themselves as chambermaids to get to see him in hotels; in Geneva, tourists spied on him with telescopes. His disaffected wife termed the craze "Byromania." When people weren't trying to get off with Byron themselves, they were outraged by him. Byron commented: "The Morning Post in particular has found out that I am a sort of Richard the Third—deformed in mind and body—the last piece of information is not very new to a man who passed five years at a public school."

The facts: Byron was literally deformed, with a clubfoot. From the shins up, though, he was pretty—and vain. He was always dieting and wore curlers in his hair at night. By the evidence of his letters, he was bisexual at least; probably gay, but he certainly gave women a shot. He even had an affair with his half sister. His affectations were legion: he kept a bear as a pet at Cambridge because dogs weren't allowed, and drank from a human skull he'd had mounted as a cup.

He became famous overnight with the publication of the autobiographical *Childe Harold's Pilgrimage*. This is the work that introduced the world to the Byronic hero—a slacker type who knocks around Europe, drawling about how pointless life is, while breaking women's hearts in a series of glamorous locations. A nineteenth-century version of a trashy bestseller, it's borderline unreadable today. *Don Juan*, however, where Byron plays the same material for laughs, is still good fun, as are his shorter lyrics, especially "She walks in beauty like the night."

Like most Romantics, Byron was a lefty. He became a real, not just Byronic, hero at the end of his life by going to fight in the Greek Revolution against the Turks. The Greeks mysteriously welcomed this novice, with the curlers and the dieting, etc., as if he were Napoleon. Although he had no military experience, he took part of the army under his control, but died of fever before he could lead his troops into battle. Thanks to this timely exit, he is still revered as a hero by the credulous Greeks.

	Importance	Accessibility	Fun
Don Juan, short poems	8	9	8
Childe Harold's Pilgrimage	2	9	2

PERCY BYSSHE SHELLEY (1792–1822)

Shelley really, really couldn't do life. At Eton, he was routinely beaten up for being a sissy. At Oxford, he wrote and circulated a pamphlet called "The Necessity of Atheism." Good-bye, Oxford. Then he eloped with a sixteen-year-old girl to free her from the tyranny of her father, despite the fact that he didn't especially like her. By this time, his own father, who was his only means of support, was barely speaking to him.

A few years later, he left his wife—with two children, and another on the way—to run away with Mary Wollstonecraft Godwin . . . and her sister Claire. Since Mr. Godwin was Shelley's most influential friend in London, this was not a sharp career move. Still worse, Shelley's abandoned wife drowned herself in the Serpentine, and the one Godwin sister he hadn't abducted, Fanny, poisoned herself. Then Shelley and Mary had an open marriage which amounted to him cheating while Mary stayed home and had a series of babies who all died. Finally he took a boat out with two friends, hit a storm, and was killed at twenty-nine. Ten out of ten!

He was probably the least successful of all the Romantic poets. Despite being good friends with international superstar Byron, he is estimated to have only earned forty pounds from all his writings. Of course, forty pounds was worth more in those days. You could still buy an okay sofa for that money, for instance. Shelley could have bought a sofa, and called it the poetry sofa, and then he and Mary Shelley could have sat on it saying, Well, this was certainly worth a whole life's work!

Shelley was the most idealistic of the Romantics. He was an egalitarian, a feminist, a pacifist, a believer in free love, and a vegetarian. His poetry is all waterfalls, Love, and Beauty, and his only mode is ecstatic hyperbole. In "Ode to a Skylark," the skylark's song is more lovely than "all that ever was joyous and clear and fresh." Furthermore, Shelley assumes that because it has a pretty voice, the bird is perfectly happy—and wise too! Specifically, it knows more about death "than we Mortals dream." If you think about it, Shelley is also suggesting it is immortal.

Shelley had a far greater interest in science than the other Romantics (although his interest clearly didn't extend to ornithology). Scientific ideas repeatedly crop up in his poems, looking a little surprised and uncertain as to how they got there. Then they're washed away by a waterfall with chunks of Love and Beauty floating in it.

Sometimes Shelley's philosophy falls into a hopeless tangle of straining thoughtness. Sometimes his images are so hyper-sublime, it's like drinking a gallon of honey. Still, the poetry is beautiful. It's beautiful, no matter how stupid it is—like a skylark, or Jessica Alba. For long stretches, it's hard to tear yourself away, even when you stopped understanding a word of it two pages before.

His short poems—"Ode to the West Wind," "Ode to a Skylark," "Ozymandias," etc.—are the place to start. For many people, they will also be the place to finish. Once he gets beyond a page, his poems become radically more challenging. His medium-length poems—like "Adonais," "Mont Blanc," and "Epipsychidion"—are still well worth deciphering. The wealth of the ideas, once you figure out what they are, more than repays the effort.

His long poems, however, are strictly for the birds, if you can get the birds to eat them. The only one of his long poems that is still read is *Prometheus Unbound*, a sequel to Aeschylus's play about the rebellion of Prometheus against Jupiter. Here, after Prometheus forgives Jupiter in his heart, he is freed magically—in fact, the whole world is freed from the chains of tyranny, and Jupiter is cast out! Whee! In the aftermath of this revolution, not only is the world freer, but everyone is good, and every face is beautiful; along with tyrants, all selfishness, stupidity, and warts are gone. If anyone could make this work, it's Shelley. Except, he doesn't.

CROWD-SOURCING SCIENCE PROJECT

Shelley's body was burned by his wife and friends, on the shore where it washed up. Edward Trelawny pulled his heart from the ashes, the story goes, and Mary Shelley kept it for the rest of her life.

The present author questions whether these people, who were not doctors, could really have been sure what they were dealing with was a heart. It could have been anything, so the present author believes, from a kneecap to a chunk of wood. This "heart," wrapped up in a page of "Adonais," was still among Mary Shelley's effects when she died. For generations, this "fact" has been uncritically repeated by critics and biographers.

I suggest that any reader who believes this story should buy a cow's heart from the butcher, roast it, wrap it in a page of "Adonais," and see how many decades it lasts.

	Importance	Accessibility	Fun
Short poems	10	6	8
Medium poems	9	2	9
Long poems	5	1	2

MARY SHELLEY (1797–1851)

While Mary Shelley had a long and varied writing career, she's remembered only for the novel *Frankenstein, or The Modern Prometheus*, written when she was nineteen. The inspiration for it came when she, Shelley, Byron, and John William Polidori (Byron's personal doctor, and later author of *The Vampyre*) were stuck indoors during a long rainy spell in Geneva. They started reading ghost stories to pass the time, and Byron suggested they all write a supernatural story themselves. Then the weather cleared up, and Shelley and Byron set off on a trip into the mountains, forgetting the whole thing. Mary Shelley, left behind as always, wrote *Frankenstein*. Percy Shelley had been trying to convince Mary to write for a long time (in between trying to convince her to sleep with his friends), so everyone was happy, except Mary Shelley, 'cause her babies all died.

The plot of *Frankenstein* is all over the place. Shelley gives it a pointless framing narrative, in the form of letters by a polar explorer who runs into Victor Frankenstein in the Arctic; she then dives into a bildungsroman section taking Victor from childhood to the point of creating his monster. The monster has his own bildungsroman section, in which he is spying on his next-door neighbors, who have their own backstory. Victor is also always going on trips, to avoid the horror that is going on, so successfully that often nothing is going on. Thus the book wanders hither and yon, only occasionally stumbling over a chunk of plot.

The monster is a hideous creature, abhorred by mankind. People flee from him on sight or attack him in hysteria. Shelley is vague about what makes the monster so grotesque, but we assume that the body Frankenstein used was a little overripe. There's also a strong sense of the monster as outcast, which is probably faintly autobiographical; the book was written at a time when Mary and Percy and Byron had all run off to Switzerland because they were social pariahs back home. The monster, like them, is a vegetarian and insists repeatedly that he was good and kind until mankind's rejection embittered him. However, we assume that Byron and the Shelleys did not, like the monster, go on a killing spree in frustration. We assume this; however, no one may ever know for sure.

THAT MARRIAGE

After Percy Bysshe Shelley's death, Mary never remarried, although she received many proposals. She refused one man—a then-famous actor—and told him that having been married to one genius, she could only marry another. His response was to attempt to convince his friend Washington Irving to propose to her. Irving didn't bite, so we don't know whether Mary Shelley thought he was a genius.

The present author feels that this would be a great premise for a romantic comedy, in which various hot men try to convince Mary Shelley (Cameron Diaz) that they're geniuses, until she realizes—after falling for regular guy Owen Wilson—that a good heart is what counts. This scene could involve the unwrapping of Percy's heart for both comic and symbolic effect.

In real life, Mary decided to "live for her son," while tirelessly promoting Percy's reputation. My movie would bury this unfortunate fact. The world would be much happier if we could all erroneously believe that Mary Shelley wised up, grew as a person, and married a nice guy who owned a hardware store. Or maybe he's a veterinarian. I haven't decided yet.

	Importance	Accessibility	Fun
Frankenstein	7	7	6

JOHN KEATS (1795–1821)

Keats was a proper London guttersnipe. He was born at his parents' inn in Moorgate, the Swan and Hoop. When he finished school, he was apprenticed to a surgeon-apothecary and completed his training before succumbing to his poetic urges. Being a physician was then a low tradesman's calling, just as it will become again once we ease the stranglehold of the survival lobby.

Keats's low beginnings were often alluded to by his many hostile reviewers.

In an essay in *Blackwood's*, "On the Cockney School of Poetry," they singled out for ridicule the now-famous opening of Keats's epic *Endymion*: "A thing of beauty is a joy forever." They added the snobbish: "It is a better and a wiser thing to be a starved apothecary than a starved poet; so back to the shop, Mr John." It's almost prescient in its perfect wrongness.

On the other hand, the quarterly's nasty review may strike a chord with anyone who's ever struggled with Romantic poetry:

> Reviewers have been sometimes accused of not reading the works which they affected to criticise. On the present occasion we . . . honestly confess that we have not read [*Endymion: A Poetic Romance*]. Not that we have been wanting in our duty—far from it—indeed, we have made efforts almost as superhuman as the story itself appears to be, to get through it; but we are forced to confess that we have not been able to struggle beyond the first of the four books. . . . We should extremely lament this want of energy, were it not for one consolation—namely, that we are no better acquainted with the meaning of the book through which we have so painfully toiled, than we are with that of the three which we have not looked into.

In his "Adonais," Shelley accuses these mean reviewers of having caused the early death of Keats. Keats's fianceé, Fanny Brawne, has also been blamed, on account of her fickle ways. The likelihood is, though, that it probably wasn't *Blackwood's*, or Fanny, or a gypsy curse, that killed John Keats, since he had terminal tuberculosis.

Although he never used his doctor's training in any other way, it served to tell Keats exactly what was wrong with him, how incurable it was, and how little time he had left. Most of his poetry includes a reference to the transience of life, and sometimes even to the special, fast-track transience of Keats's life. The worst of it was, Keats was the one Romantic who didn't even slightly believe in heaven. He was just dying dying. Well, the least we can do is read his poetry, right? Read it for Keats! He was twenty-six and in love! Let's all do our bit to ensure this poor guy's life had meaning.

BONUS GUILT TRIP

On Keats's grave, the marker reads, per his instructions: HERE LIES ONE WHOSE NAME WAS WRIT IN WATER. So sad! Dead at twenty-six, with that thought in his head!

So you see, if you don't read Keats's poems, he could be right, and it would be your fault.

Oh, and wait—before you go, the actual poetry

Thought you got away with that, did you?

As with Shelley, Keats has short, medium-length, and long poems. Short poems are always a gift to modern people, who typically have no attention span and do have cable. With Keats, the short poems are also his most perfect work. Start with the odes, like "Ode to a Nightingale" and "Ode on a Grecian Urn." Also check out "La Belle Dame Sans Merci" and the sonnet "Bright Star." From here, move on to his (medium-length) story poems: "The Eve of St. Agnes," "Lamia," "Isabella." They're macabre folk tales in verse, and hauntingly beautiful. Finally, when you can't put it off any longer, you can look at the long poems. These, frustratingly, alternate between turgid blather and lines that are ravishing. They also annoyingly revive all that stuff about the Greco-Roman gods. In *Endymion*, the moon goddess and a shepherd prince fall in love. Then we have *Hyperion* and *The Fall of Hyperion*, about the transition of power from the older Titans to the young, fresh-faced Olympian gods. These mainly consist of the washed-up Titans grumbling and snapping at one another. They were never finished because Keats died while still an Olympian.

An extra pleasure is reading Keats's letters. These range from pathetic begging letters to explanations of his literary theories. A particular high point is the explanation of his theory of negative capability. This isn't when you can't do anything, it's when you're "capable of being in uncertainty . . . without any irritable reaching after fact & reason." Not trying to know anything allows you to achieve great things, according to Keats. Contemporary people can achieve this effortlessly every time they lose their Internet connection.

	Importance	Accessibility	Fun
Odes	10	5	8
The story poems	9	5	8
Endymion and the Hyperions	6	2	4
Letters	6	8	7

JOHANN WOLFGANG VON GOETHE (1749–1832)

In the late seventeenth and early eighteenth centuries, Germany, which had been a cultural backwater, suddenly became the philosophy capital of the world. Dozens of intellectual movements sprang into being, sparred with one another and were elaborated in coffeehouses and disseminated in journals. This would all end in a Hegelian morass, which gave onto a Marxist swamp, and then a National Socialist cesspit that ... well, we all know that story. Poor Germans! Poor anybody living near the Germans!

In the English-speaking world, we protect ourselves from this dangerous intellectual movement by maintaining almost complete ignorance of it. From this complex scene, full of geniuses and madmen, the only author we know is Goethe.

The scope of this polymathic genius's career is staggering. He wrote reams of poetry and prose; elaborated a theory of color; botanized; invented the atom; composed symphonies while standing on one finger on water; built himself a wife using only rubber bands, electricity, and a woman; and whatever else he did. Anyway, it was more than enough. Oh and "Goethe" is pronounced by groaning like a mummy then making a sound like spitting out gum.

While many of his literary works are important to Germans, only two of them have mattered to English speakers: *The Sorrows of Young Werther* and *Faust*.

The Sorrows of Young Werther

The Sorrows of Young Werther is the most unalloyed, even shameless, presentation of the Byronic hero. Werther, a jobless young man whose funds uncannily materialize from thin air, goes to a pretty rural town to think thoughts. For some pages, he adores the beauty of nature and the innocent wisdom of children. Then he begins to adore the beauty of Charlotte and the innocent wisdom of Charlotte. Uh-oh! Charlotte is engaged! Werther continues to hang around, although

Charlotte shows no sign of getting unengaged. She loves Werther like a brother, or like yesterday's mashed potatoes.

Furthermore, her fiancé, Albert, becomes Werther's best buddy. So W. hangs around the happy couple masochistically, envying Albert's sensible nature and actual job, while also dismissing him as "not right for Charlotte." After a while, Werther's so inconsolable, he leaves town and finds paid work. In the new town, there's even another girl, who isn't engaged. Is Werther on the path to recovery? No. The people in this new town aren't pure enough to admire Werther properly. In a fit of narcissism, he quits.

He returns to Charlotte's side, and Albert's side—they are now happily married. In this new phase, the unemployed Werther virtually lives at their house, languishing and sniveling. It's almost as bad as living with Coleridge. At last—after a single dramatic embrace with Charlotte (i.e., pity snog)—Werther kills himself.

The success of this novel was staggering. Across Europe, Werther became a role model for youth. Everyone wanted to be like this whining reject. Scores of young men killed themselves in imitation, until Goethe was ready to go around killing them himself. For the rest of his life, Goethe was revered as the man who created Werther, even after he had written far greater books, invented colors, and created the world in six days.

FUN WITH HISTORY!

Napoleon claimed to have read *The Sorrows of Young Werther* seven times. Presumably, in his copy, some wag erased the part where Werther kills himself and wrote in a section where, in despair, he conquers Europe.

Faust

This is a Romantic/Idealist reworking of the Doctor Faustus story, in the form of two plays in rhyming verse which are totally unsuited for performance. They have nonetheless been performed hundreds of times in Germany, in front of actual audiences who were not being held hostage at the time. It is exactly as amazing as the fact that Swedes eat rotten fish. Goethe worked on *Faust* all his life, beginning Part One as a young man and finishing Part Two shortly before his death at eighty-three. In dog years, that's enough time to write a performable play, even for most dogs.

Part One of *Faust*, if not performable, is very readable. It is renowned as the great German classic. Part Two is renowned as a farrago of half-digested philosophy and jaw-droppingly stupid premises. Very few people read it. They can be recognized by their snow-white hair, trembling hands, and staring, mindless eyes. Also, to these people, *Mein Kampf* makes sense.

Goethe's *Faust* begins much like Marlowe's. The respected and beloved Doctor Faust is very bored. So he conjures the demon Mephistopheles, who offers him magical services in exchange for his soul. Done! Faust then uses his new godlike powers to seduce a poor girl, Margarete, with fancy jewels Mephistopheles gives him. Nietzsche commented: "A little seamstress is seduced and made unhappy. Surely that could not have happened without supernatural interference? No, of course not! Without the aid of the incarnate devil the great scholar could never have accomplished this." The description of the seduction, and Margarete's naïve love, are prettily rendered. Still, Nietzsche is so right.

Around this central nonevent are various lesser episodes, mostly played for comic effect. This is German comedy, which is a little like German cookery—heavy, unhealthy, meat with a side of meat. There's even something chilling about it, like a big fat Nazi pounding his fist on a table and belly-laughing, while behind closed doors the victims . . . In short, it's not funny.

Meanwhile, for the hapless Margarete, everything goes from bad to worse. She poisons her mother by mistake; Faust kills her brother; at last, she murders her illegitimate baby and is put in prison. Still, when Margarete dies, she goes to heaven. Okay, whatever. End Part One.

In Part Two, Goethe lands with a splash on the other side of the shark, looks around to orient himself, and can't. Faust makes a homunculus, which does nothing; then he goes to Greece—not our Greece, but ancient Greece, where he goes to war to defend his lover, Helen of Troy, etc. Finally, Faust dies, because of a deal he had with Mephistopheles that he would die when he acknowledged that he was truly satisfied. Why is he satisfied now? A genius needs no reasons. Then, also for no reason, Faust goes to heaven. No last-minute repentance, no good deeds. The angels just snatch him from under Mephistopheles' nose, because they feel like it, done.

Needless to say, on the pussiest day of his life, Marlowe wouldn't have sent Faust to heaven. The only excuse we can offer is that Goethe identified with Faust, was dying of old age himself, and knew he would meet a thousand Werther wannabes in hell.

	Importance	Accessibility	Fun
The Sorrows of Young Werther	10	9	8
Faust	10	4	3

ALEXANDER PUSHKIN (1799–1837)

Seemingly every Russian literary figure tells a story about discovering Pushkin, forgetting everything else, and hiding in a cupboard to deliriously consume his collected works, then emerging months later—a writer! Alexander Pushkin is by far the most beloved Russian writer; in fact, he is probably the most beloved Russian. Even the Communist Party loved Pushkin, though they expressed their love in typical joy-killing fashion by forcing schoolchildren to learn by heart not only his poetry, but his biography. The fact that Russians love Pushkin anyway proves that they really, really, are not like us.

Russians are happy to read all of Pushkin's many, many works all day and then go to one of the many, many operas based on them at night. The rest of the world has really only warmed to his stories—which range from historical romances like *The Captain's Daughter* to Gothic tales like "The Queen of Spades"—and to his masterpiece, the novel-in-verse, *Eugene Onegin*.

Like most of Pushkin's output, *Eugene Onegin* is influenced by Byron, and particularly by *Don Juan*. Eugene, a typical Byronic hero with sexy looks and no work ethic, goes to the countryside to try to conquer his ennui. Immediately he attracts the notice of the young Tatiana.

Tatiana is just as ennui-ridden as Eugene. Bored to distraction, she writes him a letter, offering herself. But unlike Byron's heroes, Eugene is not going to sleep with a woman just to spice up a poem, or to prove to readers that his author isn't gay. He gives Tatiana some song and dance about how she's better off without him. He goes on to kill his own best friend in a duel, but is disappointed to find that even this is pretty dull. Years later, he meets Tatiana again, and falls head over heels for her, presumably because she no longer gives a damn, and because he is bored.

Pushkin was giving an insider's view of the Romantic psyche; he himself died in a duel with a man who was rumored to be sleeping with his wife. If you have any Russian friends born before 1970, they can tell you the whole story in a rote, dispirited singsong.

THE SUPERFLUOUS MAN

Eugene Onegin is the first instance of a type in Russian literature known as "the superfluous man." He is "superfluous" because he can find no way to apply his talents and energies. Instead he just hangs around, making everyone nervous.

After Onegin, he reappears in Lermontov's *A Hero of Our Time*. This version regresses to a more Byronic self-regard, shallowness, and misogyny. Despite these advantages, Lermontov has never really caught on outside Russia. Other noted superfluous men are Bazarov in Turgenev's *Fathers and Sons* and Goncharov's comic hero *Oblomov*, who literally refuses to get out of bed.

As Russian literature developed, critics and writers became increasingly unsympathetic to this character. Soon they were treating the superfluous man as a spineless wreck who ought to get a job. It also wouldn't kill him to become politically active, and maybe settle down with a nice girl. The superfluous man persists in Russia to this day, although he has changed with the times, becoming the superfluous gulag prisoner in the Stalin era before finding his ultimate form as today's superfluous drunk.

	Importance	Accessibility	Fun
Stories	3	10	8
Eugene Onegin	8	7	9

ALFRED TENNYSON (1809–1892)

While Romanticism was dying, giving way to a Victorian culture too stuffy and mercantile for poetic flights, one man continued to carry its torch. All his long, post-Romantic life, Alfred Tennyson continued trying to be Keats. He never quite pulled it off, but in his best moments, no one could do lovely, lonesome melancholy quite like he could.

Today, we mainly know him as the poet who is the most uncool. The average Tennyson lover is one hundred years old, drinks sherry, and rides to hounds. He or she will be a Tory MP, from a part of England so rural that the villagers still worship badgers. Basically, collecting doilies, wearing a muttonchop beard, and liking Tennyson all have the same number of Uncool Points. Therefore, only the very cool should read beyond this paragraph.

Welcome, cool person. Nice shirt. Now: Tennyson's first two books got such bad reviews that he went into a sulk and didn't publish for ten years. The second book, nonetheless, contains some of Tennyson's greatest hits. To single out one of the most celebrated, "The Lotos-Eaters" is probably the best thing ever written about drug abuse by a non-addict. Here Odysseus's men, having eaten of the lotus, can't be bothered to sail home; they would rather just lie there: "With half-shut eyes ever to seem / Falling asleep in a half-dream." The poem conveys the strange lovesickness of the addict for his drug, but wisely omits the part where he watches *Transformers II* ten times while failing to notice that two hours ago he wet his pants—this despite the fact that Tennyson's brother was a junkie, so he'd been there. Partly because of this sure instinct for avoiding TMI, and sometimes just I, these early poems have an eerie purity.

When Tennyson published his third collection, the time was ripe for his poetry. Reviews were ecstatic, sales were huge. His next book was *In Memoriam*, a one-hundred-page poem mourning the death of his best friend Arthur Hallam. He had been working on it for seventeen years, so it's fair to say that Arthur's death hit him pretty hard. The poem's success may have balanced that sorrow out a bit. It won him the Poet Laureateship, a baronetcy, and the girl he had been courting for almost twenty years.

In Memoriam is still considered Tennyson's masterpiece. Unlike earlier poems of mourning such as Milton's "Lycidas" or Shelley's "Adonais," the grief here is personal. Tennyson's lines about the first dismal, awkward Christmas without his friend will resonate with anyone who has lost a loved one, or who has to go home for Christmas. The poem quickly gets speculative, investigating the implications of the Christian afterlife. If Arthur is in heaven, does he watch over Tennyson? Wait, maybe Tennyson doesn't want Arthur seeing what he gets up to. In fact—if Arthur is an angel now, does he still like Tennyson? On the whole, Tennyson decides: "It is better to have loved and lost, than never to have loved at all." Yes, that line was about friendship. It really isn't better to have loved and lost romantically, in case you hadn't noticed.

Once Tennyson became Poet Laureate, he lost touch with his inner Keats. Now he seemed painfully conscious of his audience, as if, just when he was settling into an ethereal trance, a voice behind him would pipe up, "Whatcha doing, Tennyson? Are you writing your poetry?" He began to embark on long, high-concept projects in keeping with his role as National Treasure. Worse still, he wrote patriotic wastepaper like *The Charge of the Light Brigade*. This solemnly celebrates a catastrophically stupid action in the Crimean War, in which soldiers rode down a valley in between two Russian artillery battalions, getting blasted at like shooting gallery ducks, for no reason. Thanks a lot, Tennyson, because we really can't encourage this kind of thing enough.

The National Treasure poems include *Maud: a Monodrama*, a long psychological poem which would be all right to read if you were in prison and it was the only book, and *The Idylls of the King*, a mournful, trance-like version of the Arthur story, which would be all right to read even if you had five or six books in prison. These blockbuster poems came at a watershed in literary history. It is the moment when people started drifting away from poetry and preferring the novel as a serious form. That's right, everyone read these works and never bought poetry again. Correlation does not imply causation, but still, where there's smoke, let's go ahead and blame Tennyson.

	Importance	Accessibility	Fun
Early poems	8	7	8
In Memoriam	8	5	6
Maud, Idylls of the King	5	5	4

ROBERT BROWNING (1812–1889)

If Tennyson wanted to be Keats, Robert Browning spent his early years straining to be Shelley. For a time, he went so far as to give up God and meat in emulation of his hero. He may have gone a little too far: his first published poem, "Pauline," had the distinction of not selling a single copy, a sales history which makes even Shelley look grossly commercial.

Browning is considered to represent a bridge between the Romantics and the modern poets in subject matter and technique. Browning also presaged the modern era in that he only lived off his family's money until he was in his thirties, whereupon he married an older, more successful woman and lived off hers.

That marriage, between Browning and Elizabeth Barrett, is the best known literary love story of the nineteenth century. She was frail and cloistered, guarded by her jealous father; he was a dashing young man who fell for her when he read her poems. They spent their fifteen years of marriage in Italy, the country that put the Roma in Romantic, as the revolutions of 1848 rose and fell around them.

Elizabeth's fame and stature as a poet grew; and Robert's grew as the person she was married to.

After Elizabeth's death, Browning returned to England. There he became a fixture of the literary scene, and his work began to grow in critical opinion, and he was finally acknowledged as one of the greats of the age. Once his poetry caught on, it never let go: the Browning Society, founded in his lifetime, still has many chapters. Meanwhile, of Elizabeth's oeuvre, all that is still read is "How do I love thee? Let me count the ways." (Eight, as it happens. It's a pretty short poem. However, she nobly doesn't include paying the rent as one of the ways.)

Browning's poems often read like finely observed, psychologically acute short stories, in vividly evoked historical settings. The language is dense, sometimes to impenetrability, and even includes some coinages of his own. Browning was largely self-educated, and had an autodidact's love of arcane knowledge, which he loves to inflict on his readers. He also has the autodidact's lacunae—one poem ends with a reference to an "old nun's twat," which Browning believed was a type of headgear.

He is best known for his dramatic monologues. The most famous is "My Last Duchess," in which a sixteenth-century aristocrat explains why his wife's undignified behavior made it completely understandable that he had to kill her. At the end, we realize he is addressing an emissary from the father of the next duchess. It's worth reading both to get a sense of what Browning does, and because it is very short.

Browning's most cited poem is "Childe Roland to the Dark Tower Came," a favorite not only of modernist poets, but also of fantasy and science fiction writers; it's inspired work by both Stephen King and Neil Gaiman. Taking off from a passage in *King Lear*, it's the story of a medieval quest through a strange apocalyptic wasteland, shot through with a feeling of existential dread. *The Ring and the Book*, Browning's magnum opus, is more interesting to discuss than it is to read. The work is based on a sheaf of legal documents from a seventeenth-century murder trial, which Browning found in a book stall in Florence. Count Guido Franceschini had killed his wife, her parents, and a priest; that was not in dispute. The trial was to determine whether he was justified in killing them since he believed his wife was sleeping with the priest. The first and last book of twelve are in the voice of the poet; the remaining ten each reveal the viewpoint of another character involved in the proceedings. When it was published, it was widely read and even more widely admired; 140 years later, it remains 21,000 lines long and seems destined to be found someday in a book stall in Florence.

Finally, anybody with five spare minutes might enjoy Browning's lively and charming version of "The Pied Piper of Hamelin." A children's poem, a high point is the only surviving rat's report to the rat world on what befell him and all his rat friends.

	Importance	Accessibility	Fun
"My Last Duchess"	7	6	5
"Childe Roland"	5	6	6
The Ring and the Book	4	4	4
"The Pied Piper of Hamelin"	4	8	8

ROMANTIC NOVELS

By romantic novels, we mean the extravaganzas of Sir Walter Scott (1771–1832), Victor Hugo (1802–1885), Alexandre Dumas, father (1802–1870) and son (1824–1895), and a handful of others who, for two centuries, have royally entertained anyone capable of suspending disbelief.

Okay, most of these aren't great literature. They have the depth of paint. However, they also have all the frivolous pleasure of really good cupcakes, without the part where you get fat.

Here we have the dawn of the historical novel as a genre. This was when writers discovered that people in the past were two-dimensional. Evil was always punished, and all girls were very beautiful. Swashbuckling hunks, witty ripostes, page-turning plots, dovetailing coincidences—it's all here.

The only thing these authors hadn't yet realized was that the public would prefer this nonsense to be written in fifth-grade English; that advance in popular fiction would have to wait until the twentieth century. Therefore, these novels have a linguistic elegance that somewhat ennobles their cheesy substance. As beach reads, these books have only one real weakness: the long descriptions. In *The Hunchback of Notre Dame*, for instance, Hugo gives us a whole chapter describing Paris in the fifteenth century, devoting a paragraph to every major building.

Some notes on the authors: Dumas père was black, or black enough to merit a thesis project. He looked black, for instance. Like, in fifties Alabama, he would have been one nervous great French writer. Victor Hugo is considered one of the poetic geniuses of French literature. In France, his poetry is more highly rated than his novels. We, however, are going to follow prevailing English custom and treat him solely as the man who gave us Quasimodo and Jean Valjean.

> **Question:** So why aren't these novels real literature, but Dickens is?
> **Answer:** Why is a tomato not a vegetable? Don't ask me. Maybe life isn't fair?

A Dozen Cupcakes

In *The Three Musketeers*, Dumas père gives us the daring derring-do of the age of Richelieu. The wars of wit in the Paris salons; the duels and sworn friendship of D'Artagnan and the eponymous three—it's to die for. In fact, it was so good Dumas wrote two sequels—*Twenty Years After* and *The Vicomte of Bragelonne* (in which the near-geriatric musketeers restore Charles II to the English throne. Pretty sure this didn't actually happen.) Also by the elder, better Dumas, *The Count of Monte Cristo* is a less funny, but equally enchanting romp. The prison break from the Chateau d'If! Smugglers! Bandits! People buried alive! This book is finger-lickin' stupid. A man after our own hearts, Dumas built himself a Chateau de Monte Cristo with his hard-earned wealth, and filled it with parasites, party animals, and random dudes he didn't recognize when he saw them in the hallway late at night.

Dumas Jr. was not so lovable. In fact, he was the sort of douche bag who chased fast girls until he got too old, at which point he began writing denunciations of fast girls. Still, he wrote *The Lady of the Camellias*, or *Camille*, which is almost as fun as his father's work. *Camille* describes—with almost admirable dishonesty and self-aggrandizement—his youthful affair with the famous courtesan Marie DuPlessis.

Victor Hugo's *The Hunchback of Notre Dame* gives us the chaotic fifteenth-century Paris of Villon, with its glum religion and jolly cutthroats; Hugo throws in the hunchback Quasimodo and a gypsy dancing girl, Esmeralda, with a gilt-horned performing goat. *Les Miserables* (in English: The Grumps) is a far more serious work, but there are still enough thrills, chills, and two-dimensional urchins to nicely cheapen its street-level view of one of Paris's bloody rebellions. (Not the big "French Revolution," one of the later off-brand ones.)

It isn't a novel, but Edmond Rostand's play *Cyrano de Bergerac* (1897) is too gloriously frothy to miss. Ugly Cyrano writes love letters for his handsome friend, who's ironically courting . . . well, you know that story. Anyway, the scene with all the brawling poets at the patisserie is the best part. Somewhat less delightful, but still, say, eight out of ten, is *Carmen* (1845), by Prosper Mérimée. The scapegrace gypsy girl of the opera is here truly abominable, hateful, in a way that takes us subtly out of Romanticism. Still, it's not quite realism; there are too many daring crimes and flowers between the teeth to cut the mustard as real life.

In England, all we really have to rival this High Silliness is Sir Walter Scott. Just to give three unputdownable unmasterpieces: there's *The Bride of Lammermoor*, a Romeo and Juliet story with Gothic overtones; *Rob Roy*, about nobly savage Jacobite rebels in the Scottish highlands; and *Ivanhoe*, set in the England of Richard Lion-Heart.

Fact: There are a hundred other Sir Walter Scott novels. Maybe two hundred.

Fact: The cocktail "Rob Roy" is named after Rob Roy. It's basically a Manhattan with Scotch instead of bourbon. Good with cupcakes and Scott novels.

Fact: Scott was offered the position of Poet Laureate but turned it down because he didn't like the connotations of sycophancy and dullness. He recommended Southey (remember Southey?), who promptly accepted.

Fact: Despite his three hundred bestsellers and his baronetcy, etc., Scott died in debt. A true knight of the pen!

CHAPTER 10

We Also Begin to Have Americans

In the seventeenth and eighteenth centuries, Americans were too busy massacring Indians, importing slaves, burning witches, and inventing democracy to have much time for that novel in the drawer. But as the nineteenth century commenced, things began to settle down. In this period, American writers helped to create the idea of Americanness as a new way of looking at the world, free from thousands of years of cultural baggage. True, they did this by ignoring the culture of the native Americans, using European literary forms, and living in Europe whenever possible. And their individualism and radical theology may seem, at first glance, to be identical to European Romanticism—but, on closer inspection, their works turn out to have American flora and fauna in the background. There is no mistaking the meaning of those turkeys, raccoons, and skunks.

Finally, the real and lasting difference is that, in Europe, Romantics were treated, at best, as impractical dreamers of dreams. In America these dreams became central to the national idea. Freedom of religion was enshrined in the Constitution, but popularized by the works of Emerson, Whitman, and Twain. The Romantic hero of Byron became the lonely drifter of every cowboy myth. America came presupplied with noble savages and tracts of pristine forest and prairie that became the theme of patriotic hymns. From political speeches to Hollywood movies, these iconoclastic ideals of personal freedom are still alive today, long after most of the forests, prairies, and noble savages are gone.

WASHINGTON IRVING (1783–1859)

Before Washington Irving's time, American literature consisted largely of sermons, and of poems that might have been happier as sermons. These glum works aimed to remind the reader of death, with hellfire close behind. In the early nineteenth century, however, authors began to write stuff you could read with your morning doughnut without bursting into tears.

Washington Irving was the first star of the fledgling American publishing industry. He became an international figure, and, in his writings, consciously promoted his brash young country to an often skeptical Europe. Most of his works were bloggy, *Spectator*-like essays and tales, written for periodicals and published under jokey pseudonyms: Jonathan Oldstyle, Diedrich Knickerbocker, Geoffrey Crayon. Nowadays, Irving's work is mostly found as selections of tales like "Rip van Winkle" and "The Legend of Sleepy Hollow," accompanied by brightly colored illustrations and published as children's literature. For an adult, reading these is like curling up under an electric blanket. Every idea is warmhearted; every sharp edge has been padded. Whether it's a ghost story or a love story; whether it comes from the Brothers Grimm or *The Arabian Nights*, it reads like Valium.

Irving's only book-length work, *A History of New York*, is an extended satire of the Dutch colony in his native Manhattan. It begins, in *Tristram Shandy* style, with the creation of the world, and incorporates parodies of philosophy, science, and classical mythology into an anarchically goofy faux history.

One can argue that this book is unjustly neglected. It's beautifully done, as engagingly written and sharp as anything by Mark Twain. On the other hand, it's been neglected so long it has acquired a certain moldy odor. It's an obscure satire about a little known part of history, and you can't help feeling as if you are alone in a deserted archive, choking on dust as you turn the pages, which crumble as you read.

A work that had more staying power, while probably deserving less, is *Tales of the Alhambra*. During his travels in Spain, Irving actually lived for a time in the Alhambra, then still populated by ragged locals who had squatted the place time out of mind. This book is a memoir of his stay, which sprawls into yarns and folk tales about the Andalusian palace, from the days of its Moorish princes to the present. Like Irving's other tales, these have a trick of turning into children's literature in your hands. Best enjoyed with a cup of hot chocolate and an overweight cat.

	Importance	Accessibility	Fun
Tales of the Alhambra	2	9	6
Other tales	6	9	5
The History of New York	2	5	6

RALPH WALDO EMERSON (1803–1882) AND TRANSCENDENTALISM

Transcendentalism is Romanticism as preached in a Massachusetts church. It centered around Harvard College and spread through a network of experimental schools, abolitionist groups, and Utopian communes, all tucked away in the still-unspoiled wilderness of New England. Many Transcendentalists were socialists and even vegans—people who would feel right at home at a Green Party rally today. The most influential was Emerson. He espoused an extreme individualism which helped to shape our idea of what it means to be American. When Sarah Palin calls herself a "maverick," she is channeling not the Founding Fathers, but the Founding Hippie.

Much of Emerson's thought echoes that of Wordsworth. Children are pure. Inspiration is better than tradition. God is not found by studying the Bible, but by looking at a sprig of burdock and thinking, "Wow ... God made you!" Emerson, though, goes much farther. Rather than prescribing any system of ethics, he tells his readers to find their own ethics in their higher selves. At his most extreme, he proposes that every individual should decide whether to obey the law.

You may ask: Won't that cause problems, since some people are just lowlifes? No, says Emerson. While Shelley dreamed of a day when everyone was pure of heart, Emerson believes that day is now: "Every man is a lover of truth." But surely some more so? No. "As a man is equal to the church, and equal to the state, so he is equal to every other man." The philosophy of the English Romantics never went in this direction, because they had all met Coleridge.

Another difference between Emerson and the English Romantics was that Emerson was squeaky clean. He wrote under the influence not of laudanum, but of prayer. When he was looking for love, he knew without being told that his sister was off limits. He did not drink from a human skull while stroking his pet ibis. In fact, he did not drink. His stoic beliefs also entailed indifference to hardship. For instance, in his final years, Emerson suffered from dementia so crippling, he couldn't always remember his own name. Nonetheless, if asked, he would say that he was "Quite well. I have lost my mental faculties, but am perfectly well."

When people talk about Emerson's writings, they almost always mean his essays. The best of them ("Self-Reliance," "The Over-Soul," "The American Scholar") are brilliant and inspiring, even at their most impractical. Read his poems, though, only if you want a cheap laugh at his expense. While admired in his lifetime, they now read like a spoof—the sort of thing a prim maiden aunt would write in a film that was going for cheap laughs. In that spirit, there is no better way to say good-bye to Emerson than with a brief quote from his "The Humble-Bee":

Burly, dozing humble-bee,
Where thou art is clime for me.
Let them sail for Porto Rique,
Far-off heats through seas to seek;
I will follow thee alone,
Thou animated torrid-zone!

	Importance	Accessibility	Fun
Essays	8	4	7
Poems	1	9	1

FREEZING MAN

The two main Transcendentalist communes were Brook Farm and Fruitlands. Brook Farm, the more famous of the two, had luminaries like Margaret Fuller and Nathaniel Hawthorne (briefly) as residents. It was founded as a joint stock company—essentially a cooperative, where every member owned a equal share of the farm and theoretically got a share of the proceeds. However, there were no proceeds. Despite its rapid growth and numerous visitors—more than a thousand annually—the farm began to rack up debts.

In an attempt to rejuvenate the project, they turned to the utopian ideas of the French communist Fourier and began to build a phalanstery—a building designed specifically for communal living, working, and socializing. However, it apparently wasn't designed for fire safety, and it wasn't insured. After it burned to the ground, the Brook Farmers were financially devastated and gradually drifted away.

Fruitlands was a much stricter community; one member was expelled for eating a piece of fish. Not only were the people at Fruitlands vegans, they wouldn't eat root vegetables, because they grew downward, and low things are bad. Nor would they exploit animal labor, and they considered the breeding of animals "debauchery." Although the one nudist was required to wear a cotton poncho, members were otherwise encouraged to follow their own spiritual paths: one man expressed his passing emotions by wailing or rolling on the ground with delight; another played music to accompany his thoughts. Louisa May Alcott lived there briefly; her father was a founding member, which suggests that *Little Women* was an early example of stability fantasies in children raised by alternative parents.

Using philosophers instead of oxen turned out to be a nonstarter. The experiment ended in hungry disarray, and Fruitlands is mainly notable as the most aptly named utopian project, and an early, much colder, forerunner of Burning Man.

HENRY DAVID THOREAU (1817–1862)

Thoreau took the idea of the noble savage more seriously than any pissant Rousseau. His great book, *Walden*, is an account of two years spent as that very savage in a drafty shack in the woods, where he grew his own food and communed with nature. His aim was to prove that the best things in life are free—the best things being nature, leisure, and solitude. Therefore everyone should get off his back about getting a real job. In short, he was a one-man Fruitlands.

Much of his book is devoted to sneering at wimps who believe the best things in life include a warm house, fulfilling work, and at least one friend. You see, it wasn't enough for him to move into a shed and live on beans while reading the *Iliad* in Greek. It wasn't enough to rise at dawn, take a swim in an icy pond, and spend the whole day pondering the infinite. Everyone else must do the same. It was not okay to enjoy a soft bed or blueberry pie; and Thoreau also thought every achievement was vain—even the relief of the poor. No wonder that, as Emerson politely put it, Thoreau was "more solitary even than he wished."

It will also come as no surprise to cynics that Thoreau took the half-hour walk to his mother's house every week to bring her his laundry and that he sometimes left his hermitage to go to parties. In many ways, he was just a nineteenth-century boomerang kid, pitching a tent in Mom's backyard because he couldn't face working for the Man.

Today, even the weakest sybarite can appreciate his work. This is partly because Walden contains great nature writing, which we appreciate much more now that we've got rid of nature, with all its horrid bugs and things. It's also because we now feel comfortable cheering at Thoreau's rants while lying on a sofa and ordering out for dinner—fearless iconoclasm in its twenty-first-century form.

	Importance	Accessibility	Fun
Walden	6	6	6

EDGAR ALLAN POE (1809–1849)

It's hard not to feel sorry for Edgar Allan Poe. All he wanted was respect and a little money in his pocket, but every time he got close to this, he promptly screwed up. He drank too much, blew job opportunities, and publicly advertised his disdain for more successful writers. Plus, he married his thirteen-year-old cousin. Even back then, when breaking the law was still legal, marrying your thirteen-year-old cousin was over the line.

His poem "The Raven" made him moderately famous, but it was a series of savagely condescending book reviews that brought him his first real attention. Poe's criticism was popular largely as blood sport. He reserved particular disdain for the "Frogpondians," as he called the Transcendentalists, but he attacked everyone. (Note to aspiring writers: "everyone" inevitably includes people who might otherwise have helped you in your career.)

Poe died young, shortly after being found wandering the streets of Baltimore in drunken confusion. The precise circumstances that led him there remain mysterious, and his death has been the source of endless fascination and speculation, by those people who like to speculate fascinatedly.

Another source of controversy is "the problem of Poe," which is essentially whether he was any damn good. Poe has enjoyed a much better reputation in France than at home, the result of translations of his work into French by Charles Baudelaire, notable for their high Baudelaire-to-Poe ratio. In the English-speaking world, some consider him a genius, others consider him a clod. Therefore, whether you love or hate his works, you're covered. However, keep in mind that there is no debate about the "thirteen-year-old cousin problem," so citing Poe as a forerunner will not help you in court, at all, at all.

The Works

Poe admired the Romantics; the public wanted the low Gothic. He compromised by churning out an unholy farrago of the two. His stories were either melodramatically morbid or preeningly intellectual, and sometimes both. Most read like what they are: overwrought one-note ideas worked up into a saleable product. (Seriously. "The Pit and the Pendulum"? "The Premature Burial"? There is probably an undiscovered story somewhere called "The Dark Place with the Scary Thing.") The prose is dense and overheated, almost gooey. However, the best of them, like "The Fall of the House of Usher," are richly atmospheric, and the specific hysteria of stories like "The Tell-Tale Heart" and "The Black Cat" is unforgettable. Poe turns these into studies of a Gothic psychology that has never exactly existed but somehow feels agonizingly familiar. There is no reason, though, to move on to his only novel. *The Narrative of Arthur Gordon Pym* is a sensational mash of shipwrecks, cannibalism, racism, and something like early science fiction. Now imagine your college roommate wrote it.

His poetry is thumping, syncopated doggerel which always ends in an early grave. For single verses, it has the naïve potency of nursery rhymes: "I was a child / And she was a child / In that kingdom by the sea / But we loved with a love that was more than love / I and my Annabel Lee." Over long stretches, it has the naïve impotence of bad poetry. Sometimes, Poe's overwrought style creates unintentional comedy: for instance, in "The Raven," when a stray bird flies into his room, the narrator gravely addresses it with the question: "Tell me what thy lordly name is on the Night's Plutonian shore?" This is just the beginning of a series of questions like "Is there balm in Gilead?" Despite the fact that the bird says one word over and over, just like a trained bird, the narrator is convinced it is a prophet of the unseen. The crowning horror of the poem is that it does not fly away. Instead . . . it just sits there. Probably it is asleep.

Poe is also famous for writing the first detective story. (Actually, another Gothic writer, E. T. A. Hoffman, got there before him, but hey. We all remember what "first" means.) His three stories featuring the condescending fallen aristo Auguste Dupin, beginning with "The Murders in the Rue Morgue," led directly to Sherlock Holmes. Poe uses Dupin to showcase what he called "ratiocination," the action of the superior mind putting together clues commoners can't see. Unfortunately, the stories are baldly contrived at best and should be approached only as literary fossils in an evolutionary line that led to something readable.

RATIOCINATION EXERCISE

Connect the dots:

Fact #1: Edgar Allan Poe has enjoyed a reputation in France much higher than he has at home.

Fact #2: Like Edgar Allan Poe, Jerry Lee Lewis, an early rockabilly star, married his thirteen-year-old cousin.

Fact #3: The other American artist who famously enjoys a much better reputation in France than at home is Jerry Lewis.

	Importance	Accessibility	Fun
Stories, Gothic	4	6	6
Stories, Dupin	7	7	5
Poems	3	9	6
Arthur Gordon Pym	3	6	4

WALT WHITMAN (1819–1892)

Whitman gives an immediate impression of greatness. This is largely because the backdrop of his poetry is always the whole universe. Whitman's favorite tactic is to show one tiny thing—e.g., a wren's egg—then pan out to show the infinite cosmos behind it. "I contain multitudes" is the alpha and omega of his poetry.

Like Blake, Whitman likes to oppose evil and good, then hug both in ecstatic acceptance. Everything is holy: "The scent of these armpits is aroma finer than prayer." Not only moral distinctions vanish: all distinctions vanish. All things are one. All times are now. All men are me, and I am good. He is like an earnest stoner trying his damnedest to blow your mind.

Whitman's downfall is that he tries to list the good things. "I believe a leaf of grass is no less than the journey work of the stars / And the pismire is equally perfect, and a grain of sand, and the egg of the wren / And the tree-toad is a chef-d'oeuvre for the highest / And the running blackberry would adorn the parlors of heaven." He can't list all the good things, because he dies of old age, but he does his best.

In short bursts, these litanies are exhilarating. However, if you try to read more than five pages at a time, it's like some freak military intelligence operation, where they try to break you by playing John Denver records over and over, for days at a time.

Leaves of Grass was found obscene by Whitman's contemporaries, largely because the poems are screaming—indistinctly but loudly—that Whitman was gay. When he is listing people, he tends to linger over the good-looking stevedore. And sometimes this triggers a scene where it seems . . . the outlines are fuzzy, but it certainly seems . . . well, what is Whitman doing to that good-looking stevedore? We can't be sure, but it appears to be something that ends with what he euphemistically calls "father-stuff."

There is no record of his sexual relationships with men, but it's hard to believe there weren't any. He seems too happy about these stevedores, and about whatever fuzzy thing happens after they are "Unbuttoning my clothes and holding me by the bare waist." He never exactly leaves the closet, but he throws the door wide open and lets us look inside. Whitman's gayness was largely ignored by the next generation, and he was enshrined in the canon as "The Good Gray Poet," an ideal of compassionate masculinity. This was probably due to his author photographs, which show him in a full white beard, wearing rustic clothing and looking like a backwoods Santa. Early twentieth-century readers basically chose to slam the closet door in Whitman's face. "Gay me no gays," they said, "Keep your Santa sex to yourself."

Appropriately for a poet who argues tirelessly that All is One, Whitman wrote a single book, which he expanded throughout his life. The first (self-published) edition of *Leaves of Grass* had twelve poems. Forty years later, the so-called "deathbed" edition had almost four hundred. For the reader who balks at a book of poetry five hundred pages long, the poem "Song of Myself" is the best place to start. It contains multitudes and is the purest example of Whitman's incantatory free verse. One favorite line: "Where the pear-shaped balloon is floating aloft, floating in it myself and looking composedly down."

	Importance	Accessibility	Fun
Leaves of Grass	10	5	8

EMILY DICKINSON (1830–1886)

If Whitman's poems are best read in small doses, Emily Dickinson's should be taken by the bucketload. They are all short rhyming lyrics and go down like potato chips. Read one, and it seems childishly simple. Read five, and they become enigmatic. At ten, eerie dimensions appear in them, and nothing is real. Read a hundred, and all you understand anymore is that this woman was a genius.

Part of this effect comes from the poetry's morbidity. Dickinson likes to give us the thoughts of buried corpses and writes gloatingly about shipwrecks with all hands lost. Half of her poems concern the moment "When everything that ticked has stopped, / and space stares, all around." These poems mix homely images with bizarre flights. Here is a typical stanza:

> She died,—this was the way she died;
> And when her breath was done,
> Took up her simple wardrobe
> And started for the sun.

Dickinson is also the bard of agoraphobia. She was, as her pen pal Thomas Higginson tells us, "a recluse . . . literally spending years without setting her foot beyond the doorstep." She explained to him that she avoided company because people "talk of hallowed things, aloud, and embarrass my dog." She only published ten poems in her lifetime, and Higginson—at the time, an important abolitionist writer—was her only contact with the literary world.

Her letters to him are worth reading in their own right. They're a rare example of a female author being aggressively brilliant and as mad as a box of frogs. She wrote about her first impulse to write poetry: "I had a terror since September, I could tell to none; and so I sing, as the boy does by the burying ground, because I am afraid."

Actually, the window of the bedroom where she spent her life looked out on a cemetery, so really all her singing was done by the burying ground. She dressed all in white, and for years her only contact with the community was when she lowered baskets of candy from her window to the local children. It's really only a matter of time before Tim Burton makes a biopic.

Of Dickinson keynotes, death is the sublime; punctuation is the ridiculous. Dickinson capitalized words at random and used dashes willy-nilly. For a long time, editors simply fixed this. Once her genius was recognized, however, that genius was assumed to extend to punctuation; the dashes became a "deliberate artistic statement." However, since the same mannerisms occur in her letters, it seems more likely Dickinson was just incurably dense about punctuation—just as many other writers were incurably dense about spelling. (Note correct use of dash.)

Dickinson asked to have her papers burned after her death. Along with letters and whatnot, a fat stash of unpublished poems was found; she had written almost two thousand. Her sister Lavinia decided to burn everything but the poetry. This one bonfire made the shy Dickinson a darling of literary fantasists, allowing them to imagine any number of lives for her without fear of being proven wrong. She has been called epileptic, and (inevitably) a lesbian; scholars have given her a late-life affair with a man, and an early-life affair with her father. The absence of information about her has only served to make biographies fatter and juicier, as fans project onto her the life they wish she had. Who knows, perhaps Lavinia was a PR genius and that was exactly what she intended to happen.

	Importance	Accessibility	Fun
Poems	10	6	8

NATHANIEL HAWTHORNE (1804–1864)

Hawthorne is the main exponent of the New England Gothic, a genre which combines sexual repression, tortured prose, and lousy weather. It is the literary equivalent of stepping in a puddle just as you leave the house. Your socks squish miserably with every step you take through Hawthorne.

His first still-read works are short stories. These are mainly high-concept parables with clear morals. Any one of them could be the basis for a *Twilight Zone* episode. To give an example, "Young Goodman Brown" is about a man living in the early days of Puritan settlement, who goes into the woods to meet the devil for a black Sabbath. At the last minute, he has second thoughts. The devil (who looks just like Brown, no horns or tail) tries to persuade him to go through with it, saying everybody is doing it; basically, four out of five Puritans recommend the devil. Brown repudiates him but ends up at the black Sabbath anyway and is terrified when he sees that all his neighbors are present—even his wife Faith. Young Goodman Brown cries out for God's help and the scene vanishes.

When he goes home, he can never look people in the eye again. He becomes a bitter, distrustful cynic, unloving and unloved. This is why you should be careful when entering the woods at night. Even with the best intentions, you may take a wrong turning and find yourself in . . . the Twilight Zone.

Hawthorne's short stories—and all of his other novels—have been overshadowed by his next work, *The Scarlet Letter*.

It is Boston in the Puritan era. As the novel begins, young Hester Prynne is led from prison and taken to stand at the scaffold, to be made a public example of to the gathered townsfolk. She has a baby in her arms and the scarlet A-for-Adultery stitched on her dress. Now Hawthorne gives us some quick backstory: Hester was sent from England to Massachusetts by her much older, very learned husband. He was supposed to follow, but he never showed up. Hester meanwhile got pregnant and gave birth to an illegitimate baby. However, she won't tell anybody who the father is.

As she stands there, Hester notices a strange figure at the back of the crowd. It's a much older man, with a learned look in his eyes. Wait, she recognizes that face! It's . . . her husband! See, these Indians were keeping him hostage and . . . anyway, he's turned up at the absolutely wrong moment.

Now the young, good-looking Reverend Dimmesdale begins to exhort Hester to admit who her baby's father was. White-faced and trembling with emotion, he begs her to confess. Even if the man will lose a high place, she should tell his name. He may not have the courage to confess—in fact, he may be right here in front of her. . . . Basically, Dimmesdale does everything he can to make it plain he's the culprit, short of saying, When I got you pregnant—I mean, when he got you pregnant. Of course it wasn't me! What a nutty idea! Ha ha!

Throughout the novel, cheap effects like this abound. The characters avoid speaking until they can use an exclamation point. Hawthorne harps on the image of the scarlet letter until it feels like being trapped in an elevator for five days with a scarlet letter. Meanwhile, his prose is flowery, circuitous, and ungainly. Try this on for size: "Doomed by his own choice, therefore, as Mr. Dimmesdale so evidently was, to eat his unsavory morsel always at another's board and endure the lifelong chill which must be his lot who seeks to warm himself only at another's fireplace, it truly seemed that this sagacious, experienced, benevolent old physician, with his concord of paternal and reverential love for the young pastor, was the very man, of all mankind, to be constantly within reach of his voice."

My apologies go out to all those forced to study this book in school. I have no explanations for you, and I cannot give you back those days of your life. It may comfort you to reflect that I have suffered too, and that I will doubtless have a score of angry Hawthorne fans denouncing me, for having the courage to speak truth to awful.

OTHER NOVELS OF HAWTHORNE'S YOU SHOULDN'T READ

A Blithedale Romance is Hawthorne's novel about the commune Brook Farm, where he briefly lived. Interesting, right? No.

The House of the Seven Gables is a straight-up Gothic tale about a family curse. The action here is minimal. Clifford is a hypersensitive invalid, broken in spirit by years in prison for a murder he didn't commit. Crass, money-minded Judge Pyncheon wants to question him about missing deeds to some land in Maine. There's your plot. And here's more of Hawthorne's classic prose: "The Judge, on one side! And who, on the other? The guilty Clifford! Once a byword! Now, an indistinctly remembered ignominy!"

In *The Marble Faun*, four people are pursued by an evil curse-like something, only this time in Rome. When published, this book was rapturously reviewed; only Emerson had the wisdom and honesty to call it "mush."

	Importance	Accessibility	Fun
Stories	5	5	5
The Scarlet Letter	9, alas!	3	4
A Blithedale Romance	2	4	5
The House of the Seven Gables	4	4	5
The Marble Faun	2	3	3

HERMAN MELVILLE (1819–1891)

"Call me Ishmael," the opening words of *Moby Dick*, are possibly the three most famous words in literature. Many authors would have been content to leave it at that, but Herman Melville kept going, adding another two hundred thousand words, until he'd written the great white whale of American novels.

Melville grew up in an impoverished branch of a distinguished family. He went to sea seeking fortune, and although he didn't find it on board ship, the years he spent there would become his literary capital. His first novel, *Typee*, based on the time he spent among cannibals on the Marquesas Island, was an immediate bestseller. Though readers loved it, they assumed the adventures were freaks of his imagination: but in fact, Melville really did abandon his ship, get taken captive by head-hunters, and go native among them. The follow-up, *Omoo*, follows the same Melvillish character through a mutiny on board a whaler, and then to Tahiti, consolidating his reputation as a writer who could deliver the exotic to your door, and was stupid enough to come back to New England from Tahiti.

Melville was now set on making a living as a writer. That living would have to be fat enough to support a wife, eight children, his aged mother, and four unmarried sisters. Unfortunately, now his literary ambitions kicked in. Where his first books were fast-paced travel narratives, with his third book, he cranked up the Melville. *Mardi: A Trip Thither* begins as another sea tale, but soon mutates into allegory, philosophy, box-office poison. Unsurprisingly, it was not as well received as his previous books, and the fourteen relatives began to gaze at Melville reproachfully. Correspondingly, the next two books, *Redburn* and *White-jacket*, were straightforward sea adventures, and, in Melville's own words: "two jobs, which I have done for money—being forced to it, as other men are to sawing wood."

With his next book, Melville's mind wandered from the bottom line, and into the deep philosophical waters that turned *Moby Dick* into the Great American Novel to beat. The story is simple enough. Ishmael, a jaded knockabout sailor, is in the whaling town New Bedford, looking for a ship. He meets up with the harpooner Queequeg, a Polynesian cannibal covered with tattoos. Despite Queequeg's frightening aspect, they become fast friends and together sign up on the *Pequod*. Her captain, Ahab, is a grand peg-legged monomaniac, ever in pursuit of the great white whale who chomped off his original, meat leg. It may seem crazy to hold a grudge against a fish in this way. It is: Ahab increasingly shows himself to be grandly mad. After a long voyage and encounters with a number of supporting cast whales, Ahab finds Moby Dick, and the showdown takes place.

What's so great about it? First, Melville added to the story everything he knew and everything he thought—histories, whaling techniques, sailor's tales, biology lessons—all carried forward by the pursuit of Ahab's bizarre vision. Melville can also be very funny, with a sharp, off-kilter humor. But, most wonderfully, he makes us feel that we're really on the voyage, with the long, eventless months at sea; the intense, claustrophobic society of the sailors; the drama of battling a sperm whale from a rowboat—all of it is unforgettably real.

Contemporary audiences, however, got bogged down in the philosophical flights and put it down in disgust, muttering, "What the hell happened to Melville?" A few critics recognized the genius here, but for the most part, even his admirers thought *Moby Dick* was best where he stuck to telling the story instead of stopping the action to explore the symbolic meaning of the whale's whiteness.

His next novel, *Pierre, or the Ambiguities*, was actually met with headlines like MELVILLE GONE INSANE! A brief look at the book suggests that he was in fact crazy—crazy to think he was writing a popular romance that would bring in a lot of money, which is what he told people at the time. *Pierre* is a melodrama in which the well-born hero gives up love and money to fake-marry his impoverished half sister, rather than disgrace the family by revealing his father's philandering. Good news: the fiancée he dumped forgives him, and the three live together. But here's the beauty part: the hero writes a novel to support them all, but the publisher rejects it. This gives Melville a stage from which to rant about how much the publishing industry sucks. Then the characters all kill themselves.

Even Melville's family wondered if he'd gone insane, and called in doctors to examine him. In fact—although he managed to escape the loony bin—he had turned into a misanthrope, avoiding his literary friends and indulging in fits of temper. It was in this period that he wrote his short masterpiece of disenchantment, "Bartleby the Scrivener." This story, with its malingering antihero, anticipates cubicle life by a hundred years and gave the world the battle cry of the passive-aggressive: "I prefer not to."

With his next novel, though, Melville continued his downward spiral. *The Confidence Man* is a strange non-story about a con artist traveling down the Mississippi, interacting with various characters, each of whom has a tale to tell. John Updike called it "crabbed and inert," and the critic R. W. Leavis said that it "seems rather to bulge and thicken than to progress."

With that, Melville officially retired from writing. With a steady job at the Customs House, and some fortunate inheritances, he didn't have to produce poorly received novels anymore. He wrote a few volumes of privately published poetry and was working on *Billy Budd* until the end, but when he died in 1891, he was considered a writer of the previous generation. The public reaction to his death was "Really? He was still alive?"

	Importance	Accessibility	Fun
Typee, Oomo	4	9	7
Mardi	5	5	4
Whitejacket, Redburn	3	7	6
Moby Dick	10	4	8
Pierre	4	5	5
The Confidence Man	4	2	1
Billy Budd, An Inside Narrative	8	5	6
The Piazza Tales (short story collection, including Bartleby)	8	5	7
Poetry	3	6	2

MARK TWAIN (SAMUEL LANGHORNE CLEMENS)
(1835–1910)

In his time, Mark Twain was world famous as a humorist and speaker. He was sharp, funny, progressive, and loved to poke fun at the status quo; a nineteenth-century Jon Stewart with added down-home Americanness. He also wrote a lot of books, one of which is considered very good.

Twain grew up in Hannibal, Missouri, the fictionalized setting for his two most popular novels, *Tom Sawyer* and *Huckleberry Finn*. He began his working life at eleven, when his father died. (Conrad and Melville's fathers also died when they were eleven. While this may seem like a trivial coincidence, our eleven-year-old readers who are serious about a writing career should take no chances. You know what you have to do.) Twain was a riverboat pilot in his early twenties, after which he headed west, where he failed to make his fortune mining gold. He started working for newspapers in California but instead made his fortune mining the quirky voice and behaviors of the locals. His short, amusing pieces bought him a reputation, travel writing assignments, and a successful career as a lecturer. He turned his travels and experiences into popular books like *The Innocents Abroad*, *Roughing It*, and *Life on the Mississippi*, then turned to writing novels.

His early fiction is sharp and sprightly; his later fiction is sharp and gloomy, but almost all of it is kid stuff. *The Prince and the Pauper*, *A Connecticut Yankee in King Arthur's Court*, *The Adventures of Tom Sawyer*—these are all snack food, best read by an eleven-year-old who has not yet tasted sin (like before you do that thing we mentioned above). Twain's place in the literary canon rests entirely on *The Adventures of Huckleberry Finn*. A sequel to *Tom Sawyer*, *Huckleberry Finn* is lifted up by its moral seriousness and its perfect snapshot of antebellum America. Hemingway is often cited as saying that "all modern American literature comes from *Huckleberry Finn*." This is obviously untrue, but Twain was the first major American author to turn away from European literary tradition and write in a distinctly American voice.

Huck Finn, rough but good-hearted son of the town drunk, was adopted into a proper home at the end of *Tom Sawyer*. At the beginning of *Huckleberry Finn*, he's snatched away by his shiftless father for plotty money reasons. He escapes by faking his own death; while hiding out on a nearby island, he encounters the runaway slave, Jim. Together, they take a raft down the Mississippi. Huck has been raised in a society that believes slaves are property, and therefore helping one escape is "stealing," which is a sin. However, he slowly begins to recognize Jim's humanity. Huck decides it is more important to help Jim escape to freedom than to do what's "right." This moral awakening is threaded through a series of colorful encounters, the most memorable being with a couple of low-life con men styling themselves the Duke and the Dauphin, who join Huck and Jim on the raft.

Toward the end, the novel becomes a grotesque embarrassment. Jim is captured and held until he can be returned to his owner. Tom Sawyer turns up in the story here, and Tom and Huck make Jim go through a series of pointless and humiliating escape schemes, purely for Tom's entertainment. Everything gets tied up when Tom reveals that Jim has already been freed, and Huck, having had his fill of this civilization crap, decides to head west.

There has been much debate about whether the book and its author are racist. If you don't like seeing the word "nigger" in print, this book is not for you. Also, despite his nobility, there is more than a hint of minstrelsy in Jim. It's hard not to see, though, that Mark Twain was doing his best to fight the good fight. When Huck decides he's willing to go to hell for the sake of Jim's freedom, it's hard not to be moved, even if it is because Huck sees Jim as "white on the inside."

BEHIND EVERY GREAT MAN

Mark Twain often got in trouble for the crudity of his language. He did not get in trouble, however, for his lifelong religious doubts, which often amounted to a cantankerous atheism. This was because he had a censor on hand, 24/7, in the form of his beloved wife. It is thanks to her influence that many of his sharpest works, like *Letters from the Earth*, were never finished in his lifetime and his angrier passages about the suffocating idiocy of nineteenth-century Christianity never saw the light of day. Twain himself was avowedly grateful to her for her guidance, although we suspect that some of the chafing Huck feels at the well-meaning Christian women who try to civilize him was inspired by Twain's daily experience with his Christian wife.

	Importance	Accessibility	Fun
Life on the Mississippi	4	6	6
Roughing It	4	6	5
The Innocents Abroad	2	6	3
The Prince and the Pauper	4	10	7
A Connecticut Yankee in King Arthur's Court	4	10	7
The Adventures of Tom Sawyer	5	10	5
Adventures of Huckleberry Finn	9	9	8
Letters from the Earth	3	8	8

STEPHEN CRANE (1871–1900)

Stephen Crane's work is the most important American contribution to the genre of Naturalism (see page 215). While other American Naturalists, such as Theodore Dreiser and Frank Norris, are now just means of making PhD students into alcoholics, Crane is still read with pleasure and interest by people who have jobs. The main reason is that he is unrivaled as a psychologist. A subsidiary reason is that his rough style—by turns two-fisted and ham-fisted—has a peculiar charisma. His prose is like Hemingway struggling to be born, but being aborted instead, and then being photographed by some sick pro-life activist.

His first book, *Maggie: A Girl of the Streets*, is a seduced-and-abandoned novel set among slum dwellers. It was written when Crane was very young and, frankly, had not yet learned how to write. A typical line of dialogue runs "Ah, we blokies kin lick deh hull damn Row." An example of Crane's imagery: "The little boy ran to the halls, shrieking like a monk in an earthquake." Here a character expresses tender passion:

> Pete took note of Maggie.
> "Say, Mag, I'm stuck on yer shape. It's outa sight," he said
> parenthetically, with an affable grin.

The plot is winningly half-baked. Maggie is a girl born into a violent, drunken family. Here every night is Domestic Abuse Night. Father beats mother; mother beats father; both beat the children; and Maggie's brother Jimmy beats her. Maggie, at the bottom of the beating totem pole, just cringes fearfully in her ragged clothes. Her love story suits these beginnings, and Crane briskly ushers her past her piggish lover on to prostitution and death.

Every character is stupid and brutalized. There is no hope or kindness. Then there's the prose, which doesn't flow so much as elbow its way past you. Crane has something ugly to say, and he turns English inside out to find an ugly way of saying it. The effect is ultimately more interesting than good writing would be.

In his later works, Crane refined his technique considerably. This later style mainly observes the rules of good journalistic prose. When he goes for a poetic effect, however, it reads like an interpolation by a maudlin slum-dweller. But again, these moments are weirdly satisfying. Somehow he seems to be channeling his least educated character and letting animal emotion break through the calm white surface of the page.

His short stories, like "The Open Boat," about a group of men trying to survive a shipwreck, and "The Blue Hotel," about a shooting in a Western town, are concise, brilliant sociological studies. So is his classic war novel, *The Red Badge of Courage*.

The Red Badge of Courage follows the inner struggle of a farmboy during his first battle in the American Civil War. The protagonist's abiding fear is that he will turn out to be a coward. Crane gives a minute-by-minute account of his several encounters with the enemy, with the focus on his thoughts and feelings. The soldiers here are terrified, incompetent, helpless kids. Even when they're courageous, Crane makes it clear that this is a meaningless reflex. Nonetheless, the experience of battle makes them what they want to be: "real men." Crane doesn't say this is a good thing, he just tells us that it makes them happy. It's a rare example of a war novel that can be read by both doves and hawks with complete appreciation. There is also plenty here for vultures: the descriptions of war wounds, deaths, and corpses are explicit and terrifying.

Crane, who never fought in a war, researched his novel by traveling to Virginia to interview Civil War veterans. The book was so convincing that he was often assumed by critics to be a much older man writing from his own experience. Other, more critical critics, made fun of him for his lack of combat experience, so Crane became a war correspondent to prove he was no coward—a typical example of life imitating art.

Crane was the son of a Methodist minister and a minister's daughter, but was himself more at home in a brothel than in a chapel. He met his common-law wife when she was the madam of a Florida bordello, the Hotel de Dream. He was destitute in his early days; he came back from his Virginia research trip on foot, in rubber galoshes, because his only pair of shoes had fallen apart. Still, he was full of self-belief, and one of his roommates remembered that Crane used to write his own name on any scrap of paper, preparing for his celebrity. *The Red Badge of Courage* won him that celebrity, but he died only a few years later, at twenty-eight, of our old friend tuberculosis.

	Importance	Accessibility	Fun
Maggie: A Girl of the Streets	5	5	6
Stories	5	8	6
The Red Badge of Courage	7	8	8

CHAPTER II

Nice Realism: The Novel Novel

Victorian novels all agree about certain pleasant truths. Love is a beautiful sentiment; children are our most precious asset; if virtue is not always rewarded here below, vice is definitely punished. What I am calling "nice realism" here is the fiction of the English in their rose-colored glasses. Often, the authors do point out that current concepts of morality are faulty: notably, we don't value love and children enough. But what luck! The author has better concepts in his back pocket, all ready to go! The world is going to be a much better place once it understands.

There are two main pieces of plot machinery here: marriage and money. Once a nice realist has started these engines, she can sit back and the novel writes itself. The most typical plot has a poor girl getting a rich husband—a plot still so beloved that if all other plots disappeared, some people wouldn't notice. When the characters have solved their money problems and gotten married, the novel is over. It is as if the novel is a board game the characters are playing, where anyone who doesn't have cash by the end of the book is dead. Any female character in her twenties needs cash and a husband. Otherwise, she becomes a dangling plotline, and you do not want to be a dangling plotline in a realist novel. Characters who defy the author's morality also find themselves in a shallow grave.

Nice realism represents itself as the literature of sanity and homely wisdom. Therefore teenagers are usually repelled by these novels, while adults are eager to foist the books on them. Generations of educators have turned youth off to reading by giving them Charles Dickens, the English department's answer to an abstinence program. The best time to read these novels is in middle age—ideally when one is sick in bed from stress brought on by too much real reality.

Because we now spend much of our lives in this state, nice realism has become the basic novel. There are no important formal differences between George Eliot, Jonathan Franzen, and Maeve Binchy. Of course, writers—a clan of broke, immoral, divorced people—have tried for decades to escape this formula. They invented modernism, but the public only accepted a few modernist works before reaching their difficulty threshold. Writers then tried returning to the eighteenth-century novel, calling it "postmodernism" to make it seem new and trendy. They tried writing books from the point of view of dogs, and books that can be read in any order, and books that can't be read, and books in the shape of dogs—anything but nice realism. The result of all this feverish effort is Jonathan Franzen and Maeve Binchy. It's bit like the escape attempts of *The Prisoner*: no matter what elaborate scheme he deploys, he wakes up in The Village again. One might come to suspect that readers really believe they are nice and deserve to find true love with an earl.

JANE AUSTEN (1775–1817)

Jane Austen's prose has an ideal eighteenth-century decorum. It's too uptight for lyricism but raises intelligence to such a pitch that it becomes beauty. The perfect prose Gibbon used for the decline and fall of the Roman Empire is used by Austen for the decline and fall of a provincial girl's vanity. Its humor feels like a by-product of its clarity—the jokes are so seamlessly integrated into the perfect fabric that we don't notice Austen making them until we have already laughed. Hers is the most elegant possible use of deadpan humor.

The main thing to know about Jane Austen's novels is that they are escapist literature. You do not need to be smart to enjoy Jane Austen, or on your toes, or prepared for a mental workout. All you need is eyes. If you leave the book on the floor, when you get home, the cat will be reading it. The public learned this long ago, and the modern Austen industry is a sprawling mass of spin-off books, biographies, movies, and TV series. So you might think no one could possibly remain to be introduced to her work. However, one large population has escaped it completely: men.

The combination of her decorous manner, the obsession with marriage, her protagonists' gender, and her gender has made generations of straight guys feel that reading Jane Austen would be equivalent to wearing women's clothes at home. We don't want to twist anyone's arm, but male readers should reconsider. Jane Austen lacks most of the features that make rom-coms unbearable for many men. Although these are love stories, Austen tends to skip the confessions of love, along with the weddings, the feelings, and the kisses. She uses the marriage plot as a simple backbone for a million snarky remarks. Really, these are more like unusually smart situation comedies set in the eighteenth-century, where the situation is "getting the daughters married off."

Pride and Prejudice is the funniest. It also has the best love story and the least clutter. The main characters, Elizabeth Bennet and Mr. Darcy, are a classic example of the couple who express their sexual tension through sparring. The heroine's father, who lives to ridicule people, is just what an Austen novel needs to get from droll to laugh-out-loud.

Emma is possibly a tighter novel, but flawed in its premises and its lack of any character who lives to ridicule people. The premises: Emma is always trying to marry off the girls around her but never thinks about men herself, until she suddenly realizes she's in love. Her secret love is a family friend twice her age whom she has seen most days since she was an infant. Austen gets away with this—barely—by never making us think about the bridegroom bouncing the baby Emma on his knee. Also, Emma occasionally shows signs of growing into a character who lives to ridicule people.

The rest of the novels are mainly a way of consoling yourself for having finished *Pride and Prejudice*. They are either too formulaic or too baggy. The beautiful writing is the same, but without a character who lives to ridicule people, it seems a waste. Here is the order in which to read them, after you've finished *Pride and Prejudice* a first, second, and third time: *Emma, Persuasion, Sense and Sensibility, Mansfield Park, Northanger Abbey*.

Finally: there is some debate as to whether Jane Austen is overrated (it's just chicklit really) or underrated (great author despised for her feminine subjects). My opinion? Chicklit is underrated and great authors are overrated. You say tomato, I say it's a vegetable. The bottom line is, there's no such thing as a bad kind of good.

	Importance	*Accessibility*	*Fun*
Pride and Prejudice	10	10	10
Emma	9	10	9
Persuasion	6	10	8
Sense and Sensibility	6	10	7
Mansfield Park	6	8	6
Northanger Abbey	5	9	6

THE BRONTËS

Like Jane Austen, Charlotte (1816–1855), Emily (1818–1848), and Anne (1820–1849) Brontë were the daughters of a clergyman, spinsters, isolated from society, and poor. Unlike Jane Austen, this turned them into very angry people. The Brontë home was a little biosphere of literary misery.

The sisters grew up with their brother Branwell in a parsonage in Haworth, a bleak Yorkshire village. Two older sisters died after a period at a gruesome boarding school. The mother also died young. (Dying young was one thing at which the Brontës excelled.) As the only middle-class family in Haworth, the Brontës had no friends. That's zero friends. No one visited them, there were no trips to London in the season, it was all Brontës all the time.

In their isolation, the Brontë children devised complex worlds of make-believe, based originally on plays enacted with Branwell's toy soldiers. Charlotte and Branwell invented a country in Africa they called Angria, and populated it with a royal family of English castaways. Because this was toy soldiers' country, the books were written in tiny print, legible only with a magnifying glass. The Angrians have names like the Duke of Zamorna and Albion; they live in the city Verdopolis and cannot go for long without breaking into rhyming verse. A sample Angrian sentence: "Oh, I abhor now, with my whole soul, every touch of beauty which appears too etherial for humanity; every shade in the colour of a cheek, every ray in the light of an eye, that has too much of the heavenly, too little of the earthly." Charlotte and Branwell worked on the Angrian chronicles well into their twenties; they eventually filled twenty-three volumes. Emily and Anne had a separate make-believe country called Gondal-land, but the chronicles of Gondal-land were destroyed. (Possibly by agents of Angria, but we have no proof.).

Even the most optimistic person will guess that these kids were not going to thrive in the outside world.

All three sisters tried schoolteaching and/or governessing to augment the family's meager income. All three hated every job they tried, and ran home. Emily was so profoundly shy she never got to know anyone outside her immediate family, and even for Anne, the most normal Brontë, life among non-Brontës was painful. Meanwhile, Branwell had begun to drink and take laudanum; his various attempts at work fell to pieces, and he too returned home to disintegrate in Angrian solitude.

Early on, Charlotte sent some of her poems to Robert Southey (remember him?) and got the famous answer: "Literature cannot be the business of a woman's life, and it ought not to be. The more she is engaged in her proper duties, the less leisure she will have for it." Disregarding this wise counsel, the Brontës soon published a poetry collection at their own expense. It was written by all three sisters, using the names Currer, Ellis, and Acton Bell. It sold two copies. Still, they persevered, and all three wrote novels. These were more successful, to put it mildly. *Jane Eyre*, published first, was an immediate bestseller and critical success. *Wuthering Heights*, though sniffed at as a cruder work, also sold in massive numbers.

The stage was now set for the Brontës to start dying. Branwell went first, from alcoholism and drug abuse; Emily checked out via tuberculosis three months later. Anne lasted another six months before tuberculosis got her too.

And then there was one. Five years passed. Charlotte published two more novels: *Shirley* and *Villette*. Tuberculosis seemed to have forgotten her. Losing her head, she married and got pregnant. Smelling a happy ending in the offing, tuberculosis got back to work. At the age of thirty-eight (that's ninety-six in Brontë years), Charlotte died, along with her unborn child.

Charlotte Brontë

Of Charlotte's novels, *Jane Eyre* is her most popular; *Villette*, her last, is most often called her masterpiece. Both are first person narratives from the point of view of a governess. They are basically told by a Charlotte who had more luck in love.

The middle novel, *Shirley*, is a baggy production about Luddism and the Woman Question. For Brontë, the Woman Question is resolved completely with the Wedding Answer. In general, this middle novel is like a middle child; directionless, trying too hard, somehow never as shiny as the others.

Jane Eyre is an odd hybrid: a bildungsroman with a Gothic romance stuffed inside. The eponymous heroine is an orphan, raised in an aunt's family. This family treats her like crap, not understanding that, in a novel, the eponymous person is always right. When Jane rebels, she is sent away to a horrible boarding school, where she continues to be treated like crap by insignificant people who will never have a book named after them.

By and by, she comes of age, and applies for a job as a governess. She will leave this stinking bildungsroman where people feed her gruel! Little does she realize that she's now booked into a Gothic novel.

The Gothic novel takes place, of course, in a semi-deserted mansion. Its name, Thornfield Hall, should alert her that this new job will be no bed of roses. Or it will be, but with the thorns left on and the blooms taken off. At first, she is alone with little Adele, the ward of Rochester, Thornfield's absentee owner. Then Rochester himself comes home. He is dark and forbidding and Byronic. A doorknob could tell he has come to have sex with an eponymous character.

For a while, the author creates artificial obstacles to keep them apart. Skipping all that, let's pick them up in Chapter 26, where they're at the church, about to get married. "Does anyone know of an impediment to this marriage?" Sure enough, a man in the back announces that Rochester is already married. Busted! They all troop back to Thornfield and go up to the attic, where Rochester has stashed the wife.

"What it was, whether beast or human being, one could not, at first sight, tell: it grovelled, seemingly, on all fours; it snatched and growled like some strange wild animal: but it was covered with clothing, and a quantity of dark, grizzled hair, wild as a mane, hid its head and face." Mrs. Rochester is incurably mad! She is always attacking Rochester and trying to kill him! And also, Rochester tells Jane, she is both slutty and stupid; even before her insanity, they never had a decent conversation. In short, she is like wives everywhere, if you listen to what married guys say when they're trying to get laid.

It doesn't work any better on Jane than it did last Thursday night at T.G.I. Friday's, and she runs out into the night—and the bildungsroman that's still going on out there. There's a long way to go before we get to the famous words "Reader, I married him," but we'll leave the home stretch to the reader. Rest assured, there's some good stuff in there.

WAIT, WHAT IS A GOTHIC NOVEL, AND WHY IS IT GOTHIC?

Gothic fiction is a broad church, which can include everything from *The Strange Case of Dr. Jekyll and Mr. Hyde* to Faulkner. Supernatural elements are helpful but not necessary; a semi-derelict mansion is preferred but not essential. The main qualification is a suppressed evil which looms, threatening to claim the heroes' lives, souls, and sanity.

Gothic novelists like to leave some mystery about this evil. It is implicitly something too dreadfully wicked or chilling to say in words. For instance, in *Frankenstein*, people scream and run when they see the monster, but his ugliness is never clearly specified. We are forced to assume there is a creeping horror there that defies description. Another ploy is to give a character a dark past that includes nameless sex acts so malignly sexual that they blight an entire extended family and its real estate. The important thing is to show people overreacting hysterically to some unspoken shadowy X.

It's called Gothic by analogy with Gothic Revival architecture, notably the sort of mansion inhabited by Horace Walpole, who wrote the first acknowledged Gothic, *The Castle of Otranto*. How exactly the word "Gothic" jumped from Walpole's house to his novel we cannot explain.

But wait—there's one more novel.

We still haven't talked about *Villette*, a book in which Charlotte Brontë revisits the bildungsroman but allows it to develop into a realist novel instead of a Gothic. The heroine, Lucy Snowe, has the personality of a mole. She's plain, she doesn't like people, she has no charm or talents, she's pathologically introverted, she's depressed. Still, we like her, partly because the average reader of Charlotte Brontë has had at least one mole year. Like Jane Eyre, Lucy is tossed about by life until, fed up with this bildungsroman crap, she runs away to Belgium. From the fact that it is Belgium, you can tell you won't get much drama here.

She gets a place in a school, and now the fun really stops. This is the truth of daily life as a plain girl with no means. A tall, handsome man appears—and uses Lucy as a shoulder to cry on, in between chasing pretty girls. She is too charmless even to afford real friends and has to make do with a student who calls her "old lady" as a sign of affection. Finally, she attracts a pompous Catholic bigot, but by the time he appears on the scene, any interest, from anyone, tastes like love.

Here virtue is rewarded, but so parsimoniously it's like a slap in the face. This reward is still miles better, however, than Charlotte's actual life.

	Importance	Accessibility	Fun
Jane Eyre	10	7	8
Shirley	3	5	5
Villette	8	7	7

Emily Brontë

Wuthering Heights is the prototype of the realist Gothic; a worthy parent to Faulkner, Flannery O'Connor, and all their gory, gloating ilk. We can immediately see how twentieth-century Gothics will differ from the *Frankenstein* kind: Emily is firmly on the monsters' side. Their monstrousness is a strange superiority; their unholiness a holy selfishness. Surrounded by dull creatures who resent or worship them, they treat these creatures with unthinking cruelty because their inferiors just don't count. In short, they are teenagers. This makes sixteen the perfect age to first read *Wuthering Heights*.

The plot goes something like this: Mr. Earnshaw, a small landowner in a desolate part of Yorkshire, comes home one day with a ragged starved urchin he found in the street. The urchin, Heathcliff, becomes his favorite child, and Earnshaw begins to neglect his own children, Hindley and Cathy. Hindley hates Heathcliff for this. Cathy, however, attaches herself to the surly newcomer. They become inseparable, and as they grow up, there is not just something sexual about their relationship, there is everything incestuous. It really makes you wonder what went on behind closed doors in the Brontë household.

Once Earnshaw dies, Hindley devotes himself to degrading Heathcliff. Treated as a lackey, Heathcliff rapidly becomes feral. He is, as Cathy says, "an arid wilderness of furze and whinstone." She keeps one foot in the world of the Yorkshire middle class, but her ultimate loyalty is to Heathcliff and to the rough, stormy moors.

Then she meets the local gentry, the Lintons, with their beautiful house, chandeliers, and fancy clothes. Selfish, carnal Cathy immediately takes to those chandeliers. The Lintons also have a son—soft pretty-boy Edgar—who is just her age. A blind man can see that she is going to marry Edgar and ruin everyone's life.

Emily Brontë buries her story in a clutter of framing devices. The narrator has nothing to do with the story; he's just renting a house from one of the characters. The person who tells him most of the story is the ex-housekeeper, whose knowledge of the story is limited to a few telling moments. The main plot is buried in a heap of minor characters, whose only role is to be crushed by the monsters. But all this is not just deadwood: obscuring the story serves in classic Gothic style to mystify it. Was Heathcliff really Earnshaw's illegitimate son, and thus Cathy's brother? Did he and Cathy ever do it? What did the monsters do to their victims, behind closed doors? The shadowy secrets turn a prosaic story about two dysfunctional families into something namelessly dark—although at times endlessly confusing.

	Importance	Accessibility	Fun
Wuthering Heights	10	8	9

ANNE AKA "THE OTHER" BRONTË

Anne was the pretty one. This, sadly, is her main contribution as a Brontë. Her novels, *The Tenant of Wildfell Hall* and *Agnes Grey*, are read for the same reason that the chronicles of Angria are read, and mostly by the same people.

As long as we're dismissing Anne, we might as well confess that the Brontës also wrote poetry. For die-hard admirers of *Wuthering Heights*, Emily's poetry is still worth reading; it has the novel's rainy, weed-strewn glooms and charms. The rest of the poems, with Anne's novels, should be consigned to a dusty shelf, along with the works of Robert Southey.

CHARLES DICKENS (1812–1870)

Dickens's childhood was notoriously unhappy, marked by an episode in which his bankrupt parents took him out of school and sent him to work in a boot polish factory. His entire adult life, however, was a raving success. From his early twenties, he was *the* British novelist, a public figure courted by politicians and aristocrats. Every British writer of the time emulated and envied Dickens.

He was also the first author to market himself as a celebrity. A keen amateur actor, Dickens inaugurated the custom of writers doing readings of their work. He earned huge appearance fees for this, which he used to bankroll his large family (ten children) and fund his acrimonious divorce. That divorce was the one black spot in an otherwise sunny and blameless life, and seems to have turned Dickens the man into a more morose personality. It left Dickens the novelist exactly the same. First and last, Dickens was the nicest of nice realists.

His heroes, and especially his heroines, are limp vanilla creatures. They want good things and feel guilt at the drop of a hat, even if the hat is not dented in the fall. Many of them are innocent children, in which case they are brutally treated by a series of heartless adults. In extorting sympathy for these urchins, Dickens twists the reader's arm unmercifully, but not always successfully. Oscar Wilde observed of Little Nell in *The Old Curiosity Shop*, "One must have a heart of stone to read the death of Nell without laughing."

These anodyne saps are surrounded by the characters everyone remembers: a host of caricatures from every height and depth of society. These characters are two-dimensional at best; they serve to make a point. When they have made their point, they make it again in every scene. This sometimes even turns into catchphrase humor. The optimistic failure Micawber from *Great Expectations* cannot appear without saying "Something will turn up!" The sycophantic creep Uriah Heep is unstoppably driven to refer to himself as "'umble." But Dickens ingeniously uses these as voices within symphonic plots; they are only crude when considered in isolation. Dismissing his works on these grounds (tempting though it may be) is like dismissing a symphony because the tuba plays the same two notes over and over.

The other objection often made is that Dickens's plots are implausible. If a character heads out her front door and walks in any direction, she will always run into the other character it would be most fun to see her meet. It doesn't matter if that character was last seen in Peru. It doesn't matter if that character was last seen being buried. Nothing matters but how much fun it would be to see them meet. One should remember that these novels were originally published as serials, which gave readers the opportunity to rest between installments, and come back refreshed and ready to suspend more disbelief.

Dickens was an angry champion of the poor, and his novels are masterworks of agitprop. All of them include some simple and compelling presentation of poverty. A recurring Dickens motif is a kindly person driven insane by hardship; nasty affluent people then sneer at his or her pathetic babblings. These scenes are as subtle as mace, but also as effective. It's not too much to say that he helped create the twentieth-century consensus that the poor deserve society's help. (Yes, it seems laughable now. But people did believe this at one time, honest.)

Here are the most famous of Dickens' novels:

Oliver Twist

Oliver is born in the workhouse. His mother dies giving birth, leaving him to be exploited and abused by one villain after another. He even falls among thieves, but is soon rescued by a good-hearted rich man who turns out to be a member of his long-lost family. This book was popularized by the musical based on it, not by its quality. It never stops cloying; it's like eating marshmallows doused in maple syrup and washing them down with cough syrup.

It also features Fagin, ringleader of a gang of child pickpockets, and one of the most anti-Semitic depictions in world literature. David Lean's 1949 film of the book actually caused a riot by Jews in postwar Berlin. (Of course these Jews might have been a little hypersensitive at that moment.)

Bleak House

This is an extended critique of the legal system, centering on an interminable lawsuit, Jarndyce and Jarndyce. Lawyers are bloodsuckers, don't get mixed up with them. Maybe you already knew this.

Like many Dickens novels, this is most famous for its minor characters, notably Harold Skimpole, a send-up of the radical poet Leigh Hunt. Skimpole is too lofty to take any interest in financial matters; he is just like a child in these matters, he says. Meanwhile, other people pay his debts. This is Dickens's trenchant exposé of authors who didn't earn as much as he did.

A Tale of Two Cities

This is a melodrama set in the French Revolution. Dickens normally loves the poor, but let them start a revolution, and, oh boy, the honeymoon is over. The moral issues here are blackest black and blinding white. This novel is often assigned in schools, presumably to discourage children from bloody revolutions.

The book has one of the most famous openings in literature: "It was the best of times, it was the worst of times. It was the age of wisdom, it was the age of foolishness. It was the epoch of belief, it was the epoch of incredulity"—etc. You will notice this is absolutely meaningless.

At the end, the dissolute lawyer Sydney Carton—whose sarcasms have been our only succor through the book—voluntarily goes to the guillotine in place of the vanilla Charles Darnay. As he goes to his death, Sydney says: "It is a far, far better thing I do today, than ever I have done before." This is a great thing to say whenever you do anyone a favor.

David Copperfield

A semiautobiographical novel about a blameless chit who is persecuted by everyone. Then he grows up, marries the wrong girl, and when the wrong girl dies, he marries the right girl. In real life, Dickens only got the wrong one, who was not, unlike her fictional counterpart, helpful enough to die young.

The first half of *David Copperfield* includes some of Dickens' most mature and thoughtful writing, notably about the nature of memory. It also has some of his most successful comic characters. The man-hating Betsey Trotwood shows her heart of gold in ways that are credible and moving; mad Mr. Dick, obsessed with the head of Charles I, is one of the most successful running gags in literature. The most beloved is Micawber, the penniless and improvident optimist, who was based on Dickens's own father. Micawber finally goes off to Australia and makes his fortune. The real Dickens Senior spent his declining years living off his famous son.

Great Expectations

Poor, abused chit Pip grows up in love with Estella, the protégée of bitter old Miss Havisham. Jilted on her wedding day, Miss Havisham still sits around in her wedding dress, plotting revenge against men, with Estella's beauty as her secret weapon. Pip's a man, therefore fair game. (Dickens starts his implausibility mill with a roar in this one.)

Then a mysterious benefactor begins to provide Pip with an income, with the aim of turning him into a gentleman. Pip is more interesting than most Dickens heroes—his new status turns him into a snob, and his love for Estella is presented as a sickness. Therefore, we actually care about what happens to him. Also, this is where Dickens finally, conclusively, throws away the crutch of credibility. The story is constructed entirely from ridiculous events, without one instance of a thing that could actually happen.

A Christmas Carol

You probably know the plot of *A Christmas Carol*. If you don't, you are a priceless resource and should not be tampered with.

	Importance	Accessibility	Fun
The Pickwick Papers	5	5	6
Oliver Twist	4	7	4
Dombey and Son	5	7	7
David Copperfield	8	7	8
Bleak House	8	7	7
Hard Times	5	8	6
Little Dorrit	6	7	6
A Tale of Two Cities	5	7	4
Great Expectations	8	8	8

(Note: While no individual Dickens novel can break an 8 for Importance, having read at least one Dickens novel is definitely a 10.)

WILLIAM MAKEPEACE THACKERAY (1811–1863)

For our purposes, Thackeray means *Vanity Fair*, a nice realist book with a twist: an antiheroine. Thackeray made his Becky Sharp a remorseless sociopath, but gave her every virtue a sociopath can have—cheerfulness, a sense of humor, self-knowledge, self-reliance, intelligence, and a boundless courage. She is capable of murder, but also of everything else. Even in the nineteenth century, people loved Becky Sharp.

Thackeray tries to bring Becky low but can't bring himself to do it: even at her lowest ebb, living in disreputable poverty in Germany, she has a great time. Soon she is back on her feet again, seducing Amelia's fat and gormless brother, and she ends the story wealthy and respected once again. "She has her enemies. Who does not? Her life is her answer to them. . . . She goes to church, and never without a footman. . . . The Destitute Orange-girl, the Neglected Washerwoman, the Distressed Muffin-man, find in her a fast and generous friend." And somehow, despite that niggling footman, we believe in Becky's kindness to these capitalized waifs.

Thackeray's other novels have their merits, but they just haven't managed to get a real toehold in the canon. However, we'll make a special plea for his early picaresque *Barry Lyndon*, where a swashbuckling male Becky Sharp tells his own story.

	Importance	Accessibility	Fun
Vanity Fair	9	7	9
Barry Lyndon	3	6	9

GEORGE ELIOT (MARY ANN EVANS) (1819–1880)

George Eliot was the first writer to successfully combine nice realism with reality. None of her people are caricatures; none of her events incredible; none of her sentiments false. Her works are "nice," in our terminology, because she is mainly interested in the inner lives of ethical, compassionate people. You couldn't get a major role in her novels if she didn't like you.

The also-ran characters are mainly flawed by awe-inspiring stupidity. They are greedy, envious, self-pitying, but their stupidity does beat all. One of her favorite techniques is describing the Chinese Whispers effect of gossip, which begins as a misunderstanding and ends as a malicious fantasy. At this point, it acquires the status of certainty and ruins someone's life.

Eliot's greatest novels are as complex and many-plotted as those of Dickens. Here is a typical plotline (from *Middlemarch*): A young heiress, Dorothea Brooke, longs to do good in the world. Therefore she marries the much-older Edward Casaubon, because she believes she can help him with his scholarly work. Literally everyone except Dorothea notices that Casaubon is a dried-up, pedantic, mediocre bore. Although she has book smarts, Dorothea is blinded by idealism. Casaubon soon pours cold water on that, and any other spark of joy in her life. Furthermore, she comes to realize his research is leading nowhere. He is actually incompetent, as well as being dried-up, mediocre, pedantic, and old. Also, his name looks like a typo. Then she meets her attractive, charming cousin Will. . . .

This is just one of a dozen interwoven plots, each of which could generate a book of three hundred pages. Taking this into consideration, at roughly nine hundred pages, this novel is a miracle of concision.

Her other novels are much simpler but, alas, not much shorter. This makes *Daniel Deronda* hopelessly baggy at eight hundred pages, many of which are devoted to digressions about the Jewish religion. (Of all things! You'd think she could dodge that bullet!) *The Mill on the Floss* uses its simplicity well (six hundred pages), but in *Silas Marner*, she tries her hand at cloying, to chilling effect, and *Adam Bede* is strictly for reading when you're in a hostel in Thailand, miles from the nearest bookstore, and it's the only book left behind by previous travelers that's not in German. (No, I don't mean "or similar situations." This is literally the only situation in which we can guarantee you'll love this book. Also, say hi to Bhichai for me.)

P.S.: ELIOT

Among the novelists of her time, critics considered Eliot the brain. She likes a pause for philosophy, and her novels are full of pithy sentences that cry out to be posted on a "thought for the day" blog. Here are a few cribbed from a thought for the day blog. Savor the wisdom!

No evil dooms us hopelessly except the evil we love, and desire to continue in, and make no effort to escape from.

That's what a man wants in a wife, mostly; he wants to make sure one fool tells him he's wise.

The important work of moving the world forward does not wait to be done by perfect men.

Opposition may become sweet to a man when he has christened it persecution.

People who can't be witty exert themselves to be devout and affectionate.

Most of Eliot's novels take place in the rural world of her youth. Farmers farm in the background of these novels, and the countryside is green. However, Eliot never forces this rustication down our throats. There is little country dialect, and livestock keeps a respectful distance. Our next author breaks down these barriers and plunges us into hard-core sheepy cowful chickenated farm porn.

	Importance	Accessibility	Fun
Middlemarch	10	5	8
Daniel Deronda	7	4	7
The Mill on the Floss	7	5	8
Silas Marner	6	6	6
Adam Bede	5	4	5

WHAT'S IN A NAME?

Mary Ann Evans took on the pen name of George Eliot for one reason only: to at least temporarily hide her gender. She famously expatiated on the narrow-minded critical responses to female writers, complaining that not only were critics unfairly negative, but they tended to reward mediocre (properly "feminine") works, while being uncomfortable and dismissive toward works of real value from a woman. Of course, in today's world of acclaimed female authors like A. M. Homes, Lionel Shriver, J. T. Leroy, Curtis Sittenfeld, and James Tiptree, Jr., we've left all that far behind.

THOMAS HARDY (1840–1928)

"I was never intended to be a prose-writer, still less a teller of tales—still, one had got to live." So Hardy assessed his career at the end of his life. He didn't mean that he was really meant to be a lion tamer, but that he considered himself a poet. Yet here he is in our novel novel section, over his dead body. (Strictly speaking, everything is happening over his dead body, or under his dead body, for readers in Australia.)

Philip Larkin, among others, agreed with Hardy that he was a great poet. The present author must confess that her poetic sense is not keen enough to perceive this greatness. To me, Hardy's poems are full of forced rhymes and mangled syntax. In a poem to his dead wife, he rhymes listlessness with "existlessness." Referring to their long estrangement, he says: "Things were not lastly as firstly well / With us twain, you tell?" In Hardy's poems, wind "oozes;" drizzle "bedrenches;" hearts are "abrim," and a poet "lips" rhymes. This seems uncannily like terrible poetry. Still, I bow to Larkin's genius and transmit faithfully to you the news that this poetry is great. Now on to the novels, whose value any dullard can see.

Like most writers of the time, Hardy published his work in serial form. The term "cliff-hanger" is thought to originate from his book *A Pair of Blue Eyes*; at the end of one chapter, a character is literally left hanging off a cliff. He set his novels in the fictional English county of Wessex (basically Dorset), and they were all tales of rural life, drawn from the experience of rural poverty into which Hardy himself was born. His parents were exactly like a pair of Hardy characters: his mother a serving maid whose favorite book was *The Divine Comedy*; his father a builder who played the violin in the local church. No one can write about milking, haying, or egging like Thomas Hardy.

His most accessible book is probably *Far From the Madding Crowd*. It's a standard mate selection novel, with lavish lashings of hay and sheep. Bathsheba Everdine takes over the family farm, resolving to run it herself although she is a woman. ("Although she is a woman" makes any plot more fun: it's the ketchup of plot devices.) Bathsheba is courted by three men. Being young, she goes for the rotten womanizer, for some Darwinian reason like he's hot. But the plot keeps rolling until the best man wins—it's all as predictable and pleasurable as it was when Cro-Magnon girls fooled around with Neanderthals, but ended up with that nice second cousin.

In *The Return of the Native*, Hardy marries the good boy to the bad girl, and the bad boy to the good girl. Then, big surprise, the bad characters are bored. This is the first of Hardy's novels which is properly sad: our favorite characters are systematically destroyed. Yet we love every minute of it, because we're made that way. Starring the red-hot Eustacia Vye (think Catherine Zeta-Jones) as bad girl. This novel also features Digory Venn, who sells the red chalk used for marking sheep and is therefore red from head to toe. A selfless, simple man who watches over the other characters, he is an early instance of the Magic Negro, before there were negroes.

The Mayor of Casterbridge begins with the scene of a drunken farm laborer auctioning off his wife in a fit of temper. Years later, having sworn off drink, he has risen to become the mayor of the title. Then his ex appears in Casterbridge, incognito and impecunious, to beg his help—with a teenaged daughter in tow. Again, the purpose of this book is to grind the mayor (and his bad girl, Lucetta) down as much as possible before killing them. By this point, Hardy has decided that what he is writing is tragedy, so the mayor is undone by the same flaws that make him interesting. His daughter, the good girl, naturally comes out fine, but who cares.

But what if the good girl and the bad girl were the same person? This is the premise of *Tess of the D'Urbervilles*. Seduced by a local rich kid, Tess has an illegitimate baby. The baby dies, and she goes to another town and tries to reconstruct her life. Now that Hardy has realized he is writing tragedy, she doesn't stand a chance. Here Tess is brought low not by her flaws, but by society's: she is a pure child of nature, an Eve persecuted by a world of hypocrites for one apple incident which may even have been nonconsensual. (Hardy's a little foggy on this point.)

She is still lucky, however, that she didn't have to be in *Jude the Obscure*. This story starts at a low point and goes downhill. As a poor orphan boy, Jude, a mason's apprentice, studies Latin and Greek in his spare time. We are absolutely sure this novel is going to be about a bright kid who claws his way into the middle classes. But no: he ends up as a disenchanted, Latin-speaking mason. Meanwhile, he marries the wrong girl; then he falls in love with his also-married cousin. The cousins become a couple but, because they can't marry, are persecuted wherever they go. Driven mad by poverty, Jude's oldest child eventually commits suicide after murdering his two siblings. At this point, we deserve a happy ending, such a happy ending that it should involve a Thai masseuse. But no, Hardy is on a roll, and who ever heard of anything rolling uphill?

While *Tess* was scathing about society's hypocrisy, *Jude* gets right to the point and beats on Christianity by name. For this, and for its frank portrayal of an extramarital relationship, it was damned by critics, and nicknamed *Jude the Obscene*. It is thought that this reception convinced Hardy to quit novel-writing, although we suspect he couldn't get another novel going, because the characters, sensing what was coming, kept killing themselves in Chapter 1.

	Importance	Accessibility	Fun
Far from the Madding Crowd	6	9	9
The Return of the Native	6	7	7
The Mayor of Casterbridge	8	7	7
Tess of the D'Urbervilles	8	5	6
Jude the Obscure	8	5	5

RUDYARD KIPLING (1865–1936)

Kipling was the first Englishman to win the Nobel Prize. This is one of two remaining reasons to take his work half-seriously. The other is the continuing status of his poem "If . . ."—perennially the most beloved poem in Britain. Here are the first few lines:

> If you can keep your head while all about you
> Are losing theirs and blaming it on you
> If you can trust yourself when all men doubt you
> But make allowance for their doubting too . . .

And so on, with many doubtless very mature things one is supposed to do and think, the reward of which is:

> Yours is the Earth and everything that's in it
> And—what is more—you'll be a Man, my son!

Note that you get not only a capital letter in your Manhood, but an exclamation point (which will doubtless stay hard even when all men doubt you). On the one hand, this poem is genuinely very inspiring. Sometimes you can only keep going by imagining yourself as a dauntless hero. When you're hungover, it's raining, and you're taking the train to your data entry job, any fortitude you can get is golden. On the other hand, "If . . ." can also make kids feel good about joining the army. While surely, at some time in the past, it was a great idea to join the army, and being a soldier was very noble, mostly this is a big fat lie. As an example I happen to have right here, Kipling's own son died in World War I, in which no one was ennobled and nothing was achieved. Kipling himself, needless to say, was never in any army, or anywhere near a war. After his son's death, Kipling wrote a poem damning World War I, with the famous lines: "If any question why we died / Tell them, because our fathers lied." He has really taken the words out of my mouth on this one.

Kipling was born in India. At five, he was sent to England to be raised—the accepted practice then among British colonials—but returned at eighteen to work as a newspaperman. After seven years working for various colonial publications, he left India once and for all, although he would write about it for the rest of his life. Among his most famous works about India are *Gunga Din* and *The White Man's Burden*. The latter reads like a recruiting jingle for colonialist oppressors:

> Take up the White Man's burden—
> Send forth the best ye breed—
> Go, bind your sons to exile
> To serve your captives' need;
> To wait, in heavy harness,
> On fluttered folk and wild—
> Your new-caught sullen peoples,
> Half devil and half child.

Even at the time, this was considered tasteless. Kipling apologists argued that it was meant ironically, but Kipling didn't. As far as he was concerned, it was a powerful expression of his sincere beliefs.

Gunga Din is an equally charming ditty about an Indian water boy. The narrator is an English soldier. He and his comrades beat Gunga Din and shower him with racist epithets, although he's hardworking and fearless. At last the water boy is shot and dies saving the narrator, who reflects that when he gets to hell, Gunga Din will still be serving him water. The final lines are often quoted: "Though I've belted you an' flayed you, / By the livin' Gawd that made you, / You're a better man than I am, Gunga Din!" This is really damning Gunga Din with faint praise. Despite its brutal content, however, this poem is very rousing, like all of Kipling's poetry, or like *Triumph of the Will*.

If you're wondering what makes this guy Nobel Prize material, reading his fiction will not solve the mystery. Those of his books that are still in print have slipped, by slow degrees, into the children's section. Meanwhile, children have slipped, by slow degrees, into not reading them. The most famous, of course, is *The Jungle Books*. Although it is really only famous in its Disney cartoon version, the original book is still truly gripping for a bright ten-year-old. For adults, the best is *Kim*, about a resourceful young street urchin in India who gets recruited as a spy by the British. Like all of Kipling's work, *Kim* has a roguish, retro charisma. Still, one can't help imagining Kipling is at this moment carrying water to the other Nobel Prize winners in hell.

	Importance	Accessibility	Fun	Evil
"If . . ."	10	0	10	5
Other poems	4	0	9	10
The Jungle Books	4	0	7	7
Kim	5	0	10	7

OSCAR WILDE (1854–1900)

Wilde told André Gide that the difference between a work of nature (bad) and a work of art (good) is that a work of art is always unique. His own greatest work, *The Importance of Being Earnest*, observes that rule to an unusual degree. Universally loved, it has never been successfully imitated. "It was written by a butterfly for butterflies," Wilde said, explaining its philosophy as: "We should treat all the trivial things seriously, and the serious things in life with sincere and studied triviality."

His characters accordingly assign maximum importance to matters like marrying a man with the Christian name "Ernest," while dismissing everything that is considered important. "If ever I get married, I shall certainly try to forget the fact," says Algernon. Lady Bracknell responds to the news that Jack has lost both his parents with the famous line: "To lose one parent, Mr. Worthing, may be regarded as a misfortune; to lose both looks like carelessness." Again and again, Wilde uses this technique of treating the serious as the trivial, and vice versa, to get laughs. Once you understand this formula, the play unfurls with perfect predictability, but no less grace. Although none of Wilde's characters ever says anything a real person would say in real life, the play leaves us feeling that we know this world—living, as we do, in a society that cares passionately about the latest fashions but is bored by the latest famines.

Wilde also wrote a few serviceable but unremarkable other comedies (*An Ideal Husband, Lady Windermere's Fan, A Woman of No Importance*) and a poetic drama (*Salome*). This last is self-consciously gorgeous, full of phrases like "Egyptians silent and subtle, with long nails of jade and russet cloaks." All of the characters speak in this heightened diction: it's a feast for people who like hearing things compared to a maiden in silver slippers.

Wilde's major prose work, *The Picture of Dorian Gray*, is only slightly less effete. Its story is well known: A beautiful young man is gradually corrupted. As he slides into vice and dissipation, a portrait painted of him in more innocent days sits in his attic. The man himself is miraculously well preserved, retaining the healthy glow and pure looks of his youth. The portrait not only ages, but is stamped with the sneering coldness of the libertine. This novel is a square inch of parable stretched out over yards of aesthetic prosing.

After *The Importance of Being Earnest*, Wilde is most famous for his imprisonment for gross indecency, at the instigation of his lover's father. The amazing thing to us today is that people had the cheek to act surprised that Oscar Wilde was gay. It's as if society had turned and prosecuted the elephant in the room. This elephant was sentenced to two years' hard labor, during which he was abandoned by all his fancy friends—including the young lover, Albert Douglas, who'd caused the fuss.

Wilde almost died from the harsh terms of his sentence. However, he claimed to be grateful for the experience, which had taught him pity and humility. In prison, he wrote two further works using these new tricks. The first is "The Ballad of Reading Gaol," a protest poem about the hanging of a man who had killed his mistress. Here is an excerpt:

> The man had killed the thing he loved
> And so he had to die.
>
> Yet each man kills the thing he loves
> By each let this be heard,
> Some do it with a bitter look,
> Some with a flattering word,
> The coward does it with a kiss,
> The brave man with a sword!

Of course, Wilde is being a little disingenuous here. Clearly a person would normally welcome being killed with a flattering word—second only to being killed with money—but object strongly to being killed with a sword.

His next work, however, is painfully ingenuous. *De Profundis* is a letter Wilde wrote to Douglas from prison. It begins with a long section in which he excoriates Douglas, blaming him for Wilde's own creative haplessness, bankruptcy, and descent into vice. But it then develops into a piece of inspirational writing, strikingly like something written by a drunk in his first year of AA. "The supreme vice is shallowness," Wilde says, with a reformed man's self-loathing. The supreme virtue, it turns out, is Humility, and, now that Douglas has been dethroned, Wilde's supreme love is Jesus Christ.

If you ever want a piece of writing to cheer you in adversity, and you're cool with Jesus, *De Profundis* is quite beautiful and even profound. It is also still read avidly by people interested in gay rights, a situation which will probably persist until gay people have equal rights. Douglas, its intended recipient, never read it. This is what will often happen if you write your ex-boyfriend a fifty-thousand word letter about your newfound love for Jesus. It also left Wilde's other partners-in-shallowness unmoved. André Gide commented that humility was "only a pompous name that [Wilde] gave to his impotence."

Why impotence? Because *De Profundis* was the last thing Wilde ever wrote. Society had managed to crush everything in him but homosexuality—which is notoriously as prone to resurrection as any Jesus. Talent, however, is sadly fragile. (Way to go, society.) Wilde went back to Douglas shortly after his release, and died shortly after that ill-judged reunion.

AFTER OSCAR

Alfred Douglas (or "Bosie," as he was called) was the coiner of the phrase "the love that dare not speak its name," in a letter to Wilde. In Bosie's case, this love was typically felt for a rent boy paid with Wilde's money. One of Wilde's mistakes at his trial was elucidating this phrase with some stirring oratory in honor of Greek love. He had forgotten that his defense was based on denying that he was gay.

Bosie outlived Wilde by many years and became a fierce enemy of homosexuals, hounding any queer people he could find through the law courts. He also went on a vendetta against the Jewish conspiracy, in whose ranks he whimsically included Winston Churchill. Clearly his attacks on homosexuals were an expression of self-hatred, but his attacks on Jews can only be due to the fact that homophobia is often a mask for being a total douche bag.

EDITH WHARTON (1862–1937)

Nice realist novels are very similar, like a brand you can depend on. Wharton is the most typical of all nice realists, like a flagship Starbucks. Her novels stand out not for any departure in form or content, but for being the most fun. These are true page-turners; airplane books you will still be trying to finish as your plane crashes.

They are set among the upper classes of America's Gilded Age. This society is shallow, obsessed with respectability while lacking every virtue. Wharton's heroines feel suffocated in this hothouse but can't live outside. The fear of being exiled drives them to criminal acts, poisons their loves, and sometimes kills them. We tend to cheer them on because we know ourselves how horrible it is to have a day job. Because this quest, however, is just plain shallow, and Wharton knows it, the treatment is witty rather than somber.

The best of all is *The House of Mirth*, about the decline and fall of a society beauty, Lily Bart. The fundless Lily hangs on as a houseguest of the rich by sheer charm, living from handout to hand-me-down. Her holy grail is a rich husband, but she is always snagged by some scruple before her gold-digging can yield a wedding band. The story of her doomed battle to escape "dinginess" is brilliantly funny and absorbing, and really makes us believe it's worth dying rather than live in a crummy apartment. Undine Spragg, the Midwestern social climber in *The Custom of the Country* has better luck but worse morals; she goes through a series of society men, and in and out of fashion, but never really loses her footing. Finally, Wharton considered *The Age of Innocence* an apology for the more scabrous *The House of Mirth*. Here the same social sphere is seen through the eyes of a man, Newland Archer, who is engaged to a nice girl but falls hopelessly in love with the faintly scandalous Countess Ellen Olenska. This book isn't much of an apology; it's the kind that would normally get tossed back in your face and land you in a hotel room for the night. In fact, the alien sterility of its moral ending leaves us thanking God society has lost these morals.

Then there's *Ethan Frome*. This turgid Gothic, set in a poor New England town, has so little in common with Edith Wharton's other novels that one suspects her muse was cheating with the mailman. If you love *The House of Mirth*, you will hate *Ethan Frome*. In fact, if you don't love *The House of Mirth*, you will hate *Ethan Frome*. If you have the ability to hate, you will hate *Ethan Frome*. It has everything that made *The Scarlet Letter* go down like a brick: heavy-handed color symbolism, a pointless frame story, dreary characters, cold weather. In the climax, the protagonists attempt suicide on a sled, yet it is not played for laughs. Basically, if you've read *Ethan Frome*, and you enjoyed it, you're asleep and dreaming. Soon you will wake up in a world where you too hated *Ethan Frome*.

	Importance	Accessibility	Fun
The House of Mirth	7	8	10
The Custom of the Country	5	8	8
The Age of Innocence	7	7	8
Ethan Frome	6	6	2

Before Harlequin

Test your knowledge! Which early writer of the romance genre produced the following sentences:

> His gleaming beauty, maleness, like a young, good-humored, smiling wolf did not blind her to the significant, sinister stillness in his bearing, the lurking danger of his unsubdued temper. "His totem is the wolf," she repeated to herself.
>
> All the time her heart was crying, as if in the midst of some ordeal: "I want to go back, I want to go away, I want not to know it, not to know that this exists." Yet she must go forward.
>
> She was tortured with desire to see him again, a nostalgia, a necessity to see him again, to make sure it was not all a mistake, that she was not deluding herself, that she really felt this strange and overwhelming sensation on his account, this knowledge of him in her essence, this powerful apprehension of him. "Am I really singled out for him in some way, is there really some pale gold, arctic light that envelopes only us two?" she asked herself.

Time's up.

It will surprise some readers to learn that the answer is D. H. Lawrence. It will surprise them more when they learn that these three paragraphs are all from the same scene—a scene in which two sisters put down their sewing and go on a walk to see the wedding of some acquaintances. At the last minute, they decide not to go into the church, and instead stand a little ways away, watching the other guests go in.

Nothing else happens.

So let's start over.

D. H. LAWRENCE (1885–1930)

Some people swear by him. I do not wish to insult these people. But if they get between me and D. H. Lawrence, they may get some pejorative on their clothes.

Lawrence is not a bad writer—always. Rather, he is one of the most uneven writers in Western literature. The first part of *Sons and Lovers*, for instance, is a thoughtful and sensitive account of childhood in a coal miner's family. But about halfway through, he takes a wrong turn—at about the point that his hero gets old enough to have sexual feelings. We are soon plunged into an endless exegesis of these feelings, which are heavy on mother issues and madonna-whore stuff, light on normal sexuality. Lawrence got his lines crossed somewhere; instead of writing his novel, he is writing the most disturbing, obsessive breakup letter in the world.

At the beginning of *The Rainbow*, Lawrence spells out his idea of the primitive life force: "They felt the rush of the sap in spring, they knew the wave which cannot halt, but every year throws forward the seed to begetting, and, falling back, leaves the young-born on the earth." Well, okay, if you like life forces, we'll allow that. But a few sentences on this has ripened into: "They took the udder of the cows, the cows yielded milk and pulse against the hands of the men, the pulse of the blood of the teats of the cows beat into the pulse of the hands of the men." Paragraphs later he is still at it: ". . . they lived full and surcharged, their senses full fed, their faces always turned to the heat of the blood, staring into the sun, dazed with looking towards the source of generation . . ."

He has still not introduced a single character. Nothing has happened, we are not entirely sure if we're on Earth or the moon. All he has said is "How about that life force!"

Despite this rather fruity beginning, *The Rainbow* is a wonderful and poetically powerful novel. Here Lawrence actually harnesses the life force and gets it to do his bidding. He has the courage of his weirdness, but also shows discretion and keeps in mind that we are here to read a story, not to hear his bizarro theories.

By the time he gets to *Women in Love*, however, he is getting life force all over himself, drooling, screaming, ranting, and eventually droning. Here, Lawrence can describe a character for an entire page, and leave you with no idea what the person is like. This is also when his usual writerly instincts desert him and he produces passages like this: "'He is such a dreadful satanist, isn't he?' she drawled to Ursula, in a queer resonant voice, that ended on a shrill little laugh of pure ridicule. The two women were jeering at him, jeering him into nothingness. The laugh of the shrill, triumphant female sounded from Hermione, jeering him as if he were a neuter." Characters, dialogue, description—all wither on the page. It's as if the characters are huddled down with their hands over their ears while Lawrence shouts his pet theories over a loudspeaker.

This is also when his lurking gayness begins to make itself felt. While it's unclear how actively gay Lawrence was (he seems to have had one male lover, but no one's sure), it's crystal clear how gay his later novels are. In *Women in Love*, the two male protagonists wrestle naked while spritzing each other with a siphon, then fall asleep, still naked, in each other's arms. The gayest part, however, is that Lawrence insists there's nothing gay about it: just good friends! Between this repression and the many gloating descriptions of male physiques, Lawrence becomes increasingly creepy. Whenever he uses the word "loins," it feels like he's licking his lips. The same goes for the word "man." The muscle-magazine homosexuality, the Oedipal material, the stalker vibe, the hovering fear of vagina dentata—it mounts until Lawrence can't talk about the weather without it feeling like TMI.

Of his later novels, the notorious *Lady Chatterley's Lover* is probably the most fun, though it now seems both very tame and very gay. The story of a lady who falls in love with a hunky, strong-silent-type gamekeeper, it could not be more obviously Lawrence's own sexual fantasy. He also wrote several extra books, with names like *Aaron's Rod* and *The Plumed Serpent* and *The Escaped Cock* and *Kangaroo* (hang on, what's phallic about a kangaroo?). Some of his short stories are justly celebrated ("The Rocking Horse Winner," "The Odour of Chrysanthemums"). Any whose names don't ring a bell, though, are probably about the helpless passion of some full-busted woman for a brute of a man of few words. And he wrote some poetry, which consisted of poems. In a cruel riposte to his other titles, one posthumous collection was published as *More Pansies*.

Finally, he painted. Here is a description of one of his paintings from the *Daily Express*: "a hideous, bearded man holding a fair-haired woman in his lascivious grip while wolves with dripping jaws look on expectantly." Sigh. Lawrence should really have hired a guy to whip him with a cat-o'-nine-tails and gotten it out of his system.

Lawrence's life was the usual round of penury, tuberculosis, wandering, and obscenity trials. To make life harder for himself, he hooked up with a German woman just before World War I, giving society an extra excuse to persecute him.

	Importance	Accessibility	Fun
Sons and Lovers	5	6	6
The Rainbow	5	5	6
Women in Love	5	4	4
Lady Chatterley's Lover	5	6	6

CHAPTER 12

Unwelcome Realism: The French and Russians Team Up to Depress Mankind

In England, the realist novel begins with Richardson, Defoe, and Fielding and develops in tiny adjustments, like a campaign to get the perfect picture on a TV set. In France, it begins with a reaction against the Romantic novel, notably against the bleeding heart liberal epics of Victor Hugo and George Sand. Their high ideals and pretty sentiments looked hollow after five revolutions, the Napoleonic wars, and syphilis (which all French realists had). Basically the French in this period were a pack of cankered degenerates, who murdered one another and burned down churches every time the wind changed. They weren't Romanticism material.

French realism is therefore characterized by extreme misanthropy. There's something forensic about its painstaking attention to detail. All the magnifying glasses and tweezers in the world, however, cannot find a worthy impulse in its characters. Occasionally, some good-heartedness seems to appear, but by increasing the magnification, the author reveals this to be vanity or ignorance.

This movement's leading lights were syphilitic grumps, who never married and never wanted to. Typically they hated their parents, and their parents hated them back. They had friends, but these were other French realists, to whom they could write long letters about their disgust with the human race. They were basically haters.

The Russians realists, while no less depressing, are far more tenderhearted. Mankind is essentially flawed and doomed, but at least the author is sorry. The author is so sorry, but no point mincing words: we're doomed. Now let's watch some flawed but essentially lovable people being doomed. Ha ha! Look at their funny little struggles! They want to stop torturing one another, poor little critters! Almost seems a shame they can't.

Rather alarmingly, the unwelcome realists are known for their psychological acuity. The shoe fits, but it's a really ugly shoe. Sometimes it's a pair of concrete boots. Reading a slew of these novels is as good as psychoanalysis. It will introduce you to dark places in your heart you didn't know existed. You will come out with insights into not only yourself, but the human condition. It's much cheaper than psychoanalysis, but remember, your family can't sue Flaubert if you hang yourself after reading his books.

STENDHAL (MARIE-HENRI BEYLE) (1783–1842)

Stendhal claimed he learned his flat style from daily reading of the Code Napoleon. He derived his plots from Romantic novels, and his facility from years of experience as a hack writer; over the years, he ran through more than one hundred noms de plume. In an obituary he wrote for himself, he reports that he "learned to understand men and their baseness" as a schoolboy. In the same auto-obit, he says that he "respected one man alone: NAPOLEON" and lists six women he loved "passionately." This mixture of swaggering, romanticism, and hatred for all men but Napoleon flavors all his work.

He was hated right back. Stendhal himself predicted that his work would begin to be appreciated in the year 1880. In fact, it took nowhere near that long. People simply waited for him to die before bursting out in appreciation. Maybe it just happened that way, but it's hard to escape the impression that people just weren't willing to admit they enjoyed his novels while Stendhal might find out.

He is best known for *The Red and the Black*, his compulsively readable novel about the social climber Julien Sorel. Sorel is a carpenter's son, despised by his family for his book smarts. He escapes from these troglodytes by entering the Church. From here, he becomes the tutor in the family of the local mayor and then the lover of the mayor's wife. His career is launched! From now on, he will be a pawn of various powerful men and women, but a pawn which is rapidly advancing across the board.

The novel is fascinating for its unflattering psychology. First and last, Sorel is motivated by egotism. His loves are symptoms of self-love. His political zeal centers on the fact that carpenters' sons can't rise now as easily as they could under Napoleon. In short, Sorel is a realist's portrait of a Romantic. Stendhal himself said the novel was about the "immense vanity which has become almost the only identifiable passion in this city." That word "become" is significant: Stendhal had been a follower of Napoleon. He believed the post-Napoleonic world was one of petty bureaucrats and banal self-interest. It was also one in which Stendhal lost a sweet diplomatic job in Italy, but we're sure that had nothing at all to do with his bad attitude.

His other great novel, *The Charterhouse of Parma*, is set in Italy, about which Stendhal could still wax semiromantic himself. Since his story is about Italians, Stendhal loves his characters. Every few pages, he lets drop a scathing remark about how much better the Italians are than the French.

Larger than life, crafty as a Bond villain, the heroine, Gina, effortlessly manipulates the ordinary people around her until she is the de facto ruler of Parma. She is breathtakingly beautiful, as is her nephew (and beloved), Fabrice; everyone they meet falls instantly in love with them. When Gina is stuck in her scheming, a poet-brigand appears out of nowhere, confesses his love and offers to do anything for her. Problem solved.

Of course, bad things happen to them too. Fabrice, whose only fear is imprisonment, is naturally thrown into prison. His last impression before being locked up is the lovely face of Clélia, the daughter of the prison warden. Since she lives in the prison compound, he can see her through the bars of his tower window in her aviary, when she goes to feed her birds. The two begin to communicate in sign language, fall in love, and this situation continues for nine months in which the hero is idyllically happy, despite the constant attempts of the Prince of Parma to have him poisoned.

This is that rare treasure, an adventure story for smart people. It's a special use of realism, where the only real thing is that the characters are really, really selfish. It's also miraculously lighthearted, considering the circumstances in which it was written. Stendhal completed it in fifty-two days. It was dictated, because he was undergoing a particularly noxious treatment for syphilis that left him so weak he couldn't hold a pen.

THE BLACK AND THE BLUE

Seven years after writing *The Red and the Black*, Stendhal started a novella called *The Pink and the Green*. It was later abandoned, presumably because Stendhal just couldn't live with those colors.

	Importance	Accessibility	Fun
The Red and the Black	10	8	8
The Charterhouse of Parma	8	7	10

HONORÉ DE BALZAC (1799–1850)

Like many great writers from the Renaissance onward, Balzac was intended by his parents for a lawyer. He was so ill-suited to this that in his first job as a clerk, he received a note saying: "M. Balzac is requested not to come to work tonight because there is a great deal of work to be done."

As a writer, Balzac started as a hack, producing nine abysmal pulp novels under pseudonyms. He also started various businesses, all of them failures, but never lost faith that he would someday be rich and famous. Then, one day, he had an idea for a series of novels which would give an encyclopedic account of human society. Thrilled, he ran to his sister's house to announce, "I'm about to become a genius!" Some of our readers may have brothers like this and feel a little weary at hearing it again. However, as never ever happens with your brother, Balzac was totally right.

The novels he then produced are collectively known as *La Comedie Humaine* (*The Human Comedy*, for people who are really backward at decoding French). As works produced with riches in mind, these books are pandering, page-turning potboilers. Characters reappear from one book to another—notably the criminal mastermind Vautrin—making the whole series a long soap opera in book form. Unusually for French realism (but inevitably for soap operas) there are occasional good characters, all selfless virgins. Everyone else is cankered through and through with astonishing vices.

Sometimes, as in *Eugénie Grandet*, where the miser is crushed by his own blindness, the sinful are punished. Just as often, though, they go on to brilliant careers. For instance, in *Père Goriot*, Balzac's version of the King Lear story, the selfless father Goriot dies in penury while the unscrupulous Rastignac launches a brilliant career, and the dastardly villain Vautrin escapes to corrupt the young another day. (To add spice, Vautrin is a homosexual who corrupts youth to satisfy an infernal itch.)

Balzac is a crowd-pleaser rather than a fine stylist. Instead of the factual simplicity of Stendhal, here we have all the florid absurdities of nineteenth-century pulp. This is from *A Harlot High and Low*: "By a rare circumstance, if indeed it is ever found in very young girls, her hands, incomparably formed, were soft, transparent and white like those of a woman brought to bed of her second child." Who can forget those transparent hands you get when you're giving birth to a second child?

While his portraits are hyperbolic and tacky, they often have a certain deadly aim. While the machinations of the eponymous character in *Cousin Bette* are completely unbelievable, her motivations—envy, sexual frustration, jealousy—are so palpably real that the novel is full of electricity. Furthermore, those improbable plots (as is well known) spare you the effort of turning the pages. They also spare you the effort of getting any sleep or getting to work on time. You come back to yourself ten hours later, with the pages all turned and a crick in your neck. Because of the salacious plots, Balzac is never as depressing as the more convincing French realists, but still don't expect to come away uplifted. True love is always betrayed. All marriages are for money or titles. Good will always be punished. Evil may be rewarded, though sometimes it is punished too, because what's more fun than watching someone's body disintegrate from a weird Brazilian toxin?

Like most French realists, Balzac detested his parents and was hated by them. He did manage to marry, although the story is a classic example of the life of a French realist. He tied the knot in Kiev when he was already gravely ill, then headed home, in terrible pain. When the carriage arrived at his house, no one answered the knock, although there was a light in the window. He was left out in the cold night, suffering, a circumstance that pushed him over the edge into his final decline. As could only happen to a French realist, earlier in the day, the housekeeper had gone insane.

	Importance	Accessibility	Fun
Eugénie Grandet	7	8	6
Père Goriot	8	9	8
Lost Illusions	5	8	7
A Harlot High and Low	4	5	6
Cousin Bette	6	8	7

GUSTAVE FLAUBERT (1821–1880)

Flaubert's favorite saying was *La vie est bete*—"Life is stupid." By this, he meant that events have no significance. History is not leading to anything, and any patterns we discern are figments of our imagination. In his greatest novels, the narrator has the voice of an indifferent God; he just doesn't care what happens to anyone.

During his lifetime, this impartial stance was box office poison. Critics who happily swallowed sentimental portrayals of adultery were disgusted by *Madame Bovary*. "There is no goodness in it," squawked Sainte-Beuve, while Matthew Arnold peeped anxiously, "It petrifies the feelings." Though it lacks a single sex scene, the novel was the subject of an indecency trial. The prosecutor said that the book was offensive not only because of its content, but because "You cannot tell what is going on in the author's conscience." From Flaubert's point of view, it would have made as much sense to complain that you couldn't spot the author's unicorn.

While the public were shocked by his morals, Flaubert was obsessively refining his lucid, unadorned style. He was the origin of the cult of *le mot juste*—"the right word." The right word was not the most beautiful one, but the simplest and most accurate. Later generations caught this mania, and now it is common for an author to labor for hours to produce a sentence like "The doctor's office was on the first floor."

This deep participation in his fiction meant that Flaubert was content not to have a life. He lived with his mother in the country and had only one serious love affair, which was a flop. Apart from that, love for Flaubert was a narrow path from the brothel to terminal syphilis. His friends were writers with whom he corresponded about writing. This lonely dedication to his craft has blighted the lives of countless Flaubert wannabes. Every year, a new crop of hopefuls gives up career, family, and ski vacations in order to enrich the world with their own, perfected version of "The doctor's office was on the first floor."

Here are his major works:

Salammbo

Flaubert said that in him, there existed two writers: the realist and another who "loves lyricism, great eagle flights, the sonorous phrase." This is from Flaubert's sonorous side, a historical novel about Carthage. It's tacky, sleazy, cheesy, gaudy, gooey, and yet it isn't fun to read. It even manages to feel creepily racist, although most of the groups he is describing (Carians, Gauls, Cantabrians) no longer exist. Here is a typical piece of dialogue from the heroine, talking to her heathen gods: "Dead! All dead! No more will you come obedient to my voice as when, seated on the edge of the lake, I used to throw seeds of the watermelon into your mouths! The mystery of Tanith ranged in the depths of your eyes that were more limpid than the globules of rivers." This is what comes of feeding your gods on watermelon seeds. What was she thinking?

The Temptation of Saint Anthony

Another sonorous work, which Flaubert considered his masterpiece despite dogged attempts by friends to get him to reconsider. It's written in the form of a playscript, and depicts the night in which Saint Anthony was tempted by the devil, in the form of Lust and Death and the Queen of Sheba, among others. This is Anthony, reminiscing to himself: "Nevertheless, this one was taller . . . and beautiful . . . prodigiously beautiful! (Passes his hands over his forehead.) No! no! I must not think of it!"

Nothing sets the pulses racing like an ellipsis . . . then an exclamation point!

Despite how easy it is to poke fun at his excesses, Flaubert had the rare quality of remaining interesting even when the book completely stinks.

Madame Bovary

Bored with her inadequate husband, Emma Bovary cheats with other, sexier, inadequate men. She has a child she doesn't love and spends money she doesn't have. At last, in a fit of justifiable despair, she eats poison.

The story is based on a real case, and Flaubert is unsparing in his description of the banal events. Sometimes we think Emma is weak and selfish; sometimes it seems that society has no place for her better capacities. Ultimately, it is both. Emma is no good; people are no good; things are no good; good is no good. What is this "good" you speak of? Life is stupid and then you eat poison.

At the same time, Flaubert's writing is so good, the book is not nearly as disheartening as it should be. The detached elegance of his mind also makes us feel that Flaubert inhabits a purer sphere, until we remember that he lived with his mother, when he wasn't at a brothel getting icky diseases.

A Sentimental Education

This is an autobiographical novel about a young man's love for a woman twelve years his senior. Here Flaubert, who considered his use of a dramatic plot in

Madame Bovary pandering, turns to an episodic form to further distance the reader. The result is so arid that even the loveliest sections make life seem piercingly empty. If you read it aloud in a forest, birds will fall down dead around you.

As with Madame Bovary, this book is never entirely gloomy, because it's coupled with such intellectual grace. However, Flaubert's ascetic style feels less appropriate in a book about callow youth; it's truthful, but it doesn't feel real. It's like watching first love through a powerful telescope. Perhaps for this reason, *A Sentimental Education* has been much admired, but never popular.

Bouvard and Pecuchet

Here Flaubert sets out systematically to depress the hell out of us. His original title for this work was: *The Two Woodlice*. But again, this book has a grace that makes it rise above its generally depressing subject matter. Also, it's funny.

The story begins with Bouvard and Pecuchet working together as copy clerks. They are middle-aged bachelors, content with their monotonous, limited lives. Those lives are interrupted when Bouvard comes into a large inheritance and decides to share his wealth with his best friend.

Freed from the need to work, they move to the countryside, where they set out to lead the perfect life. The perfect life, however, is a moving target. One month they take up science; then they throw their energies into creating a beautiful garden; or they adopt disadvantaged children. Flaubert carefully demonstrates how every effort leads to crushing disillusionment. Nothing works, primarily because the world is no damned good. Religion, art, politics, love—all are empty and meaningless. They do not, however, try living with their mothers and going to brothels at night, so perhaps they missed a trick.

	Importance	Accessibility	Fun
Salammbo	5	7	6
The Temptation of Saint Anthony	5	4	6
Madame Bovary	10	10	8
A Sentimental Education	7	7	7
Bouvard and Pecuchet	5	7	7

EMILE ZOLA (1840–1902)

In cognitive-behavioral therapy, people are taught to avoid "unhelpful thoughts"—thoughts about one's worthless nature, the miseries of the world, and our helplessness in the face of cruel fate. Naturalism is a form of realism that consists entirely of unhelpful thoughts. Here all human desires are base, and we are slaves to these desires. It is only justice, then, that we are doomed. Science proves this, sorry. Still, enjoy the moment, because the world is getting inexorably worse. Also, there's no heaven. People with a history of mood disorders should avoid naturalist works at all costs.

The main European practitioner is Emile Zola. He wrote a series of twenty interrelated novels called the *Rougon-Macquart* series, after the family who serves as its antiheroes. He intended to show "how the race is modified by the environment," which was by going from bad to worse. The Rougon-Macquarts all inherit a "ravenous appetite," which may be for money, alcohol, or just plain murder. The archetypal Zola heroine, *Nana*, destroys every man she meets—one stabs himself with scissors, another immolates himself in a barn—before getting smallpox and ending her career as "a shovelful of putrid flesh." In *La Bête Humaine,* Jacques is tormented by an unquenchable yearning to murder women for no reason: a "perverse need to throw the female over his shoulder, dead, and carry her off like prey." Needless to say, he will scratch this murderous itch before the novel is finished, and he will not be the only one.

Like Balzac, Zola had a tabloid sensibility; like Flaubert, he was a perfectionist about research, becoming an expert on the ghettos of the poor, the lives of railway workers—any milieu where a Rougon-Macquart might fall into bad company, commit brutal crimes, and be dismembered. What makes Zola worth reading, for the constitutionally resilient, is his magical skill at creating a complex social world and infusing it with trashy life. He wrote grippingly convincing scenes of the life of the alcoholic poor, a miners' riot being violently suppressed, a catastrophic train wreck—seemingly anything that will send the vulnerable into a spiral of suicidal ideation. Zola seizes on depressing material with such gusto in these books, there is something invigorating in their bleak negativity.

Naturalism also became an important element in American fiction, particularly in the works of Stephen Crane (see page 178) and Theodore Dreiser (see some other book, by somebody who thinks people should read Dreiser).

THE ZOLA TECHNIQUE FOR GETTING RID
OF UNWANTED FRIENDS

One day, the artist Paul Cézanne received a package in the mail from his old friend Emile Zola. What's this? Why, it's Emile's new novel, *The Masterpiece*. Its hero is one Claude Lantier, a Rougon-Macquart boy who becomes a painter uncannily similar to Cézanne, an innovator who is maligned by the critics. In the novel, Lantier gradually finds his genius falling into incoherence, struggles to find his way again, but fails catastrophically. Realizing his work is crap, he finally hangs himself.

Cezanne wrote Zola a polite thank-you letter, and never spoke to him again.

THE DREYFUS AFFAIR

This was a controversial trial that divided French society for years, something like the O.J. murder or the Rosenberg trial, only a hundred times worse. Friend turned on friend. Fistfights broke out. Family members stopped talking to one another.

It was basically a heated debate about whether Jews could be trusted not to betray the French government. Given that France had a revolution every few years, you'd think nothing could be more French than betraying the government, but they didn't see it this way.

Captain Alfred Dreyfus, a Jewish artillery officer, was accused of giving military information to the Germans. He was convicted and sent to Devil's Island. Two years later, French army officials found out somebody else did it. They suppressed the information and even had someone fabricate new documents to cover it up. This was a fairly open secret, though many people refused to believe it, dismissing it as a crazy conspiracy theory.

This was when Zola stepped up. He published an open letter to the president, known as the "*J'accuse*" letter, in which he laid out the campaign against Dreyfus. It culminated in a series of sentences beginning with "I accuse . . ." Zola named everyone involved in the cover-up and specified their part in it. He challenged any of them to sue him for slander, knowing that a trial would lead to a reexamination of the Dreyfus case.

In the wake of the scandal that followed, Dreyfus was re-tried . . . and again found guilty. Oops! However, he was given a pardon and released, putting an end to the furor. Meanwhile, the French may have learned a little something. They stopped both overthrowing the government and persecuting Jews, realizing they had a whole nation next door, ready and willing to take both jobs off their hands.

	Importance	Accessibility	Fun
Germinal	6	6	6
Nana	6	6	5
La Bête Humaine	4	7	6
L'Assomoir	4	7	5

JOSEPH CONRAD (JÓZEF TEODOR KONRAD KORZENIOWSKI) (1857–1924)

Joseph Conrad was born a Polish aristocrat living under Imperial Russian rule. He was a naturalized English citizen and English was his third language. This makes him something like a concert pianist who performs wearing two pair of mittens. It also makes his fiction a distinct mix of nice and unwelcome realism.

In Conrad's novels, men are faced with a dauntingly, almost tauntingly un-caring universe, which batters them until whatever flaws they have are exposed. There is redemption, though, in manly loyalty to a cause. Nobody is so good as a simple sailor who doesn't desert his post, and no one is so bad as the European slackers who infest the outposts of Empire, shirking their way through life.

Conrad went to sea as a teenager and worked his way up through the briny ranks. He retired from the sea to write at thirty-seven, fed up with being valued and remunerated. Almost all of what he wrote was based directly on his experi-ences at sea. If you've been through a storm at sea with Conrad, you'll feel like you've actually been through a storm at sea. Afterward, though, when you go outside, you'll blink up at the sky, disappointed to find it is not swollen with meaning.

Charles Marlow, a stand-in for the author, often narrates the stories. In the novella *Heart of Darkness*, he is a steamboat pilot who heads upriver through the Belgian Congo to find the trader Kurtz, who is breaking all records with his provision of ivory. Once an enlightened exemplar of Western civilization, Kurtz has gone renegade and set himself up as the local warlord. Worse, he's shacked up with a black girl. The horror! The jungle drums! The prose excesses! (For a quick and dirty look at the Belgian Congo, see the sharp and deadly short story "An Outpost of Progress," sort of dry run for *Heart of Darkness*. All the horror, none of the emoting.)

Marlow also tells the story of *Lord Jim*, about a young ship's officer who dreams of glory. When the crunch comes, though, Jim lacks cojones and leaves eight hundred passengers to die on a sinking ship. Except it doesn't sink. Eight hundred people can tell this story many, many times. Jim goes into hiding, moving from port to port with the shame nipping at his heels. He finally finds peace and respect among some Malay villagers, who accept him as their "lord." This book is psychologically acute, and stylistically brilliant, but takes a sharp left turn at the end into pulp adventure territory.

Another favorite is *Nostromo*, a complex political novel set in a fictional South American nation. Here the thing that exposes men's flaws is their lust for the silver that comes from the mines of Señor Gould. The book takes us through revolutions, doomed love, and the usual macho escapades—this time mostly on dry land—then takes a left turn at the end into pulp romance territory.

In the first half of the twentieth century, discussion of Conrad's work focused on style, symbolism, and narrative technique. More recently, attention has turned to his treatment of race, particularly since 1975, when Chinua Achebe gave a speech denouncing *Heart of Darkness*. Its Africans were symbols, not people; their gruesome deaths mere scene-setting for the story of white men. Conrad's basic criticism of colonial genocide is that it corrupts white morals. It's like a German novel about the bad influence Auschwitz had on Rudolf Hess.

"Oh, get a life" is the reaction of Conrad's fans, who point out that Conrad was in the vanguard of then-progressive opinion on this. It seems unfair to single him out, when Kipling is standing right next to him. However, race issues are inescapable in discussing the last book I will mention, *The Nigger of the "Narcissus."* Go ahead, try and discuss it without thinking about the race issue. The title was a problem even back in 1897; it was published in America as *Children of the Sea*. The N-character, Jimmy Wait, is a sickly sailor who comes on board the *Narcisssus* and promptly takes to bed. The crew's reactions to him form the meat of the book, but Jimmy is also a fully realized character rather than a dusky backdrop. The book wouldn't have been significantly differently had it been *The Dago of the "Narcissus,"* except that it would probably be among Conrad's most read books today.

	Importance	Accessibility	Fun
Lord Jim	9	5	8
Heart of Darkness	9	4	7
Nostromo	7	6	8
The Nigger of the "Narcissus"	6	6	8

NIKOLAI GOGOL (1809–1852)

Gogol is the bard of the petty officialdom of the Russian Empire, with all its dusty squalor, bribe-taking, and moral dissolution. In Gogol's world, most men live lives of very noisy desperation. The occasional quiet type is a quiet insect who will be squashed, and no one will care, because he has no soul. Luckily, it's all played for laughs—though the non-Russian reader may sometimes find it hard to smile through the misery.

His short stories provide the easiest access, and "Diary of a Madman" is probably the easiest of all. Its hero is a shabby petty official who develops the uncanny ability to hear the conversations of dogs. Soon he is convinced he is the king of Spain, and he ends his adventures in an asylum. Also popular is "The Nose." This begins with a barber finding a nose in his morning roll. He is horrified to recognize it as that of one of his clients, Kovalev, and hurries to dispose of it. Across town, Kovalev wakes up and is horrified to discover his nose missing. The runaway nose takes on an independent life, and adding insult to injury, it is more successful than its owner.

Gogol's classic play, *The Government Inspector*, is almost disappointingly conventional by comparison. A man visiting a provincial town is mistaken for an inspector from the capital. A host of corrupt officials descend on him, currying favor, offering presents, trying to marry him to their daughters. For a brief period, he lives the life of Reilly, until, inevitably, the real government inspector shows up.

In Russian serfdom, peasants were actually the legal property of landowners. Serfs were called, in the aggregate, "souls." When a landowner said he had two hundred souls, he did not mean that he was possessed by legions of the dead, but that he had a big farm with lots of workers. So, while *Dead Souls* sounds like a particularly indigestible example of Russians trying to depress us, it is in fact comedy.

The hero Chichikov is a scammer buying up dead serfs who have not yet been officially registered as dead and struck off the rolls. When he has gathered enough, he will use them as collateral for an enormous loan, thereby becoming rich overnight. But of course, he is also (as Nabokov points out in his *Lectures on Russian Literature*) a petty agent of the devil, buying the (dead) souls of the landowners with whom he deals.

With this premise, Gogol takes us on a tour of the various types of petty Russian gentry. The specimens he presents are so well pinned and aptly taxonomized that their names have entered into the Russian language. Russians now say someone is a *Korobochka*, or moan about rampant *Nozdrevism*. They strike a non-Russian differently, inevitably, because they are types we lack, making the book a touch more phantasmagoric and a touch less touching for the unRussian.

This is one of the many books intended to mirror *The Divine Comedy*, although (typically for these enterprises) Gogol only published the hell part. He did write the purgatory section, in which Chichikov is reformed, but burned it in a fit of religious mania and literary criticism. This is admirable in comparison to all the weak-willed writers who asked other people to burn their works, as if it was just too much for them to stumble to the fireplace with a manuscript in their arms.

This religious mania progressed, leading Gogol to subject himself to an increasingly harsh mortification of the flesh. Eventually he stopped eating altogether and died. Or so it seemed. When his body was later exhumed, it was discovered lying facedown, suggesting that Gogol was buried alive. Still, given the way he spent his declining years, being buried alive probably only scored a 5 on Gogol's scale of bad days.

	Importance	Accessibility	Fun
Stories	8	6	8
The Government Inspector	6	7	7
Dead Souls	8	4	9

WESTERNIZERS AND SLAVOPHILES

In Russian cultural history, Westernizers (*zapadniks*) were those who saw Russians simply as underachieving Germans. For generations, the Russian gentry had spoken French at home and considered their own country to be a backwater. It was common for a well-off Russian to spend most of his or her life in Western Europe, returning to Russia only occasionally, in order to look down on people. Russia's absolute monarchy was medieval; its serfdom barbaric; its people louse-ridden and illiterate; there were only two seasons, winter and mud. While the mud wasn't strictly speaking the government's fault, the fact that most roads were made of it was. Even hotel rooms in Moscow often had dirt floors.

Slavophiles, on the other hand, believed in the superiority of Russian ways and the Russian soul over any godless Western society. They were typically devout Russian Orthodox Christians, who believed that Russian peasants were closer to God than any other people in the world. To an outsider, the idea that Slavs are God's Chosen People has to be encountered a few times before you realize it's meant seriously. However, some of the greatest writers of the time subscribed to this, including Gogol, Dostoevsky, and Tolstoy. (Gogol was not technically Russian, but Ukrainian, a fact which matters to Ukrainians. For non-Ukrainians: Ukrainians are the same as Russians, except that they hate Russians.)

In prerevolutionary days, both Westernizers and Slavophiles tended to be communists, though Gogol, unusually for a person smart enough to tie his shoes, was a fan of serfdom and absolute monarchy. Dostoevsky also came around to believing in the tsar, after not believing in the tsar got him four years in Siberia.

LEO TOLSTOY (1828–1910)

Although *Anna Karenina* is everyone's favorite, Tolstoy's great, and also huge, novel was *War and Peace*. It established, and still maintains, his reputation as a thinker. It's not just because the public has an exaggerated respect for long books (they do) or that books about war are disproportionately admired (they are). This book evokes a million moments of lived experience, and incorporates them all within a unified philosophy. There are hundreds of characters, of every age, sex, and personality type, all embroiled in the Napoleonic wars (of Tolstoy's grandparents' generation) with such transparent realism that afterward, we feel a personal nostalgia for those wars. As Isaac Babel said after reading it, "If the world could write by itself, it would write like Tolstoy."

Tolstoy is doing all this to show we are all pawns in the hands of God. Everything is predestined. We do not—repeat, DO NOT—have free will. Napoleon only wanted to invade Russia because God wanted him to; Natasha falls for Anatole because God wanted her to; and you are only reading this book because God wanted you to. Someday, Tolstoy says, we may be able to understand God's will as reflected in history. In the meantime, the main thing is to remember that Napoleon was not a great general. Napoleon was a pawn like everyone else, in fact more so. Also, a dirty Frenchman.

Tolstoy could have demonstrated this theory just as well without dragging Napoleon into it, and many readers will wish he had. In *War and Peace*, the war parts are notoriously less interesting than the peace parts. Don't get us wrong, the battle scenes are often terrific. But Tolstoy stops the action again and again to lecture us about our misconception that Napoleon had free will.

A crafty publisher could do a service to lazy readers everywhere by coming out with *Peace*. An even more appealing redaction would result in *Godless Peace*, excising the many, many religious experiences, prayers, and speeches about Christ's love. This book would then consist entirely of romance, domestic disputes, and hunting scenes. In short, it would be *Anna Karenina*.

Anna Karenina is one of the most readable classics. It was even an Oprah book choice (causing widespread eye-rolling when Oprah's name was larger on the new edition than Tolstoy's). A page-turner about adultery among Russian aristocrats, *Anna Karenina* is full of dances, hunts, love scenes, and agrarian reform. (Yes, but the agrarian reform parts are much shorter than the war parts in *War and Peace*.)

It begins with the famous sentence: "All happy families are alike: every unhappy family is unhappy in its own way." He has 99 percent of readers hooked right there. It's like one of those lifestyle articles in the *Times*: STANFORD COUPLES STUDY: "ALL HAPPY FAMILIES ARE ALIKE." Oh my God, how? I must know how immediately!

Like most happiness studies, Tolstoy's advice amounts to telling you to like really boring things you will never like. Since you can't, Tolstoy adds, you only have yourself to blame if you end up under a train. However, we have a lot of novel before Tolstoy throws us sinners under the train. The novel is mostly about the unhappy, and therefore includes many, many things we do like, all of them marvelously evoked. It's acknowledged as Tolstoy's perfect work, and there is no shame in reading this while putting off reading *War and Peace* until an improbably long vacation that never comes.

In both his great novels, Tolstoy jerry-rigs an ending to force us into the conclusion that the only worthwhile life is that of a family man who works alongside his own peasants. You might object that you do not have any peasants to work alongside. Tolstoy had an answer to this. Even more ideal than the life of the peasant-owner was the life of the peasants themselves. These simple laborers were the closest to God. In an ideal society, everyone would be one. Tolstoy himself, of course, wasn't. He worked alongside them, but quit whenever he felt like staying at home to write a thousand-page novel. Furthermore, his nights were always spent in the comfort of his mansion, where he was waited on by house peasants, whom he also showed no sign of joining. One of these peasants was actually his illegitimate son, whom he employed as a coachman instead of adopting, or freeing, or anything.

This practice-preaching gap finally got to him. At the age of eighty-two, he set out to become a simple pilgrim, leaving his mansion, his peasants, and his family behind. He did bring along a porter carrying trunks, however, and a private physician. With this little entourage, instead of tramping the roads in the eternal fashion of Russian pilgrims, he took the train. It was like The Leo Tolstoy Hypocrisy Tour.

This perfect comedy setup unfortunately ended in tragedy. Tolstoy fell ill at a railway station and spent his last few days in a makeshift bed in the station waiting room, with a mob of unruly disciples and reporters behind the door.

	Importance	Accessibility	Fun
Anna Karenina	10	10	10
War and Peace	10	7	8

FYODOR DOSTOEVSKY (1821–1881)

Dostoevsky was the first to fully realize the rich subtexts of the Gothic novel as masochism. Usually, in the Gothic novel, a mysterious evil gradually engulfs a seemingly blameless person or family. Of course, this evil is latent in all of us, and the monster/curse that embodies it is a metaphor for how we will all inevitably be punished for being human. When you disguise the evil as a shambling monster or a malevolent castle, it's less depressing. Dostoyevsky went in the other direction.

He burst onto the Russian literary scene with *Poor Folk*, a straightforward realist novel about the squalid lives of the intelligentsia in St. Petersburg. While it doesn't stint on grimness, the novel has a relatively happy ending, as most of the poor folk become folk who are less poor. It was embraced by the crowned heads of the Russian literocracy, notably the reigning critic Belinsky, a socialist who thought Dostoevsky was the great white hope of agitprop. Dostoevsky was invited to parties, feted, etc., but he was not a charmer. Vain, irascible, and neurotic, he alienated everyone with his posturing and tantrums.

He put the last nail in his social coffin by making his next book, *The Double*, a morbid Gothic novel instead of the realist work his fans expected. In *The Double*, a government clerk gradually goes insane, convinced that a doppelgänger is usurping his place and using this position to ruin his life. It's unclear throughout whether there really is a doppelgänger; or if the clerk is ruining his own life. Anyway, there isn't any trenchant social commentary, so Belinsky and his crew were totally disgusted.

Still, things could have been much worse. We know this because things then got much worse. Dostoevsky had become involved with a group of revolutionaries. It was really more like a meet-up than a cadre, but they got as far as buying a printing press and producing a single revolutionary pamphlet. The Russians to this day have not managed to put anyone in charge who sees the funny side of this situation.

Here's an example of what a Russian leader does find funny. Having arrested everyone connected with this ineffectual band, the tsar cooked up a great prank. They were assembled in front a firing squad, with a cart nearby apparently piled high with their coffins. They were blindfolded and the countdown began. At the last minute, a horseman came galloping in with a pardon from the tsar. Heads of state just don't have that zany sense of humor anymore.

The revolutionaries were then packed off to Siberian prisons, and Dostoevsky spent four years in freezing, pestilent barracks with two hundred criminals, many of them murderers. The conditions were harsh enough to kill some of his fellow revolutionaries. Dostoevsky's sentence required him to enlist as a common soldier on his release. In all, it would be almost ten years before he wrote another book. This sentence was particularly hard on Dostoevsky, since murderers and soldiers found him just as unlikeable as the Petersburg literati had. Those years are at the heart of his mature writings, however, which draw on the criminal characters he met, the revolutionary fervor, and his own grappling with issues of guilt and atonement.

This nightmare is described in realist terms in his account of his prison years, *The House of the Dead*. For people who like being morbidly depressed, it's interesting to compare this with accounts of the later Soviet prison camps. Everyone else should skip it and pick Dostoevsky up again when he starts writing his masterpieces, from the relative comfort of civilian poverty.

Those masterpieces:

Notes from Underground

This is generally considered the great existentialist novel. Nietzsche himself said it "cried truth from the blood." It begins with a long diatribe on human nature, essentially explaining why we will never be happy or good. Unfortunately for those of us who still held out some hope for our children, "cries truth from the blood" pretty much nails it.

The book then goes on to detail some of the Underground Man's adventures in the real world, in which he behaves like a craven scumbag, driven by a host of neurotic impulses which readers immediately identify with. Mysteriously, this identification is quite heartening: at last, someone is willing to carry the torch for us as we really are, in our scumbag hearts. What is eventually somewhat depressing is the fact that Dostoevsky's hero has no friends, no love, no family—his life is completely empty. While stating that the Underground Man represents all contemporary people who think, Dostoevsky has failed to show him as he usually exists, in the midst of a pack of other underground men, women, and children. However, he will remedy that omission in his later books.

Crime and Punishment

The hero Raskolnikov is a penniless intellectual who convinces himself to murder and rob a despicable old lady. There is no reason this person should live. No matter how he looks at it, it's obvious he ought to kill and rob this horrible person. It's actually, if he thinks about it, cowardly not to kill this person. Also, he is broke.

He screws up his plan, getting nothing of value and killing a bystander as well as the evil crone. Then he is tormented by guilt. He gives all his money away and goes around acting as guilty as he can. The people around him, though, have their own existential angst to fry. In the seething mass of guilt and degradation that is a Dostoevsky novel, Raskolnikov doesn't really stand out.

In fact, everyone is so messed up that some other random person confesses to the murder, trying to steal Raskolnikov's punishment! Jeez. Who does a guy have to screw to get sentenced to hard labor in this joint? At last, however, Raskolnikov finds his way through a maze of challenging subplots to arrive at the promised land: Siberia.

The Idiot

The idiot of the title, Prince Myshkin, is considered idiotic first because of his epilepsy (from which Dostoevsky himself suffered) and second because of his Christ-like goodness. This is a subtle version of a story Dostoevsky loved: what would happen to Jesus if he returned? In this telling, some people recognize Myshkin's saintliness but still can't help rejecting him because people hate themselves more than they love anything else. The Magdalen figure, for instance, refuses to be saved by him, running off with a scumbag because that's all she deserves.

The hysteria of the characters here is a little overplayed, even campy. If you give one of these people a hill of money, they immediately throw it in the fire. A woman will only sleep with a man when she is certain she loathes him. If two characters meet, they will never ever talk about restaurants or current events. Instead, they threaten suicide, confess their darkest secrets, then one of them tries to stab the other, after which they exchange crosses and swear eternal friendship. It's like a game where the author hands the characters cards at random with different emotions written on them, which the character then has to avow, regardless of anything that's happened before.

The Possessed

This is Dostoevsky's scathing treatment of an anarchist cell. The Russian title is *Biesy*—literally, Demons, which gives you an idea how the revolutionaries are portrayed.

Again, the characters speechify, strike doomed poses, and attack one another. However, they are actually plotting political crimes, for which they can all be hanged, so this is quite reasonable. Furthermore, it's played for laughs. Many of the scenes are extremely funny, particularly in the subplot about the local patroness of the arts and her self-important parasite, Stepan Trofimovich.

Despite its subject, this novel isn't about politics per se, but about power struggles between individuals. These struggles take (surprise!) a perverse and bloody turn, and no one gets around to doing anything political. Instead they slap one another, shriek, "I only say I love you because I despise you!" and announce that, by committing suicide, they will become as God.

Because the plot works, this is all ten times more interesting and believable than it was in *The Idiot*. There is also no saintly character gumming up the works and stumbling around in confusion because he was told this gig was for a Tolstoy novel.

The Brothers Karamazov

The dissolute and clownish Fyodor Karamazov has three sons: the sensualist Dmitri, the intellectual Ivan, and the devout Alexei. He also has a servant, Smerdyakov, who is rumored to be his illegitimate son. Finally, he has a woman, the man-trap Grushenka, for whose somewhat soiled affections his son Dmitri is his rival.

One of the sons will kill him by the end of the book. A different son will be punished for the crime. In the meantime, the characters grovel in front of monks, brag about how base they are, and throw away money.

This book is famous for Ivan's Grand Inquisitor speech, another version of the Unwelcome Jesus story. Here, it's literally Christ coming back, in a poem Ivan once tried to write. Christ is instantly imprisoned by the Church, and the Grand Inquisitor figure delivers a long speech to Him about how the Church now deals exclusively with Satan, because Christ has no idea of mankind's real needs. People need bread, rules, and miracles, not free will. Giving them free will just ends with most of them damned to hell, and makes them miserable while they are still alive. Happily, the Church has done away with all that. At the end, Christ silently, lovingly kisses the Grand Inquisitor instead of answering. Christ doesn't want to encourage him to get started on Napoleon.

	Importance	Accessibility	Fun
Notes from Underground	10	7	8
Crime and Punishment	10	5	7
The Idiot	6	4	5
The Possessed	6	5	8
The Brothers Karamazov	9	5	8

Realist Drama

This continues the depressing tradition of unwelcome realism, while inaugurating a new tradition of depressing Scandinavians. The great grandfather of depressing Scandinavians was the Norwegian Henrik Ibsen (1828–1906).

Ibsen's plays nowadays seem like the most conventional of dramas. The early political plays, like *A Doll's House* and *The Enemy of the People*, often even have happy endings. The plot proceeds through a series of conflicts and revelations, all centering around a burning issue of the day. The characters are distinct and nuanced, and their relationships are changed forever by this controversial issue. It is the prototype, in short, of the average Oscar movie.

When Ibsen began to write his plays, however, the typical drama was still written in verse. Romanticism was the mode, historical settings were the rule, and the plots of the plays had not changed much since the time of Shakespeare.

In the work of Ibsen and his cohort, settings were contemporary. Actors spoke lines that were just like the real speech of ordinary people. Everything on stage mirrored the lives of members of the audience. While the plays often ended with a suicide, it took place offstage, and the characters' reaction to it was muted. There was no declaiming about the pitiless gods over a heap of corpses. Instead, there was someone saying, "Oh, dear, it seems Peter wasn't joking about that gun. Who's going to tell his mother?" CURTAIN.

In later life, Ibsen turned to darker, more psychological works like *The Wild Duck* and *Hedda Gabler*. The latter has become a perennial favorite for its charismatic heroine, bored into sadism by her feminine role. Both plays end with the woman killing herself, which represents the meeting between feminism and realism in the late nineteenth century.

While Ibsen was inventing the realist drama, August Strindberg (1849–1912) took it one step further and opened the door to experimental theater. He is most famous for his pressure-cooker drama *Miss Julie*, in which an aristocratic girl sullies herself with a servant. The power shifts back and forth between the two of them, and wherever it is, it is always abused. *Miss Julie* still takes place in the real world, although it is a drunken, hysterical corner of it. In *The Ghost Sonata*, however, Strindberg enters Ionesco territory. Ghosts interact with the living dead; a woman turns into a human parrot; honest statements literally kill the people unlucky enough to hear them. Finally, *A Dream Play* is literally that. The hero morphs, proliferates, and postures around "Indra's daughter," a central female Christ figure. Strindberg wrote it after a psychotic episode, and it has the uncensored earnestness of mental illness. This may sound forbidding, even embarrassing. And it is, but that's what makes it worth the price of the ticket.

In Russia, Anton Chekhov (1860–1904) was writing his own Ibsenite plays. The characters are unlike any others in Russian literature; hostages not to masochism, sin, or politics but to the sheer banality of life. In a subpar production, therefore, they are just banal, and richly deserve the boos that greeted the opening night of *The Seagull*. When they come to life, they create the same sad conundrum posed by Chekhov's stories (see below): man as a cockroach with an immortal soul. Chekhov found his great interpreter in the legendary director Stanislavsky, whose Moscow Art Theater redeemed *The Seagull* and went on to successfully produce *Uncle Vanya*, *The Three Sisters*, and *The Cherry Orchard*. Note: Chekhov mysteriously called *The Seagull* and *The Cherry Orchard* "comedies." This has left generations of baffled theatergoers straining to find laughs in these gloomy plays.

	Importance	Accessibility	Fun
IBSEN			
A Doll's House	8	9	6
An Enemy of the People	5	9	7
Hedda Gabler	8	8	6
The Wild Duck	7	8	6
STRINDBERG			
Miss Julie	8	6	8
The Ghost Sonata	5	5	4
A Dream Play	5	4	7
CHEKHOV			
The Seagull	8	6	6
Three Sisters	8	7	5
The Cherry Orchard	8	6	5
Uncle Vanya	7	6	6

MORE ANTON CHEKHOV

There are two Chekhovs. There's the one known to theater-lovers and thespians, the kook who believed *The Cherry Orchard* was a comedy. Then there's the Chekhov who is a god to short story writers.

The soul of every Chekhov story is the horror of life's banality and mankind's indifference to suffering. Each story offers a brief haven of love and meaning . . . and then tramples on it. The quintessential Chekhovian stories either show a fresh, idealistic person being swallowed and digested by pitiless banality—"Ionich," "Anna on the Neck," "Big Volodya and Little Volodya"—or show the world from the point of view of a person already in thrall to banality—"The Grasshopper," "Rothschild's Fiddle," "In a Country House."

Here's one example: "Ward Number Six," one of the most relentlessly humane stories ever written. It's about a provincial doctor whose duties include overseeing the local insane asylum, indistinguishable from a badly run prison. The few inmates are beaten and mistreated, and Chekhov describes them carefully so that we know just what this means to each individual. The doctor becomes fascinated by one patient, who despite being mentally ill is brilliant, caustic, and more interesting than any of his comfortable provincial friends. The patient derides the doctor for his callous collaboration with the system's brutality. Still the doctor keeps coming back.

His long conversations with this patient soon attract attention. Rivals for his position spread rumors that the doctor's own sanity is compromised. Eventually he is thrown into the asylum himself—beaten, robbed, stripped of his human dignity—and Chekhov carefully describes the first day of his imprisonment so that we fully understand that thousands of days like this will now constitute his life. Furthermore, he deserves this hell, because his callous collaboration with the system's brutality was real, and unforgiveable. It is also our own.

No, there's nothing funny about it. Really, absolutely nothing. Go ahead and turn the page.

	Importance	Accessibility	Fun
Short Stories	8	10	8

CHAPTER 13

The Messy Twentieth: Finally Over

We are now going to dip our toe in the twentieth century, and then retreat, shivering, to the safety of our beach hut. We will only deal with authors who have been properly canonized; those works that have begun to ossify in a suitably grand pose. A comprehensive look at twentieth-century literature would expand beyond the scope of this book. Therefore, we will concentrate on the essentials, The Big Ten, or The Big Twelve, or The Big Number Established by a Person Who Counted the Authors in This Chapter.

These same number-obsessed people may notice that we include here some writers who are chronologically part of the nineteenth century. This is because they are twentieth-century writers in spirit, who arrived early and had to wait a round, making conversation until James Joyce showed up. But what makes an author twentieth-century, if it's not just a number?

First, the twentieth century is an age of –isms. No self-respecting writer could pick up a pen without an –ism to guide it in its flight. Modernism, symbolism, imagism all flourished and floundered. Even where the author didn't cite a word that ended in –ism, innovation was the rallying cry. The main innovation, though, was that authors spouted meta, which always explained why their books were better than any previous books, and why if you hated them, you must be stupid.

Also, it is here that literature gets deliberately confusing. Up until this point, most writers tried to be understood. When we find them difficult, it is usually due to their obsolete language and topical references, or because they're boring (a form of difficulty that every generation invents anew). But, as the twentieth century begins, people start intentionally writing books you need a computer chip in your brain to understand, then patting themselves on the back when no one gets it.

There are three main types of difficulty here.

First, there are works (especially poems) that make their own kind of sense—the kind laypeople call "nonsense." The prose poems of Rimbaud and Mallarmé take place in a world that is not quite ours. As you familiarize yourself with it, its logic begins to become clear. It is simply logic you didn't have in Kansas, because there you didn't need to eat your husband and turn into a rooster. This kind of difficulty varies, on a continuum from Kafka (elementary) through Apollinaire (intermediate) to the Russian futurist Khlebnikov (brains worn on the outside of the head, squawking gibberish, cuckoo! cuckoo!). These works create a metaphorical language for feelings and intuitions, then use that language to try to create new feelings and intuitions that no one has had before. They also attack the chains of reason that keep us in the bondage of knowing what's happening. Finally, some of these writers had been smoking hashish for five days straight without getting any sleep.

Secondly, there are works, like those of Marcel Proust and Henry James, that use such labyrinthine sentences to express such subtle ideas, that they require an extraordinary feat of concentration to follow—although the story is just about an unhappy love affair, taking place in the garden variety real world. The style here aims to convey the rich complexity of experience, as experienced by a person with a brain the size of a watermelon.

Finally, there is a heartless corps of writers who purposely leave out information that is necessary to understand their books. Reading these authors is like listening in on one half of a telephone conversation with constant lapses into church Latin, after which the person laughs as if they just heard the funniest joke in the world. Ezra Pound is the worst offender here, followed closely by James Joyce.

These writers assume that you will not read, but rather study them. Their books are only comprehensible with the aid of copious notes. Joyce famously said, "The demand that I make of my reader is that he should devote his whole life to reading my works." Surprisingly, Joyce's demand has been met by many readers. In our capitalist system, we even pay people called professors to do this, because . . . well, it's something to do with the invisible hand. Market forces want James Joyce read properly because . . . Go ask an economist.

The bad news is that these difficult writers are still worth reading. However, I will try in the following pages to chip away at some of the difficulty, without writing the sort of literary analysis for which incomprehensible authors were merely blazing a path.

CHARLES BAUDELAIRE (1821–1867)

Charles Baudelaire was a key influence on the French symbolists, who in turn influenced everything else. (That's right, everything, from William Faulkner to punk to advertising. Even Hallowe'en costumes are a little different because of the symbolists.)

Baudelaire invented for himself the cult of the "dandy," and "*dandysme*"—a devotion to foppish artificiality from which the French are only now beginning to recover. The dandy was a man who had evolved beyond the natural, which was anathema. Dandies had existed in England for a long time—hence the English term—but they were just men in flamboyant clothes. No one there had thought of making it an existential principle.

As suits this philosophy, Baudelaire's poetry fabricates more than it describes. Victor Hugo, one of the few people who recognized him in his lifetime, wrote that Baudelaire gave readers *un frisson nouveau*—"a new shiver." While that shiver is now more than a hundred years old, the poetry's grandiose negativity still has an uncanny power.

Baudelaire was not a happy bunny. He had such a miserable life that learning its details is probably a mistake. In overview: He was poor, his poetry was overlooked until it was suppressed, he hated people and they hated him, women demanded pay to sleep with him. His life was most effective as a breeding ground for syphilis; in his later years, even his opinions have a syphilitic odor. He describes his great love, a black actress/prostitute called Jeanne, in the language of sickness: his love for her is like the craving of "worms for carrion." All his feasts are on rotten fruits, all his roses shriveled. No one could make Bohemianism sound quite so gross.

His great work is the poem cycle *Fleurs du Mal, Flowers of Evil.* In the world of these poems, the poet is an accused pariah, straying among beauties, decayed flesh, the world's hatred, and private exaltation. Baudelaire loves luxury words: he is always happy when he is listing costly balms and perfumes: spikenard, myrrh, frankincense, with a little gangrene thrown in for flavor. Angels and grave-worms are as common here as actual people. Horror, rapture, and despair are the only possible feelings. Baudelaire did not know what it was to calm down.

They say you can tell an incurable disease by the fact that it has hundreds of treatments. Likewise, *Fleurs du Mal* exists in countless English translations, none of which quite capture the original. Baudelaire wrote in the peculiarly French verse form of rhyming alexandrines—lines with six stresses, which notoriously only sound good in French. In this form, his nasty flowers are subtle and incantatory; they seem to float in the air, haunting and hinting and flaming and fading. If you have any French at all, read these in a dual-language edition. If you have no French, to some extent, the beauty of these poems will remain a rumor. Often Baudelaire translations come across like a magician chanting a spell while wearing a wizard hat made of silver paper and a purple polyester robe with felt moons glued to it.

It's also worth looking at Baudelaire's *Journaux Intimes*, which are full of sour aphorisms; often faintly Nietzschean, always dandyish. "The belief in progress is a doctrine of the lazy, a doctrine for Belgians." "The most prostituted being is God, because he is the most loved by every individual, because he is the common, inexhaustible reservoir of love."

Here we get to know the dandy, Baudelaire's superman of artificiality. And superwoman?—you may ask. No. Baudelaire was a bitter misogynist—with the handy excuse of a man who is dying slowly and painfully from cooties. He writes in *Journaux Intimes*: "I have always been amazed that women are allowed to enter churches. What conversation could they have with God?"

	Importance	Accessibility	Fun
Fleurs du Mal	10	4	7
Journaux Intimes	2	9	8

The Damned Poets

Paul Verlaine coined the term *les poetes maudits*, "the damned poets," for the French symbolist writers, outcasts who destroyed themselves with syphilis and absinthe while writing poems with Poe-inspired (and drug-induced) imagery of grave-worms, flesh both alluring and rotting, and hellfire. A reader could be forgiven, though, for thinking it is because their damned writing makes no damned sense.

This is the point in history where poets first wrong-foot you by not trying to make sense. Savants will be savvy to it and ignoramuses can ignore it. If the poem made sense to you, in fact, you're not getting it. You should get some cool person to explain it to you, so the poetry stops making sense to you too.

This has created a certain mystique around these poems, which can be used as a snob's shibboleth. However, this technique is also used in the lyrics of a host of important contemporary musicians, like Bob Dylan and Beck, and also by Oasis in "Wonderwall." In short, the only thing the average bloke needs to love Rimbaud is a catchy guitar part.

ARTHUR RIMBAUD (1854–1891)

Rimbaud has become the best-known symbolist outside France because of his cool biography. The bulk of his work was written before he was nineteen; he gave up writing forever at twenty. As a poetry-writing teen, he was a vagabond, tramping from town to town, deliberately filthy, long-haired, and grotesquely rude. As a houseguest with the older poet Paul Verlaine, he mutilated an heirloom crucifix, shocked the neighbors by sunbathing in the nude, and boasted about his lice. When Verlaine took him to a poetry reading, Rimabud punctuated every line with "*Merde!*" When someone tried to eject him from the reading, he stabbed the man. Meanwhile, he sought poetic illumination in a systematic derangement of the senses, achieved through various sins, including absinthe, hashish, and sex with Paul Verlaine.

Verlaine responded as legions of readers have done ever since: by falling head over heels in love. Under the rotten influence of his boy lover, and absinthe, Verlaine became abusive to his wife and child. The two men also quarreled, and Verlaine finally shot Rimbaud in the wrist and went to prison for it. Verlaine never really recovered, descending into drunken dereliction. Rimbaud tramped around for another year or two, with repeated pauses for R & R at his mother's house, then abandoned poetry, Bohemianism, and homosexuality to become a businessman in Africa.

It's worth reading Rimbaud's earlier, more traditional work—rhymed verses which include many filthy pasquinades—and keeping him company as he enters and experiences his derangement. Even his earliest poems are brilliant and surprising. As he turns into the hairy walking insult of the Verlaine years, he creates some of the most painful beauty in world literature. Poems like "The Stolen Heart" and "The Drunken Boat" are rare examples of French poems that translate into English with hardly a scratch.

He broke out of sense entirely with the prose poetry of his later period. In the prophetic, railing *A Season in Hell*, Verlaine becomes the Infernal Bridegroom, and Rimbaud is the Foolish Virgin deceived by false promises. This has stunning passages, although the incoherence gets boggy; it's very hard to see by the light of Rimbaud's lightning bolts and hellfire.

Happily, in his later prose poems, collected in *Illuminations*, he transcends all his and our limitations. Here Rimbaud seems to be trying to say something too good to be contained in words. The words therefore sometimes fray; the diction sometimes collapses into prosaic, almost bathetic, awkwardness. But this seems like a failure of the language rather than of the poet. What Rimbaud communicates here is the hope of a revelation greater than any merely possible experience, and which can paradoxically only be reached by a snot-nosed kid sneaking out the window from one debauch to another.

When *Illuminations* was published to great acclaim, the publisher listed it as by "the late Arthur Rimbaud." He was not dead, although he was dead to poetry. When a friend asked if he was still thinking about literature, he shook his head with "a half-amused, half-irritated smile, as if I had asked him: 'Do you still play with a hoop?' and simply answered: 'I do not mind about it anymore.'" However, his various merchant ventures—included some gun-running in Ethiopia—were all failures. He also, very disappointingly, constantly complained that Africa was boring, a backwater in which even Abyssinian concubines apparently were not enough. He did, however, manage to become good friends with Haile Selassie's father, which is not nothing. He died at thirty-seven from cancer, without having written another line of poetry.

	Importance	Accessibility	Fun
Early poems	6	5	6
A Season in Hell	7	4	6
Illuminations	7	4	7

RAMBO V: A SEASON IN HELL

Note: Rimbaud is pronounced "Ram-BO"—exactly like a French person talking about the Sylvester Stallone character. Please, please, Mr. Stallone, make a movie that brings these two together, preferably a buddy movie involving a time machine and an African war.

Other Damned Poets

COMTE DE LAUTREAMONT (1846–1870)

The Comte was actually a Uruguayan guy named Isidore Ducasse who wasn't a count at all, just a daring fabricator of pen names. His great work is the *Chants de Maldoror*, prose poetry about a figure of perfect evil set loose in a gory/voluptuous evilscape. He intended to go on to sing of the good, but somehow never got there. Just as well, since undoubtedly no one would have read that part. Lautreamont inaugurated, among other things, the open use of plagiarism (nowadays called "appropriation"), twisting the words of many great French authors to suit his evilscape. Often funny, often scary, he was a major influence on the surrealists.

GERARD NERVAL (1808–1855)

A precursor who wrote poetry similar to the symbolists' because he was incurably insane. Had a pet lobster named Thibault whom he took for walks. (Wait, how well can lobsters walk? Perhaps he was dragging this lobster?)

TRISTAN CORBIÈRE (1845–1875)

Incantatory, lovely—and crucially, easily compared to fellow incantatories like Rimbaud or Mallarmé.

PAUL VERLAINE (1844–1896)

After his cataclysmic affair with Rimbaud, it's fair to say Verlaine was a broken man. In this period, he wrote many of his poems in the hospital, where he would land after his binges. As an obituary in the *Yale Literary Magazine* put it, he "died in a garret, penniless, steeped in absinthe, and yet famous." The glass in which absinthe is served is sometimes called a *verre* Verlaine. His poetry is more formal, old-fashioned, sweet, than his amant Rimbaud's; awww-inspiring rather than awe-inspiring.

JULES LAFORGUE (1860–1887)

Known for his puns and portmanteau words. Due to this wordplay, English translations lack a certain *je ne sais quoi*, or a *vous ne savez quoi* if you don't read French. His poetry (like Verlaine's) may seem a little overpopulated with Pierrots to suit contemporary taste. He was a major influence on T. S. Eliot, among others, although his hyper-romantic moons, swans, and hearts were left behind by his modernist admirers.

STEPHANE MALLARMÉ (1842–1898)

Best known for the poem "*L'apres-midi d'une faune*," which is itself best known for the Debussy piece based on it. This is another poet who used sound effects in his poetry as if he specifically didn't want them to be that great in English. In his "*Un coup de dés*" ("A throw of the dice") he also uses typographical elements, to produce a poem that can be read in different ways, much in the manner of an advertisement printed like: "BUY three WIDGETS, and get the fourth one free TODAY only."

ALEXANDER BLOK (1880–1921)

The main Russian symbolist poet, known primarily for his poem about the October revolution, "Twelve," in which the Bolsheviks are somehow being led by Jesus.

	Importance	Accessibility	Fun
Lautreamont	5	5	6
Nerval	4	4	7
Corbière	3	6	7
Verlaine	5	7	6
Laforgue	5	4	5
Mallarmé	5	3	6
Blok	3	5	5

(Note: All Fun ratings in this section are based on a reader who knows no French. For French speakers, give every French writer an extra two Fun points, and subtract one Fun point from Blok, just to put him in his place.)

DADAISM, SURREALISM, FUTURISM: OR BASICALLY, JUST READ APOLLINAIRE

In literature, all of these movements are closely related to symbolism and very similar to one another. (In the visual arts, it's a different story.) There are some piddling differences. The Dadaists explicitly claimed that nonsense would liberate us from the prison of the past. The surrealists took Freud seriously. The futurists were Italians. All of these later movements dropped the rotting corpses and spikenard, and favored free verse. For the most part, they didn't produce important writing even when they produced wonderful writing. Andre Breton's *Surrealist Manifesto* and F. T. Marinetti's *Futurist Manifesto* are more commonly read than almost any surrealist and futurist poetry.

The exception to this rule is Guillaume Apollinaire (1880–1918). His poetry has the beauty of Baudelaire's without the adolescent posturing, carrion, and unguents. He is funny, open-hearted, ingeniously peculiar, calling the crucified Jesus "the first airplane" but then falling into religious raptures. Next thing, it's a bird that lives upside-down and makes its nest in air. A *Selected Poems* is probably the best way to go here, as his individual books are just too short. He also wrote anarchic, sex-obsessed prose, notably *The Poet Assassinated*. A friend of Gertrude Stein, he appears in various silly episodes of her *Autobiography of Alice B. Toklas* (see page 244).

WILLIAM BUTLER YEATS (1865–1939)

Yeats is a modernist that the average person can get behind. He expressed the normal feelings of a normal person in poetry which sounds pretty even to the least discerning ear. This accessibility was so welcome that Yeats got the Nobel Prize before he wrote any of the poems that are now anthologized. The Nobel Prize committee may also have been indulging in that political do-gooding for which they have since become notorious.

Yeats was immersed in the world of Irish nationalism from his early youth. He was one of the leading lights of the Irish Literary Revival and a founder member of the Abbey Theatre, conceived as a launching pad for Irish drama on Irish themes. His first full-length work was a treatment of an Irish epic, the Fenian saga, in verse. He could not have been more steeped in Irishness without actually being a leprechaun.

The other major influence on his intellectual life was his interest in esoteric religion. Yeats was a member of the Rosicrucian Order of the Golden Dawn, a celeb-filled cult which practiced conjuring of spirits, divination, and related humbuggery. Although his participation fell off, Yeats never really got over this nonsense. Even in his old age, he and his young wife were practicing automatic writing and talking seriously about spirits. Really, Yeats was always half-nightingale, half-dodo.

The great love of Yeats's life, and the name that always comes up in connection with him, is Maud Gonne. She was an Irish nationalist, feminist, and noted beauty. When they met, he was a rising literary star; but he apparently just didn't light her fire. After ten years of pursuing her, he finally got to sleep with her—once. Soon after, she was writing letters to him about the beneficial effects of celibacy on artists.

He proposed to her first in 1891, and then again in 1899, 1900, and 1901. In 1916, he proposed to her one final time, at the age of fifty-one (she was then fifty). After receiving a final refusal, he proposed to her twenty-one-year-old daughter, who also said no. So he married some other random twenty-something—and then cheated on her every chance he got. (This is what you get when you marry a guy who's on the rebound from his One Great Love and her daughter.)

In his fifties and sixties, with the Nobel Prize looking down from his mantelpiece, Yeats produced the poems everyone quotes. They are miracles of concision and lyricism, with a spooky overtone of Golden Dawnness which gives them staying power. This is the era of "what rough beast / its hour come round at last / slouches toward Bethlehem / to be born?" and "only God, my dear, / Could love you for yourself alone / And not your yellow hair" and "how can we tell the dancer from the dance?"

These poems often dwell unhappily on his advanced age. The young see him as a "comfortable kind of old scarecrow." Soldiers go to civil war cracking jokes "as if to die by gunfire were / The finest play under the sun," while old man Yeats is left at home, complaining about the weather. He protests "I too had pretty plumage once" (though Maud Gonne doesn't seem to have thought much of it). In his later years, Yeats dealt with the aging process in the time-honored fashion, by sleeping with young aspiring poetesses, and trying not to think about what his plumage looked like in the morning.

	Importance	Accessibility	Fun
Poems	10	4	7

HENRY JAMES (1843–1916)

H. G. Wells once said that a novel by James was "a magnificent but painful hippopotamus resolved at any cost upon picking up a pea, which has got to the corner of its den." This is a reference to the fact that, while James's writing is elaborate and grand, James's characters are typically hung up on some teeny-weeny scruple. This scruple paralyzes any life that was threatening to break out in their midst. The life they do have is the life of the mind; they spend the novel thinking rather than doing or even talking. Furthermore, these characters have thoughts no one ever had, and do not ever have the thoughts that everyone has. For instance, they never think "Nice body." They never have any thoughts of any kind about bodies, to which they are stone blind. They never worry whether someone likes them, or think about what they're going to eat. They have no neuroses, and therefore never think about how worthless, ugly, or fat they are; they never think about how brilliant or good-looking they are, either.

Instead, they like to think about what other people are thinking. They wonder about one another's surmises, while dreading one another's willingness to suppose. James's characters are so practiced at this that they often simply know what other people are thinking. When their telepathy fails them, they impotently wonder what other people knew, when, about what someone believed about the question in Verena's eyes.

The other Jamesian keynote is the convoluted sentence. These sentences are a sort of literary Great Wall: while other, similar, structures exist, none are quite so long with so little apparent reason. (In fact, some sentences in *The Golden Bowl* can be seen from space). Multiple feelings and perceptions are layered in each of them, in a syntax that seems to flow in every direction but forward. To give you an idea, here's one from *The Ambassadors*: "Nothing could have been odder than Strether's sense of himself as at that moment launched in something of which the sense would be quite disconnected from the sense of his past and which was literally beginning there and then." You will never catch Henry James writing "The dog barked." It will always be: "Had the dog not been, from the moment at which she entered the room in the perplexed flush of expectation in which she had been left by the hints of Mr. Westcott, barking . . ."

James's works are usually divided into three periods. The early period consists of readable, pacey romances like *The American* and *The Portrait of a Lady*. Here, the characters sometimes perform feats of Jamesian telepathy, but none of the sentences feels like a problem in epistemology. These novels have a recurring theme in which unworldly, pure-hearted Americans are led astray by corrupt, sophisticated Europeans. These Europeans are usually motivated by a lack of folding money. (All Americans in Henry James novels are heirs to great fortunes.) Even the louche Europeans, however, are not so depraved as to notice anyone's body.

The middle period includes James's *The Turn of the Screw*, in which a governess tries to save two children from evil ghosts (evil = noticed each other's bodies, when they had them). In books like *The Spoils of Poynton* and *What Maisie Knew*, James deepened his studies of consciousness, especially the consciousness of guilt. Sometimes the guilt is sexual; sometimes it is greed. Always it is something the reader would do without a second thought. However, the vicarious high-mindedness of James is very satisfying. The pleasure is even, weirdly, voyeuristic.

Because the guilty person is too corrupt, some innocent person is forced to fix the guilt for them. Sometimes Innocent just walks out on Guilty and moves in with Other Innocent. However, sometimes Innocent has to renounce Other Innocent and stay with Guilty forever in a loveless marriage. Otherwise, two rights might make a wrong, by having sex while rich.

In James's third period, his themes and conflicts remain the same, but he turns them into sprawling obstacle courses of obfuscation. *The Ambassadors, The Wings of the Dove, The Golden Bowl*—by the time you have finished any of these, you can feel every muscle in your brain. All of James's energy goes into fractal sentence structure. The plots are static, and the only changes are in what Innocent thinks about what Other Innocent knows about Guilty's guilt. When he can no longer prevent things from happening, James manfully tries to prevent the reader from discovering what they are. Meanwhile, the nonevents the Innocents endure change them subtly, from people who think in long sentences without getting any, to sadder-but-wiser people who think in long sentences without getting any. Sometimes, the shock of finding out that someone got some kills them. In the denouement, there is a question left unanswered, a niggling dangling plotline. Closure, to James, would be too much like getting sex.

UNTIL PROVEN GUILTY

No one knows whether James himself ever had sex. Whether he did or didn't, it was probably homosexual in orientation. If there was no sex, it may (or may not) have been because of an injury to his testicles, received in his duties as a volunteer fireman. If there was sex, he lied about it, describing himself once as "hopelessly celibate."

This celibate tag has stubbornly adhered to James, though history teaches us that most people sneak out for some sex, sometime, and even the most distressing injury does not stop most people from doing something to someone that would kill a James character stone dead.

	Importance	Accessibility	Fun
The American	4	7	8
The Europeans	4	7	8
The Portrait of a Lady	8	5	6
The Bostonians	7	5	6
The Spoils of Poynton	7	5	6
The Turn of the Screw	10	5	6
What Maisie Knew	6	3	6
The Wings of the Dove	10	2	8
The Ambassadors	10	2	8
The Golden Bowl	8	2	7

GERTRUDE STEIN (1874–1946)

Gertrude Stein once memorably reproved Hemingway by saying, "Remarks are not literature." However, her most popular book is enduring proof they could be. *The Autobiography of Alice B. Toklas* is a compendium of brilliant remarks and madcap antics from the brilliant Paris of the madcap twenties. Of course, it's no autobiography—at best, it's an autobiography that Stein put into her long-term partner Toklas's mouth. This Toklas only thinks about Stein and her famous friends; it's an exercise in making your own Boswell.

The beating heart of the book is Gertrude Stein's salon—an informal but historically crucial meeting of artists, writers, society beauties, and assorted greats at Stein's house in Paris every Saturday. Before becoming the essential meeting of minds of the Modernist Era, it was a home-away-from-home for the artists who exhibited at the Salon des Independants. At the time, these artists included Picasso (Stein's best friend), Matisse, Braque, and Juan Gris. Here they are shown screwing up their love lives, imitating circus routines, dropping casual bon mots—being twenty-something geniuses together. If this is the Lost Generation, can we be lost too, please? Please? Uncannily well written and drop-dead cool, the *Autobiography* is the greatest twentieth-century contribution to that disreputable but delightful genre, gossip.

Among the remarks with which Stein herself enriched us was: "There is no there there." (Oakland, California, in this case.) This alone is worth an encyclopedia entry; but fans also credit her with being the ultimate brains behind modernism, and behind the sparse style of much contemporary fiction. Her pronouncements were respected by figures as disparate as Apollinaire and Ernest Hemingway. Her works have resisted a full revival mainly because the best are very difficult, and we just don't have the stamina to deal with another James Joyce situation. It's easier to keep her exiled from the canon and turn back to the ongoing work of getting rid of Ezra Pound. However, even the most hostile scoffer at her experimentalism will admit that Stein had a magical affinity with language.

Let's start with stuff any fool can read. Her first published work was *Three Lives*, a set of short stories based on Flaubert's *Trois Contes*. Radical at the time, these now seem beautiful but relatively mainstream, perhaps due to the generous flood of Steinism that has entered that stream. The only clue to Stein's later degenerate narrative is the fact that they do not proceed in an orderly fashion from beginning to end, but loop back, repeating premises and phrases, to create litanies of concrete life. The most famous, "Melanctha," is about a black woman in Stein's fictional town of Bridgepoint. This was considered a sympathetic portrayal of African-American life at the time—by Richard Wright, among others—but now the language has a troubling ring. When Stein says one character is "a big black virile negro" or talks about the "earth-born, boundless joy of negroes," we feel a certain ick. Or take: "Rose Johnson was a real black, tall, well built, sullen, stupid, childlike—" okay, stop right there. Richard Wright can go soak his head. This is racist. And in fact, in 1938, Stein (who was Jewish) headed a campaign to award the Nobel Peace Prize to Adolf Hitler.

Let's pause and take a deep breath. You may feel reassured to learn that this is the last we will hear of Stein's political views, and be willing to accept her art on its own terms. You may also just want to skip to the next author, cursing Gertrude Stein and all her works. No one will blame you either way.

After *Three Lives*, Stein took a sharp turn in her writing and produced the thousand-page behemoth *The Making of Americans*. This is her first book in the extreme hermetic style for which she is famous, and continues being widely unread to this day. Here she out-experiments everyone around her, leapfrogging a hundred years with a single bound.

Giving you an idea of this work is giving understanding repetition. Always repeating is understanding, more and more repeating what is true of every one gives loving repeating in such a one's living. Now again to begin. Some have it as being to love the repeating that is always in every one coming out from them (as Stein might put it).

Some find this style to be like Chinese water torture. Stein says in the early pages of this book, "If they get deadened by the steady pounding of repeating they will not learn from each one." If you can endure the steady pounding of Stein's abstract sentences, glimmers of profundity grow behind them. There is philosophy here, and a genuine aesthetic intimately connected with it. There is also a music in the language, and its ingenious syntactical strategies subtly turn English into something else; it's like the language of a million people speaking at once, or the voice of Whitman's leaves of grass, or like the voices you begin to hear in your head after hours of Chinese water torture.

Most people will prefer to grapple with Stein in smaller chunks. Both her much-beloved book of poetry, *Tender Buttons*, and the collection *Geography and Plays* will be easier to enjoy. These have all the witty bliss of *The Autobiography of Alice B. Toklas*, but in the form of garbling deluxe. They also offer up little pungent koans to the reader. Here's a quick one:

WATER RAINING.

Water astonishing and difficult altogether makes a meadow and a stroke.

These can also give you the sense that Gertrude Stein invented all of contemporary poetry's most befuddling movements, saw them take root, and walked off laughing. However, even if you can't stand this kind of thing, there is something breathtaking about watching someone do anything for the first time, and so lightly and so well.

A ROSE BY THE SAME NAME

The line "A rose is a rose is a rose" has come to represent the repetitive frustrations of Stein's work. She recycled this line in several of her writings; in its first occurrence in the poem "Sacred Emily," it was "Rose is a rose is a rose is a rose," where the first Rose was a woman's name.

Stein commented on the ridicule it had attracted: "Now listen! I'm no fool. I know that in daily life we don't go around saying 'is a . . . is a . . . is a . . .' Yes, I'm no fool; but I think that in that line the rose is red for the first time in English poetry for a hundred years."

Hemingway, after his acrimonious falling-out with Stein, rendered this as:

"A bitch is a bitch is a bitch." Stein might have rebutted that "A copycat is a copycat is a copycat," since, as Hemingway himself semi-admitted before their falling-out, his whole literary style was lifted from Stein's *Three Lives*. (See page 269.)

	Importance	Accessibility	Fun
The Autobiography of Alice B. Toklas	6	8	10
Three Lives	10	8	8
The Making of Americans	4	−1	2
Tender Buttons	8	2	8
Geography and Plays	4	2	8

FRANZ KAFKA (1883–1924)

In his day job in an insurance office, Kafka acquired a precise, unassuming style, which made bizarre events seem as clear as the liability in the case of a missing guardrail on a chicken combuster. Thanks to this quietly declarative prose, his fiction is completely convincing, making surreal premises feel simple and inevitable. An ape writes *A Report to an Academy*, about his capture and gradual process of education into human ways; a scholar of the mice writes the history of the great mouse artist Josephine the Singer. Both have the air of someone sincerely, painstakingly trying to explain a problem that has been bothering him for some time.

The most famous story, "The Metamorphosis," begins with the famous sentence, "Gregor Samsa awoke one morning from uneasy dreams to find himself transformed in his bed into an enormous insect." The insect—which appears to be a cockroach, though Kafka is too sensitive of his hero's feelings to call it by name—is Everyman seen through the lens of Jewish guilt. Kafka kick-starts this preposterous trope, then leaves it isolated in a world of petty worries (I'm going to be late for work!) and tacky domestic objects. Samsa's family are not only grief-stricken, but thrown into practical difficulties. The servants leave; the lodgers give notice. Soon his sister is saying, "We must get rid of the idea that this is Gregor. If it were Gregor, he'd realise human beings can't live with such a creature, and would have left himself." Unfortunately for all of us, there's something painfully familiar in her attitude.

Kafka spent his life in the heart of a bourgeois Jewish family, under the thumb of a dictatorial father. As a direct result, the fuel of most of Kafka's fiction is guilt. This is most clearly expressed in his novel *The Trial*. Here Joseph K. wakes up in his boardinghouse one morning to find that he's been placed under arrest. An inspector has set up shop in the bedroom next to his; but instead of inspecting anything, he simply informs K. of his arrest, without offering to explain what crime he has committed. Nor is K. being apprehended; in fact, he is encouraged to go to work. The rest of the novel concerns K.'s fruitless effort to discover the nature of his crime and defend himself against the accusation. Of course, his life falls apart, and although he never gets his explanation, he does receive his punishment.

The Castle takes place in a similar landscape of futile, fatal officialdom. The hero (another K.) has come to a small town that is dominated by the castle, an inaccessible and quasi-mythical realm of bureaucracy. The villagers hold the business of the castle in awe, insisting its workings are flawless. However, K. is constantly witnessing malfeasance and blundering by its representatives. Pointlessly, hopelessly, K. attempts to gain access to the castle, and the official Klamm, throughout the novel.

The more cheerful, slapstick *Amerika* is about a young immigrant to the United States named Karl. Kafka apparently knew next to nothing about America and carelessly concocts a nation that suits his imaginative needs. His star invention is the Nature Theater of Oklahoma, a thinly veiled scam luring people into menial jobs in the West. Kafka intended Karl to eventually find his happy ending there, but Kafka died before it was finished, so we will never discover how Kafka would have handled joy.

While Kafka's works have glaringly obvious political overtones, he saw them primarily as religious parables. The officialdom is somehow that of the Jewish God, and our guilty verdict is built into the fabric of creation. Someone, somewhere is presumably finding salvation, but where we live, it is only a persistent rumor. When asked if he really believed there was no hope, Kafka replied, "Plenty of hope! An infinite amount of hope! But not for us."

Almost all of Kafka's works were published posthumously; his three novels were all unfinished to varying degrees. He is one of the many writers who asked to have his works burned, specifically directing his friend Max Brod to do so. Instead, Brod published them all. Really makes you wonder if we've lost a score of masterpieces because their authors had friends who believed in keeping a promise.

ENTOMOLOGY AND ETYMOLOGY

While the creature in "The Metamorphosis" is usually called an insect in English translations, the German word Kafka uses, *Ungeziefer*, simply means "vermin." Some people therefore suggest that Kafka did not want us to assume the creature is an insect, although it has many legs, likes to hang from the ceiling, has difficulty turning over when on its back, and has a carapace.

Likewise, our readers may assume that the term "Kafkaesque," usually applied to surreal excesses of bureaucracy, originates with the author's name. However, since there is no proof of any such connection, it is best to assume it's a remarkable coincidence.

	Importance	*Accessibility*	*Fun*
Stories	10	6	7
The Trial	10	6	7
The Castle	6	4	6
Amerika	5	5	7

T. S. ELIOT (1888–1965)

In Eliot's poetry, all the loveliest dreams of our civilization are lost—both in the sense that they are gone forever and, perversely, in the sense that the dreams are blindly stumbling around in the poems, bumping into things. His poems are full of quotes and echoes from the literature of at least three cultures, in at least five languages.

Eliot's absolute favorite thing is litter. While his women languish in rooms cluttered with art, jewels, perfumes, from which they are powerless to escape, his men wander unswept streets, feeling inadequate and small, with scraps of Dante and Shakespeare washing around in their brains. Here, the absence of beauty is more beautiful than beauty. When the narrator of "The Love Song of J. Alfred Prufrock" says: "I have heard the mermaids singing, each to each; I do not think that they will sing to me," he is more poignant than any crass Odysseus. Soon one feels only a wimp would die heroically; a great soul stares insignificance right in the eyes and ends with a whimper.

When published in 1922, Eliot's "The Waste Land" caused a sensation and helped create an audience for modernism. The poem was heavily edited by Ezra

Pound, who Eliot said had "done so much to turn 'The Waste Land' from a jumble of good and bad passages into a poem." There were apparently many bad passages, as Pound cut four hundred lines. It was also originally entitled "He Do the Police in Different Voices." While it's hard to imagine it being a big sensation under that title, it does describe the collage form of this poem quite well. Random voices succeed one another: two working-class women talking in a pub, a quote from *The Tempest*, a bit of Eliot's commentary, a few lines from a popular song, all stitched together. Sometimes a story line emerges, but Eliot will abandon it the next moment, along with the entire reality it belongs in. The poem ends in actual glossolalia, babbling:

> Quando fiam uti chelidon—O swallow swallow
> Le Prince d'Aquitaine à la tour abolie
> These fragments I have shored against my ruins
> Why then Ile fit you. Hieronymo's mad againe.
> Datta. Dayadhyam. Damyata.
> Shantih shantih shantih

The reader is supposed to make sense of all this herself, since the poet pointedly didn't. This is the dawn of an era when the poem/fiction stops being able to communicate on its own, and authors increasingly rely on criticism—either by themselves or helpful scholars—to supply a key to the work. The poem provides the ingredients, while someone else provides the recipe and the reader cooks the meal. Readers (who are often already too lazy to cook for themselves) have been unenthralled by authors' move to outsourcing their work. "Let me get this straight," they say, "You made this hard for me on purpose?" Avant-gardists simply smile insufferably and say, "No pain, no gain. And also, vellum ЖӘль bicycle."

Eliot's other famous poem—and the twentieth-century work which is perhaps most often quoted—is "The Love Song of J. Alfred Prufrock." Prufrock stands for the Everyman of the twentieth century, and this is not a love poem, but a poem about the futility of expecting love, or heroism, or meaning, in a world of Prufrocks. The best known quotes summarize the vie de Prufrock:

> Do I dare to eat a peach?
> I have measured out my life in coffee spoons
> No! I am not Prince Hamlet, nor was meant to be
> I grow old . . . I grow old . . . / I shall wear the bottoms of my
>   trousers rolled.

This poem is wonderful, and the most accessible work of Eliot's; even the most unskilled person can cook it in five minutes.

In midlife, Eliot converted from Unitarianism to Anglicanism. As he said, "I am an Anglo-Catholic in religion, a classicist in literature, and a royalist in politics." His politics we can dismiss, lumping them together with his love of whoopie cushions and exploding cigars, as the inevitable boneheaded part of an otherwise brilliant mind. His religion, however, became a crucial theme in his later poetry. "Ash Wednesday," for instance, is a Marian poem—one about the poet's feelings for the Virgin Mary. (This struck George Orwell as so ridiculous, he insisted Eliot was putting it on. Alas, no.) *Four Quartets*, which Eliot considered his masterpiece, is a series of religious poems that deal with issues of time, salvation, and modernity. Here, the abstract language can be off-putting. Lines like "Distracted from distraction by distraction" just don't have that oomph. Still, it has its moments, and it's a deep expression of Eliot's religious feeling, and . . . Okay, it's boring.

P.S. ABOUT AN S

T. S. Eliot has been called anti-Semitic for poems like "Burbank with a Baedeker; Bleistein with a Cigar" and lines like "The red-eyed scavengers are creeping / From Kentish Town and Golders Green" (traditionally Jewish parts of London).

In fact, he was anti-Semitic. But what seems more important to us today is that, as the poet Tom Raworth has pointed out, without the initial S in his name, it would spell "toilet" backwards.

	Importance	Accessibility	Fun
J. Alfred Prufrock, The Wasteland, The Hollow Men	10	6	9
Ash Wednesday, Four Quartets	7	4	5

WILLIAM CARLOS WILLIAMS (1883–1963)

While T. S. Eliot was probably the most successful poet of his time, Williams was far and away the most influential. The bulk of modern poetry has its source in this unassuming obstetrician who lived and died in New Jersey.

While he was a friend of Pound and Eliot, Williams disapproved of their allusive style and their quotes from Latin, French, Carthaginian, etc. As Marianne Moore put it, Williams wrote in "plain American which cats and dogs can read." An oft-repeated line in Williams's poetry is "No ideas but in things." This belief in the thingness of ideas, and the abstract aura of things, is exemplified by his much-anthologized poem:

> so much depends
>
> upon
>
> a red wheel
>
> barrow
>
> glazed with rain
>
> water
>
> beside the white
>
> chickens

This is a great example of ingredients literature. Instead of telling you anything, Williams poses the question: "So what is it that depends on a red wheelbarrow glazed with rain water beside the white chickens, exactly? How does it differ from the thing that depends on a red wheelbarrow glazed with rain water beside the brown chickens?" This specificity (no ideas but in things) is the stuff of his poetry. Take this other much-anthologized ditty, entitled "This Is Just To Say":

> I have eaten
> the plums
> that were in
> the icebox
>
> and which
> you were probably
> saving
> for breakfast
>
> Forgive me
> they were delicious
> so sweet
> and so cold

This poem gains its power from the specificity of the moment it takes place in. For instance, any fool can see it would be a different poem if it were about a cheese danish, as it would then be about the end of a marriage.

You may say (many have said), "In what way is this poetry any better than notes I leave when I eat other people's stuff out of the fridge?" It is what it is: you can pause over it, and experience the moment of the poem, and laud it as great art. Or you can claim that your apology notes kick Williams's poetry's ass. In any case, for better or worse, not all of Williams's poetry is as simple as this. There are many ideas in things, it turns out, and some of them are, paradoxically, very abstract. Try this extract from "The Descent":

> The descent beckons
>> as the ascent beckoned.
>>> Memory is a kind
> of accomplishment,
>> a sort of renewal
>>> even
> an initiation, since the spaces it opens are new places
>> inhabited by hordes
>>> heretofore unrealized,
> of new kinds—
>> since their movements
>>> are toward new objectives
> (even though formerly they were abandoned).
>
> No defeat is made up entirely of defeat—since
> the world it opens is always a place
>> formerly
>>> unsuspected. A
> world lost,
>> a world unsuspected,
>>> beckons to new places
> and no whiteness (lost) is so white as the memory
> of whiteness

Most cats and dogs would struggle with this. But a human who has struggled with this, and claims not to see anything in it, should go back and struggle again.

A book of Williams's poetry includes both these excursions into philosophy and many, many just plain things which humbly escort them. Although a *Selected Poems* is fine, getting one of his books is strongly recommend. The most famous are *Spring and All* and his book about the New Jersey town where he spent his life, *Paterson*. Any idea that Williams is a simple-minded or unpoetic poet will vanish after a few pages of these richly populated and deeply contemplated works. Also, you will never look at an obstetrician in quite the same way again.

THANK GOD

Williams didn't believe in God in any ick way like T. S. Eliot, nor did he believe in any ick dictators like Ezra Pound did. He did consider himself a socialist, but this is hardly worth mentioning, since socialism is as common in American poets as long ears in rabbits.

THE GREAT AMERICAN NOVEL

This was the title of Williams's only novel, the story of a little blue Ford car who falls in love with a Mack truck, among other things. Worth a look, if only because it proves obstetricians can also be funny.

	Importance	*Accessibility*	*Fun*
Spring and All	10	5	8
Paterson	8	3	8

EZRA POUND (1885–1972)

Ezra Pound was more important as a literary impresario than as a poet in his own right. As the aider and abettor of Eliot, the tireless promoter of Joyce, and literary counsel to a score of other major modernists, he changed the face of literature by sheer force of will. He was one of the most successful autodidacts in history, growing from an opinionated, insulting youth from Nowhere, Idaho, into an opinionated center of cultural life in Europe. Pound put the bray into abrasive, leading less by example than by the beloved sound of his own voice. He was an

Imagist, then a Vorticist—two short-lived but seminal movements dedicated to scrubbing the Victorian fripperies out of literature.

His works of popular criticism, *ABC of Reading* and *Guide to Kulchur*, are a good introduction to the good parts of his mind. They're offensive, offbeat, brilliant; also brilliantly stupid. Here's a taster: "It is my intention in this booklet to COMMIT myself on as many points as possible, that means that I shall make a number of statements which very few men can AFFORD to make, for the simple reason that such taking sides might jeopard their incomes (directly) or their prestige or 'position' in one or other of the professional 'worlds.' Given my freedom, I may be a fool to use it, but I wd. be a cad not to." His tone is consistently that of a troll on an Internet bulletin board.

It's not surprising that, in his final transformation, Pound became a Fascist. In World War II, he worked for Mussolini, making radio broadcasts against the U.S., Jews, and the international banking conspiracy. After the war, he was prosecuted for treason. He pleaded insanity, and spent twelve years in an insane asylum as a result. Nowadays we would say that Ezra Pound had a personality disorder, which is what modern clinicians have come up with to avoid saying the patient's an asshole.

He is most famous for the work that is least read, the *Cantos*, a fat book full of vocabulary words, attacks on the banking system ("usurocracy"), anti-Semitic barbs, and appropriated passages from sources including the Federalist Papers, Homer, Adam Smith, Dante, Propertius, a Carthaginian explorer called Hanno the Navigator, and the Tatar ruler Oulo. Pound loved to quote foreign languages in his texts, including some he did not speak: when he breaks into Chinese ideograms, the reader should not feel cowed, since Pound himself did not understand them. *The Pisan Cantos*, written in detention at the end of World War II, are generally considered to be the most interesting, and can be read separately, by those people who can read them at all.

Most people glance at the *Cantos*, then turn to Pound's short lyrics. The most accessible and rewarding are his loose translations of Chinese poetry, collected in *Cathay*. Here, his tendency to hysterical erudition is held in check by the austere simplicity of the originals. Because he had an astonishing lyrical gift (which he usually buried under cuckoo economics and obscure allusions), these poems are limpid, fine, and often the best versions of the Chinese originals in English, even where Pound got the details wrong. (He wrote them on the basis of Ernest Fenellosa's rough translations; unfortunately, Fenollosa himself had learned Chinese with a Japanese teacher.)

Pound's other short lyrics are by turns ravishing and frustrating. A good *Selected Poems* will serve as an introduction. For any approach to Pound, bring every dictionary you possess and expect to spend more time looking at dictionaries than you do reading the actual text.

FASCIST PERSONALITY DISORDER

Here's a quote from a letter written late in Pound's life: "The NAACP is being run by kikes not by coons." This meant that the Jewish usurocracy was behind racial unrest in the U.S., for some obscure usurocrat reason. Pound obviously missed his historical moment. If he had lived long enough, he could have become a crippling embarrassment to the Tea Party Movement.

ON THE OTHER HAND

Here's his most famous, and briefest, poem, about the surprise of seeing three beautiful people in a row in a passing crowd at a train station.

In the Station of the Metro

The apparition of these faces in the crowd;
Petals on a wet, black, bough.

	Importance	Accessibility	Fun
Guide to Kulchur, ABC of Reading	2	9	8
Short poems	5	4	6
The Cantos	5	1	4

JAMES JOYCE (1882–1941)

Joyce spent his life writing. As a result, his biography isn't exactly a gripping tale. He lived in many different cities—Dublin, Paris, Trieste—where he sat and wrote. His lifelong partner, Nora, was a loving companion but a relatively simple woman who was irritated by his later works. Their first date was on June 16, immortalized as Bloomsday, the day on which the events of *Ulysses* occur. However, the most important fact to know about Joyce is that for most of his life, he was supported financially by the feminist editor Harriet Shaw Weaver, out of a pure love of literature. She also created a press purely in order to publish his works. Without this patron, we would not have *Ulysses* or *Finnegans Wake*. This allows frustrated readers to curse a whole extra person for the headache they get while trying to read James Joyce.

Joyce wrote one play, *Exiles*, and a volume of poetry, usually published as *Chamber Music*. These are early and unimportant, which is a relief, since they aren't much good. Joyce was not one of those depressing writers who peaks at twenty-one and is washed up at thirty. Once he got going, though, he produced four whole books that have each become an Everest every would-be intellectual has to scale.

Dubliners

This is a collection of good but run-of-the-mill realist stories. They are slices of life from the Dublin of Joyce's youth, written in language that is sometimes simple, sometimes lyrical, always normal, seldom fantastic. The gutsy approach in many scenes contrasts well with the elegiac tone of the characters' inner lives, and some of these ("Araby," "The Dead") are very finely written. Still, they're pretty boring compared to anything else Joyce did, or to similar stories by Flaubert or Chekhov. In fact, *Dubliners* is like the first room in the retrospective exhibition of a great artist, where you find the derivative paintings done when the artist was twenty-one and hadn't yet found his style.

People love to say *Dubliners* shows that Joyce was a writer who only produced masterpieces. This is despite the fact that the book is patently not a masterpiece; presumably there's something irresistible about that first hyperbolic step across the line between true and false. These same fibbers like to call it a "good intro-duction to Joyce." In the sense that these stories are much more accessible than his later works, yes. On the other hand, these stories are less like *Ulysses* than they are like humming, or like spending the day at Bloomingdale's, or a balloon animal. Since "Joyce" really means *Ulysses*, these stories will only give you the il-lusion of knowing something about his work.

Portrait of the Artist as a Young Man

Now you're talking. Many people read this as a sort of *Ulysses Lite*. It's not exactly that, though it does have the mixed tone of lament and send-up that constitutes the Joycean chemical signature. It's a bildungsroman; like most such works, it's autobiographical, and contains accounts of Joyce's aesthetics which will fascinate people who can care about anyone's aesthetics.

The plot is Joyce vs. the Jesuits. It begins in the depths of childhood, where we find little James (here named Stephen Dedalus) trying to puzzle out his life in the midst of bullies, priests, and lessons. Catholic boarding school was never so poetically evoked. By the time Stephen Dedalus has decided that his vocation is not for the priesthood but for writing poetry and chasing girls, we are almost sorry.

The good news is that *Portrait of an Artist* can be read by everybody. That's not to say it's always easy: people who aren't familiar with Irish history, or Catholics, should choose an annotated version. But, unlike with Joyce's later works, you don't have to carry around a whole other book to explain the book you're reading. It is also, though, just a great novel. It's not a kind of literature the world has never seen before. It won't force your brain to grow entire new neural networks in the brain's doomed attempts to understand it. It's not so much *Ulysses Lite* as it is gateway Joyce.

STEPHEN HERO

This is an early version of *Portrait of an Artist* which is closer to Joyce's real youth and farther from delicious. A must for Joyce worshippers; for everyone else, it's something to put on your to-do list if you're going to live for eleven thousand years.

Ulysses

Pretentious, garrulous, gorgeous, relentless, *Ulysses* is both a milestone in our literature and a millstone around its neck. Many people hate it because the subtext in every word is "I'm smarter than you." For the same reason, many people revere it, even those for whom it was as much fun as swallowing rocks. Finally, some people genuinely love it. These people should keep their heads down, though, since nobody will believe them.

There is reason for that love: *Ulysses* is a life-changing experience for many people, and not only because it offers some youths their first experience of feeling smarter than everyone else. No one ever spent quite so much talent in one place. Every page abounds with puns, keen impressions, cool ideas, psychological depth, and twenty other things I've forgotten. Also, *Ulysses* is a comic novel, and one that is actually very funny. Of course, you have to get the jokes before they can be funny, which is not child's play.

You could say Joyce just came up with an interesting way to make it really hard to read a realist novel. However, the difficulty is the point; the novel itself is only backdrop. If you have the patience to work through the difficulty, *Ulysses* is like a scoop of neutron star; it has a higher density of entertainment than any other single thing.

It has been an influence on many, many writers, and generally a bad influence. With this book, literature turns into a pissing contest. Just as the Romantics taught generations of kids to believe they could live on dreams, Joyce taught generations of budding writers that the more unreadable your book was, the more likely it was to be read for a thousand years.

In fact, *Ulysses* is a string of terrible ideas, redeemed by the overwhelming force of a particular kind of genius. Other authors can only imitate the bad ideas; they cannot produce the particular genius, if indeed they can produce any genius. As a result, the more directly a writer was influenced by Joyce, the more likely he is to be marginal today. Even Joyce cannot always write himself out of the fixes he gets into. Let's start by looking at those fixes.

Odyssey

Joyce based the structure of the book on the *Odyssey*. Stephen Dedalus (yes, the same Joyce stand-in from *Portait of the Artist*) is Telemachus. Leopold Bloom, a Jewish advertising canvasser, plays the part of Odysseus. Every chapter (except one, randomly) mirrors a section of the *Odyssey*. This mirroring is very, very loose. If no one told you it was there, you would not notice it.

Also, the *Odyssey* has nothing at all to do with Joyce's story. Even Ezra Pound, one of Joyce's greatest supporters, pronounced this an "*affaire de cuisine*," meaning something that is important to the chef but not the diner. The best thing we can say about the *Odyssey* stuff is that it can provide harmless entertainment to people who feel like puzzling it out.

The one correspondence that matters is in the relationship between Leopold Bloom and Stephen Dedalus. For readers who are familiar with Homer, Bloom's position as a surrogate father for Stephen does have dramatic power, especially at the end. Every single other correspondence is absolutely meaningless, which makes Joyce look kind of prattish if you stop to think about it. Here's where we all have to pitch in: don't stop to think about it.

Joyce named each chapter after the episode in the *Odyssey* it corresponded to. However, these chapter titles were left out of the book. The chapters are still called by these names, however, by literary critics. We too will use these names, because there are no other names, and the chapters aren't numbered, and everybody's doing it. (Please don't stop to think about this. Thanks.)

Hamlet

There are countless references to *Hamlet* in *Ulysses*, including actual arguments about the meaning of the play. There is also a second set of correspondences here, where Stephen is Hamlet, haunted by the idea (ghost) of fathers. This shouldn't work at all, it has no right to work. But it does; the theme feels absolutely natural, and unlike the *Odyssey* material, it's something that exists inside the book (in Stephen's head, in conversations) instead of being visited on the characters by an author who doesn't care about their needs.

Pastiches

In some chapters, but very few, Joyce spoofs various styles of writing or oratory. For instance, the Oxen of the Sun chapter is written in a series of pastiches of literature, arranged in a timeline from Old English to the present and showing how each style could have been more difficult to understand. There is Middle English; there are bits mimicking Lawrence Sterne; there is a Gothic apparition.

These pastiches are nothing to do with anything. The explanation usually given for the Oxen of the Sun pastiches is that since the scene is set in a maternity hospital, these pastiches show the gestation and development of English literature. We can only hope Joyce didn't actually intend something as mortifyingly tasteless as that.

Likewise, there is no essential reason that Leopold Bloom's visit to a pub (the Cyclops chapter) should break into journalese and Irish epic, etc. These random detours into pastiche just feel self-indulgent. However, they are so brilliantly done that for the most part (not always) it's an indulgence for the reader too.

Circe

Aka the Nighttown sequence. Here, in the middle of the book, Joyce writes a 150-page dream sequence in the form of an avant-garde playscript. OH MY GOD IS THIS PART HARD TO GET THROUGH. Until the very end, there is no plot information at all. In the "real world" of the novel, the characters are in the red light district getting drunk. In the dream sequence, they are being elected dictator, building fantasy cities, being berated by their parents' ghosts, being turned into women and sexually humiliated, and so on and so on. It would take a page to list all the things that happen, except that they're not really happening.

The only excuse for the Nighttown sequence is that it acts out the subconscious dramas within the characters. To some degree that's reasonable, but for the most part it reads like Joyce showing off to no purpose. It's brilliant, it's impressive. But no one can show off irrelevantly for 150 pages without getting on your nerves.

Scat

Joyce stays with his characters continuously, which means that he also accompanies them to the bathroom. They do numbers one and two. They also fart. Many early readers rejected *Ulysses* for this reason alone. For the squeamish, these are not parts of *Ulysses* which you will treasure and read over and over with rapt appreciation. However, the experience of elimination is so accurately rendered that it's surprisingly interesting. And after all, this is stream of consciousness; life as it is lived. We might wish that our consciousness stopped as we got to the bathroom door and only picked up again once we were washing our hands. Unfortunately . . .

Stream of Consciousness

This needs its own box. Can we get a box here?

THANK YOU

Most of the book is written in stream of consciousness. Mainly it is from the points of view of Dedalus and Bloom, but it occasionally shifts into the minds of other characters too. Joyce's stream-of-consciousness style is radical, and radically hard to understand. As a means of representing consciousness, it is fatally flawed, since people do not find it challenging to understand what they themselves are thinking.

For instance, in real life, when you think of Randolph, you implicitly know whether Randolph is your brother, your cat, or a brand of soap. A passing thought like "Randolph's fallen in the bath" automatically has meaning. In *Ulysses*, a phrase like this can only be decoded by piecing together cryptic references to Randolph, bath mats, and kibble on pages 116, 289, and 551.

Also, in real consciousness, passing impressions come pre-labeled as memories, feelings, thoughts, imaginings. The only way to represent this labeling in fiction is via words like "he thought" and "he remembered." Joyce didn't want this deadwood cluttering his style. Therefore, in reading *Ulysses*, it's often impossible to tell if something is happening now, decades in the past, or in the land of make-believe.

Also, nonverbal impressions (sounds, smells, sights) are represented alongside thoughts like "Must get kibble on the way home," without any distinction. Put all this together, and a Randolph section might run:

Must get kibble on the way home. In the carrier from Macklin's, that spring. Cradled starfish-fashion in the palm, claws in out breathing like. White? White. Some say they can be toilet-trained.

Blaring strains beside came, Jessop skipping sideways. Blue slippingly as the tram passed.

When you first read Joyce's stream of consciousness, it's like being trapped in the head of a dementia patient. You only gradually become adept at piecing it all together. It is written at the pace of thought, but can only be read at the pace of a snail, and a snail who keeps circling back to pick up something he's lost.

Now let's look at the story which is hiding behind these narrative experiments. The action all takes place on the 16th of June, 1904. Stephen Dedalus gets up in the morning, interacts with his frenemy Buck Mulligan and the Englishman Haines. He then goes off to see Deasy, the man for whom he works as a teacher. Deasy entrusts him with a letter to the editor about foot-and-mouth disease. Later, he stops by the Quaker library, where he has an argument with various literary types about Shakespeare. We see him later at the maternity hospital, where he runs into Leopold Bloom for the first time. Let's switch to Bloom.

On the same morning, Leopold Bloom learns that his wife Molly is going to be visited by a man, Blazes Boylan, with whom she will probably have sex. He doesn't do anything about this, and we learn that he and Molly have not had sex for a long time, since their infant son Rudy died. Bloom goes out and makes a few business calls, with this on his mind. At a pub, he is assaulted by an anti-Semitic drunk; retreating to a beach, he masturbates clandestinely, watching three young girls nearby. He then visits the maternity hospital, where a woman he knows is having a baby, gets caught up in the company of a group of drunken students, including Stephen Dedalus, and ends up in the red light district.

Here Dedalus gets into a scrap. He is injured and Bloom takes him back to Bloom's place in a cab. Dedalus and Bloom have a friendly conversation, but Dedalus turns down the offer of a place to stay for the night. The last section of the novel is from Molly Bloom's point of view: she thinks about her sex with Boylan earlier in the day, then about various other sexual escapades in her life, and ends by remembering her acceptance of Bloom's marriage proposal: "yes I said yes I will Yes."

This may not seem like much story, considering the insane difficulty of understanding it. There is probably no reader of *Ulysses* who is never weary of straining every neuron in her head, chapter after chapter, in order to discern that, once again, a group of Irishmen are getting drunk. Most readers will be conscious, at all times, of how many pages are left to the end of the book.

However, most readers find the experience worthwhile. And sadly, there is no way of knowing whether you are one of them without reading at least three hundred pages of the book.

BRAGGING RIGHTS AND WRONGS

Outside of certain rarefied groups, it is almost never a good idea to say you've read *Ulysses*. If you say you didn't like it, people will hear "I wasn't smart enough to understand it, and I'm too vain to admit it." If you say you liked it, they will hear ". . . because I'm smarter than the average person." If you take pains to say you definitely understood it, but still didn't like it, even if they believe you, all they'll hear is "I'm so smart, I'm smarter than all the eggheads who like *Ulysses*." Under no circumstances can you tell someone you've read *Ulysses* and have them hear only "I've read *Ulysses*." It's like announcing you belong to Mensa.

Just as with Mensa, the only good time to say you're in the *Ulysses* club is when someone else says it first. Even then, it might be a good idea to pretend you haven't read it, in the hope that this poser won't bother you again.

Finnegans Wake

Nowadays, it is generally agreed that with this book, Joyce went too far. Taking seventeen years in the writing, *Finnegans Wake* is a string of puns immersed in wordplay, pastiche, and little else. It begins in the middle of a sentence and ends in the middle of the same sentence. It includes words from sixty-odd languages; parts of German words are welded to parts of English words, or French words are spelled so that their echoes of similar English words are made punningly obvious. The sound of it is quite remarkable, but often that's all there is. Here's a snippet, taken at random:

> Nuboletta in her lightdress, spunn of sixteen shimmers, was looking down on them, leaning over the bannistars and listening all she childishly could. How she was brightened when Shouldrups in his glaubering hochskied his welkinstuck and how she was overclused when Kneesknobs on his zwivvel was makeacting such a paulse of himshelp!

It is 650 pages long, and every page is like that.

So few people read *Finnegans Wake* in its entirety that those people who write dissertations about it may be the majority of its readers. It is ideal for dissertation writing, for reasons that should be obvious. There are entire books written by these dissertationists which offer a key to *Finnegans Wake*. It's probably vain to expect to understand it without such a guide. Here's Jorge Luis Borges confessing his failure:

> I have examined it with some bewilderment, have unenthusiastically deciphered nine or ten calembours, and have read the terror-stricken praise in the N.R.F. and the T.L.S. The trenchant authors of those accolades claim that they have discovered the rules of this complex verbal labyrinth, but they abstain from applying or formulating them; nor do they attempt the analysis of a single line or paragraph. . . . I suspect that they share my essential bewilderment and my useless and partial glances at the text. . . . *Finnegans Wake* is a concatenation of puns committed in a dreamlike English that is difficult not to categorize as frustrated and incompetent.

Mee-ow! And kudos to him for saying it first.

	Importance	Accessibility	Fun
Dubliners	9	7	6
Portrait of the Artist as a Young Man	10	5	8
Ulysses	10	1	8
Finnegans Wake	5	1	4

MARCEL PROUST (1871–1922)

Proust's masterwork, *In Search of Lost Time*, is famous for its size: at seven volumes, it makes even *War and Peace* seem like a sketch. Its sentences are built to scale, winding from thought to thought in tireless, gorgeous excursions that cover half a page. Sometimes he seems to have crammed every idea he ever had into a single sentence. Sometimes finding the sentence's meaning is like chasing a cat around a room full of folding chairs. Once you get used to the exercise, though, these sentences become like a series of Fabergé eggs. Each one is ingenious, faintly comical, and so beautiful it's hard to believe they're only made of words.

The first volume, *Swann's Way*, is the most commonly read—mainly because it is the first, but also because it is the most perfect. It begins with the notorious madeleine, the taste of which sparks a flood of memories, which in turn spark the writing of the book. This passage also sparks many excited young people to buy madeleines, only to be disillusioned to find they are really just empty Twinkies.

We step off this empty Twinkie into the narrator's childhood, where we find him neurotically desperate that his mother should kiss him before he goes to bed. Meanwhile, downstairs, the adults entertain a family friend, Charles Swann. Proust then leads us, via the prolonged amazement of early childhood, into a novella about Swann's destructive love affair with the courtesan Odette.

Swann falls in love with Odette for no reason; even against reason. She is not his physical type, being too skinny and pale. She is dull, dishonest, and has mediocre taste, while Swann is a wit and connoisseur, beloved by the hostesses of the aristocratic Faubourg Saint-Germain. He is so urbane, in fact, that only the über-urbane Proust could have written him. Once Swann loves his bony hooker, though, he turns into a chowder of ill-judged feelings. His gradual descent into the mess of love presages the later adventures of the narrator himself.

This narrator (called by name—Marcel—only once in the course of the book) is and isn't Proust. While Proust was both gay and Jewish, in his book both qualities are projected onto other characters. They are projected in abundance. The book is especially full of clandestine gayness, notably that of the Baron de Charlus, whose amours are described with homophobic relish by Marcel. It's worth reading to the end just to see Proust lose all control and identify virtually all the male characters, whom we have known for six volumes, as closeted homosexuals. The great love of Marcel's life, Albertine, is also suspected of lesbianism. (The character of Albertine was based on Proust's chauffeur and inconstant lover, Albert; interestingly, the fictional Albertine is given a driver who abets her in her infidelities.)

As Marcel begins to grow and fall in love with "girls," he also becomes a fixture in the fashionable set of the Duchess of Guermantes, and in the up-and-coming salon of Mme. Verdurin. The life of this latter salon has a biography of its own, and its gradual rise to prominence is one of the most fascinating aspects of *In Search of Lost Time*. As an actual denizen of high society, Proust was in a unique position to demystify this world. No sociology degree will teach you more about human relations than you can learn from the progress of the Verdurin salon from gauche outsiderdom to vogue—without having essentially changed in the transition. Dozens of lives pass through these salons; meanwhile Marcel grows from a boy to a man. Finally he returns to society after a long absence to discover that he is now one of the old folk.

Along the way, there is love, and again love, and more stupid love. The central passion is Marcel's obsession with that cheating Albertine. Endless tracts in volumes five and six are devoted to this love affair. There is even a section in which you could swear that Proust is drunk and writing the same few pages over and over. Marcel's futile attempts to control his lover, his boredom whenever she's true to him, and the boundless, causeless despair he feels once she is gone, are repeated and extended and embellished with the monomania of real infatuation. Yes—you have already guessed—it sends you to sleep. But it's a sweet doze, not the headachey, disgruntled sleep that comes from reading Milton.

It takes anywhere from three months to a year to read *In Search of Lost Time*. You may wonder if it's worth devoting a year of your life to any single book, no matter how great. All one can say is that it will make that year a better year. It's like a book you wish would never end, except then it doesn't end. In fact, it's a little like being in love.

	Importance	Accessibility	Fun
In Search of Lost Time	10	4	10

VIRGINIA WOOLF (1882–1941)

While many female writers had written great works and even won fame, Virginia Woolf was the first to try to reinvent a genre. It's probably no coincidence that she was an ardent feminist, and it's certainly no coincidence that she had independent means.

She makes both points herself in her classic essay "A Room of One's Own." Here Woolf explains the underachievement of women as artists: a person with no education and no leisure time is unlikely to dash off *Paradise Lost* on the nights when she can't sleep. Education and leisure apparently aren't enough, though: Woolf's preconditions for intellectual effort include the solitary room of the title, but also an independent income, servants, and fine wines. Woolf also proposes that female writers will create a new kind of literature, because their minds are essentially different from men's. This, for example, is a female sentence. This one was written by a male confederate. Female sentences will express something women experience and men don't, and then we'll find out what that is. (Woolf is a little fuzzy on this point.)

The most salient feature of Woolf's mature work is not femaleness, but shifting points of view. Time flows continuously, but passes from one consciousness into another, often without warning. If Nancy is passing the salt to Reginald, we hear her thinking, "He doesn't notice. That absent-mindedness of his, foolish of course to take it so personally." Then, in a new paragraph: "Oh, salt, Reginald noticed. What's that for?" We might stay in Reginald's consciousness now for pages on end, or for a single paragraph. And even the most pompous windbag is shown (from the inside) beset by Big Questions, twinges of compassion, and abysses of self-doubt.

In *To the Lighthouse*, the first novel of this mature style, the stars are the conventional materfamilias Mrs. Ramsay and her houseguest, the painter and liberated woman Lily Briscoe. Through them, through the Ramsay family, and through anyone else who passes by, Woolf gives us a day at the Ramsays' summer house. Then she accelerates time, and ten years pass in a brief second section.

Trees grow and World War I is fought. Mrs. Ramsay dies in a parenthesis. Then we're dumped back into real time, and the summer house, but with most of our points of view gone. The stripped-down, lonely nature of this latter day is a powerful representation of a bereaved family. The remaining people can't think or feel enough for us, and consciousness itself seems widowed.

The eponymous heroine of *Mrs. Dalloway* is a less maternal, more brittle version of Mrs Ramsay. Her day (here there is only one day) is centered around the party she will give that evening. Meanwhile, her old flame Peter Walsh has come back from India to help her reminisce about their youth. A third, unrelated, character, Septimus Smith, has come back from World War I and fallen into psychosis. We follow these three, often via the consciousness of innocent bystanders, from morning to night. Although Septimus doesn't make it all the way, the novel still ends on a life-affirming note, with Mrs. Dalloway reflecting that she's glad that young man killed himself, because it makes her appreciate life more. Thanks a lot, lady.

The Waves is a more experimental work the mannerisms of which are so improbable we can only represent them with a quote:

> "I love," said Susan, "and I hate. I desire one thing only. My eyes are hard. Jinny's eyes break into a thousand lights . . . Though my mother still knits white socks for me and hems pinafores and I am a child, I love and I hate."
>
> "But when we sit together, close," said Bernard, "we melt into each other with phrases. We are edged with mist. We make an unsubstantial territory."
>
> "I see the beetle," said Susan. "It is black, I see; it is green, I see; I am tied down with single words. But you wander off; you slip away; you rise up higher, with words and words in phrases."

As you may have guessed, "said" here doesn't mean said. It doesn't even mean "thought." It indicates a melded all-consciousness that precedes both thought and speech. The entire book is written in this form. It follow six friends through their lives, as represented in this "saying," which is pregnant with metaphor. In fact, it's nine months pregnant with metaphor, so that it can hardly walk. At first, this is risible and pretentious, but as you become accustomed to it, it becomes a successful representation of preverbal life.

One early book of Woolf's has had a second life, primarily because of its status as a gender-bending classic. *Orlando* is better than its hype. Written for Vita Sackville-West, briefly Woolf's lover, it tells the story of a young man born in Renaissance England; he lives for hundreds of years, in the course of which he unexpectedly transforms into a young woman. While the gender stuff is definitely there, there's also magical realism, postmodernist jokes about the fact that this story is being told, and all the pleasures of a historical novel. It is pure joy.

THE BLOOMSBURY GROUP

Woolf was one of the most illustrious members of the Bloomsbury Set. This was a group of friends who lived in Bloomsbury and got together a lot. There is no other meaning to it, so don't waste time looking for one. The other really important members of Bloomsbury were John Maynard Keynes and E. M. Forster. The common intellectual thread between Keynesian economics, Woolf's prose experiments, and Forster's graceful, conventional novels is that they were all written in English by people who walked on two legs.

AND THAT FASHIONABLE MADNESS

Virginia Woolf, despite being happily married, well-off, and lauded by her contemporaries, and having servants to bring her fine wines, killed herself. She had suffered from mental illness intermittently since late childhood; when she felt it descending again in her fifties, she gracefully checked out. Drowning was her chosen method, and she showed a pragmatic streak by providently weighting her pockets with stones. (Of course, nobody saw her, so she might have been trying to drown herself for hours and kept floating to the top.) Anyway, if you're drowning yourself: stones in pockets does the trick.

ERNEST HEMINGWAY (1899–1961)

Above, I make the provocative claim that Hemingway's fiction is so derivative of Gertrude Stein's that really he is no better than a copycat. Of course this is a vast oversimplification, which is what made it fun to say. While Hemingway himself acknowledged his debt to Stein, he also copied from Sherwood Anderson, Guy de Maupassant, and Pound, among others, and—I suppose it is no secret—had something of a distinctive literary voice himself.

Hemingway is most vividly remembered as a he-man writer. Almost single-handedly he created the type of the macho novelist who writes with one hand while punching a punk's lights out with the other. He hunts bears with a fork and is most at home in no-man's-land. It is sad to reflect that this tradition of masculine posing may have been the fault of Hemingway's mother, who dressed him as a girl for the first two years of his life. It didn't hurt that, as a young man, Hemingway was heart-stoppingly gorgeous; there is no mystery about his perennial appeal to women.

Hemingway's plain, adverb-less style, with its heavy dependence on the word "and" and on the repetition of words like "big" and "good," was for a time the favored style in American prose, especially for men. Adjectives were out; grunts were in. Prose was supposed to be "lean, muscular, athletic." A sentence that used the vocabulary of a first grader simply had more truthiness. Some male authors still got away with the florid style of Faulkner (see page 276), but only if they came from the South, had a favorite fishing fly, and stank of whiskey.

This style is all about not saying. One of Hemingway's favored techniques was to write a story without mentioning the most important event. The most famous example is "Hills Like White Elephants," where a young couple plan an abortion without ever calling it by name. Hemingway thinks he's invented this trick out of thin air, but of course our insightful readers will recognize it as an interesting twist on the Gothic Unmentionable, aka Don't Mention the War. (In "Big Two-Hearted River," it is literally the war.)

Despite this little obfuscation trick, Hemingway's dictum was that "A writer's job is to tell the truth." The truth meant the events, not anyone's feelings or thoughts about them. This technique gave his characters—male and female—a certain macho flatness of affect, like an action-film assassin character with the sobriquet "The Maintenance Man." It is not that emotions are never to be mentioned at all. But they should be described in an inarticulate, understated, man way, to wit: "When his wife and children died in that fire, Jake figured he felt about as bad as he could feel. He felt that bad feeling for a long while, though it was something a man didn't speak of. Yet there was no *desgracia*, and so the bad feeling did not change his heart." (I made this one up.)

Hemingway first gained a reputation with his short stories, which received some critical acclaim. But his first big hit was *The Sun Also Rises* (published in Europe as *Fiesta*), a spare, sad portrait of the Lost Generation wandering around

Pamplona. Here his main character suffers from literal as well as symbolic impotence, and the story mirrors this, almost loving, almost happening, but always drooping again in a way that commands more attention than a successful act. (The impotence wasn't autobiographical. Don't even get your hopes up.) Then came *A Farewell to Arms*, a beautifully understated love story based on Hemingway's experiences as an ambulance driver in World War I. In both novels, the laconic style sometimes makes the characters seem glassy-eyed with boredom. This conveys the generation's lostness, hints at existential crisis, and handily also makes them cool.

For Whom the Bell Tolls was about the Spanish Civil War, and another love story set therein. It notoriously introduced the idea that when sex is real love, the earth moves. "But did thee feel the earth move?" Robert Jordan asks Maria. Happily, Maria not only felt the earth move, she also "died." (Jordan didn't die, but then it's only etiquette to let the woman die first.) Here Hemingway tries for big emotions, and his blank style makes the characters seem inappropriately wooden. It's like love and war among cigar store Indians. However, for long patches, the book works because of its subject, one of the great lost causes of history, which gives room for lines like "If you have not seen the day of Revolution in a small town where all know all in the town and always have known all, you have seen nothing."

His last important novel was *The Old Man and the Sea*, where a simple, aged Cuban fisherman struggles for three days to land a marlin in a sailboat half the marlin's size. At last, he has the marlin lashed to the side of the boat, where it is eaten by sharks as he sails back. (Although he has been fishing in these shark-infested waters all his life, this possibility never occured to him.) This novel reads like a children's book for people in their second childhood. The old man is provided with a perfectly loyal boy, who does everything for him out of simple reverence for his fishing wisdom, who can only have been based on Hemingway's last wife.

Hemingway's short stories are among the classics of the genre, and his style generally works better here. There are many famous ones, such as "The Short Happy Life of Francis Macomber," about a weak cuckold who becomes a real man via big game hunting—only to be shot by his wife, who does not want any non-cuckold husband. The most famous of all is probably "A Clean, Well-Lighted Place," which is about how you sometimes go to a coffee shop just to get out of the house. Here Hemingway famously named the thing we are then fleeing as "nada": "It was all a nothing and a man was nothing too. . . . Some lived in it and never felt it but he knew it all was nada y pues nada y nada y pues nada."

He also wrote nonfiction, notably *Death in the Afternoon*, a fan's account of bullfighting, and *A Moveable Feast*, a self-mythologizing memoir of his happy youth in Paris, written in Hemingway's final years. The latter is notable for its negative and pitying portraits of Hemingway's rival authors, notably Gertrude Stein and F. Scott Fitzgerald, and for the version of himself as a wholesome servant of truth. Still, it has an enduring charm. "This is how Paris was when we were very poor and very happy," as Hemingway ends the book. The happiness is infectious.

Note: In his later years, Hemingway went by the nickname "Papa." For the present author, this has the embarrassing ring of a married couple who call each other "Mother" and "Father." Anyway, referring to "Papa Hemingway" is a neat way of evoking all the things that made the guy ridiculous, so thanks to whoever first called him that.

THREE HEMINGWAY MANLY FICTION TRICKS

- Make a generalization about a class of people that is so specific it literally cannot be true. Example (from "Mr. and Mrs. Elliot"): "They did not try [to conceive a child] very often on the boat because Mrs. Elliot was quite sick. She was sick and when she was sick she was sick as Southern women are sick. That is women from the Southern part of the United States. Like all Southern women Mrs. Elliot disintegrated very quickly under sea sickness."

You can't tell the author anything new about Southern women on boat trips, no sir. He is a man of the world!

- Refer to an experience that is universal. Make sure everyone immediately knows what you're talking about. Then treat it as a mystery only known to the initiated. Here Hemingway nails it in *A Farewell to Arms*: "I tried to tell about the night and the difference between the night and the day and how the night was better unless the day was very clean and cold and I could not tell it; as I cannot tell it now. But if you have had it you know."

And if you have not had it, you also know, because he just told you.

- Use the point of view of a simple man of the soil and have him expound his philosophy. Remember—simple men are different from you and me! Don't give your character any thoughts we might have. Here is Santiago in *The Old Man and the Sea*: "The fish is my friend too," he said aloud. "I have never seen or heard of such a fish. But I must kill him. I am glad we do not have to try to kill the stars. Imagine if each day a man must try to kill the moon, he thought. The moon runs away. But imagine if a man each day should have to try to kill the sun? We were born lucky, he thought."

The key to this technique is to imagine Arthur Rimbaud has had a massive stroke. Now write one of his poems, using only the few words he remembers. This is how peasants think all the time, because they are close to the poetry of the earth.

FOUR WEDDINGS AND FOUR FUNERALS

Hemingway's first wife Hadley is sweetly portrayed in *A Moveable Feast*, where he darkly hints at the rich people who spoiled their innocent love. By the rich people, we understand, he meant his rich second wife, Pauline Pfeiffer. Their marriage was made under an unlucky star: Hemingway got anthrax on their honeymoon, and his major work of the Pauline period was a short story collection entitled *Men Without Women*.

Hemingway, however, was not a man to be without women, and he left Pauline only once he had legendary journalist Martha Gellhorn in his bed. She lasted a few years and finally ceded her place to another journalist, Mary Welsh, who stayed to the end, aided by her willingness to turn a blind eye to Hemingway's many dalliances with young girls.

Their marriage ended only with Hemingway's suicide. This suicide could be seen coming a long way off; not only because of Hemingway's many mental and physical illnesses, but because Hemingway's father, brother, and sister had also killed themselves.

	Importance	Accessibility	Fun
Stories	10	10	8
A Farewell to Arms	8	7	7
The Sun Also Rises	9	8	8
For Whom the Bell Tolls	6	7	7
The Old Man and the Sea	7	10	4
A Moveable Feast	5	10	10

F. SCOTT FITZGERALD (1896–1940)

Shabby genteel but precociously talented and (don't say it doesn't matter) very good-looking, Fitzgerald left the Midwest to go to Princeton, where he was a big literary man on campus. He enlisted just in time to miss World War I, and met and romanced glamorous deb Zelda Sayre. Unfortunately, he wasn't up to her financial standards and had to publish his first novel, *This Side of Paradise*, before he could win her hand. It made him famous, they married, and together the two crazy kids became the poster couple for glamorous Jazz Age youth. Scott drank, Zelda had mental problems, Scott drank, finances became a problem, they ran with the fast literary crowd in Paris, Scott drank, Zelda was hospitalized, Scott drank and wrote dozens of short stories for glossy magazines to support them, complaining that they kept him from his important work. At the end Fitzgerald was washed-up, scraping by miserably in Hollywood until he died of a heart attack, aged forty-four.

There are many novels people think are boring because they were crammed down their throats in high school. With many novels, they are absolutely right. However, this impression is glaringly wrong in the case of Fitzgerald's master-piece, *The Great Gatsby*. Exquisitely written, thoughtful and romantic, it is a prof-iterole of a novel, gorgeous to look at and filled with delicious whipped cream. It is also, not incidentally, the least autobiographical of Fitzgerald's four novels. It tells the story of Jay Gatsby, a mysterious wealthy character who throws grand parties at his estate on Long Island. Nick Carraway—Gatsby's neighbor and our narrator—eventually learns that, rather than the heroic patrician he claims to be, he is really Jay Gatz, a nobody from nowhere who made his fortune bootlegging. With his money and fancy shirts, he's hoping to win over the beautiful Daisy

Buchanan, a genuine patrician, who is already married and as shallow as they come. Lots of well-handled plotting passes quickly, involving love affairs, the wealthy revealed as pigs, a big pair of glasses that symbolically watch over everything, and a tragic car accident that leads to Gatsby's death. Disillusioned, Nick leaves the upper classes to rot on Long Island, and the upper classes don't notice, because they are different from you and me.

None of Fizgerald's other novels offer the perfect blend of craft, smarts, and froth you find in Gatsby. Here's a roundup:

This Side of Paradise
Glamorous, idealistic young man from the Midwest goes out into the world, is rejected by beautiful girl, becomes disillusioned, drinks.

The Beautiful and Damned
Glamorous, well-born young man waits to inherit, wastes his life, marries, sinks into dissolution with his wife, drinks.

Tender Is the Night
Glamorous psychiatrist moves to the South of France with formerly insane wife, has affair, loses wife, falls apart, drinks.

The Last Tycoon
Glamorous movie producer falls in love with an extra. The book is unfinished; one assumes he would otherwise become disillusioned and drink.

Fitzgerald's short stories range from silly claptrap written to pay the rent to ingenious little gems. Some of the silly claptrap is still wonderfully entertaining; written about the part of his autobiography where boy met girl amid Jazz Age glitz and disenchantment. The most famous of these is "The Diamond as Big as the Ritz," where the hero is transported to the secret luxury compound of the family who are sitting on said diamond. Fitzgerald's last works, *The Pat Hobby Stories*, are a smart, funny, rueful series about a washed-up screenwriter scraping by in Hollywood, written at a time when that description fit him like a glove.

	Importance	Accessibility	Fun
This Side of Paradise	5	9	7
The Beautiful and Damned	5	8	6
The Great Gatsby	10	7	10
Tender Is the Night	8	6	7
The Last Tycoon	5	9	8
The Pat Hobby Stories	4	10	9

WILLIAM FAULKNER (1897–1962)

Faulkner is the greatest exponent of the Southern Gothic. His people are haunted wrecks, damned by the original sin of slavery, brought low by their loss of the Civil War, and embarrassed by the fact that Aunt Rose ran away with a traveling salesman. Every story Faulkner tells is about this doomed South, and every unpleasant thing that happens to his characters, even bad teeth, is the reaping of what was sown by the War Between the States.

His style can be quite simple. In books like *Light in August*, there is a clean flow of Hemingway-like prose, with only an occasional baroque image floating in it like a mannequin discarded in its store-tired frippery and back-flung disgrace. Much of his work is also stream of consciousness, notably *As I Lay Dying*, where the point of view circulates among a series of characters, and each chapter is headed with the name of the consciousness streaming. In this book, Faulkner melds modernist lyricism with backwoods dialect, ranging from sentences like "It wasn't nothing else to do," to "Against the dark doorway he seems to materialise out of the darkness, lean as a race horse in his underclothes in the beginning of the glare."

Other novels—notably *Absalom, Absalom*—are written in a high modernist style characterized by syntactic complexity, Gothic flights, and overripe vocabulary, which sometimes crosses the line into hot mess. In his passion for piling on adjectives, he falls into redundancies like "stubborn recalcitrance" and "incredulous amazement." When we read: "What creature in the South since 1861, man woman nigger or mule, had had time or opportunity not only to have been young but to have heard what being young was like," we are torn between pity for the mules robbed of their childhoods, and wonder at the Mississippi black people who were apparently neither men nor women. A character innocently says he doesn't need the electric light to read an old letter. His father replies: "Perhaps you are right; maybe even the light of day, let alone this which man had to invent to his need since, relieved of the onus of sweating to live, he is apparently reverting (or evolving) back into a nocturnal animal, would be too much for it."

If you suspend your incredulous amazement, this style can be very rewarding, allowing Faulkner to maintain an almost hysterical emotionality through a series of completely improbable events. But readers—and plaudits—have tended to gravitate toward those Faulkner novels that leaven this high style with simpler passages, like *As I Lay Dying* and *The Sound and the Fury*.

Underneath the layers of adjectives, all of his novels are a rollicking freak show. Idiot brothers abound in Faulkner, as do doomed fallen women and men with a skeleton in the closet which turns out to be that of a black grandfather. *Sanctuary* includes a rape-by-corncob, murder, and sexual slavery; *Light in August* has bootlegging, murder, arson, and castration. Then there is the Snopes trilogy, *The Hamlet*, *The Town*, and *The Mansion*, featuring the rise of the evil, squalid Snopes family to ascendancy in the town of Jefferson. In the first novel alone, there is arson, bigamy, prostitution, and an idiot son who is in love with a cow.

A final warning to the reader: none of Faulkner's characters ever had a happy moment. If they laugh, it is the forced, hysterical laughter of the doomed. They have no happy memories and no hopes. If they enjoy anything, that thing is a murky business cloaked in taboo, probably involving sex with a vegetable or a barnyard animal. They will pay for that thing, either in blood or by living under a fearful interdiction from all men women niggers and mules. In some cases, the family may opt for castration. When they die, they are mourned either not at all, or for the rest of an embittered spinster's life. Where Adorno famously said "After Dachau, no poetry," Faulkner's motto was "After slavery, here's a noose." Also, although in his avowed politics Faulkner was anti-racist, in his fiction he is often channeling the racist assumptions of his homeland. He uses not only the N-word, but the underlying N-beliefs on page after page.

	Importance	Accessibility	Fun
As I Lay Dying	9	5	9
The Sound and the Fury	9	3	7
Absalom, Absalom	6	1	7
Light in August	6	6	7
Snopes trilogy	6	2	6

CHAPTER 14

Conclusion: Beyond Western Lit

Of course, literary history has moved on since the days of William Faulkner. Sometimes it moves in circles, sometimes it takes to the sea and treads water, and at other times it just moves from the bed to the refrigerator, and then slumps back to bed again. The fact is, despite a really stirring determination to produce new and radical forms, writers have essentially been reproducing forms created and perfected in previous centuries—but with the addition of contemporary slang and black characters who can think.

This has not stopped critics and writers from announcing a literary revolution every few years. The postmodern novel was touted as a cutting-edge expression of the fragmentation of twentieth-century consciousness, despite its origins in the eighteenth century. Some avant-gardists posed as rebels by using "appropriations"—long, uncredited quotes from other writers, mingled into their own texts. This was often attacked as plagiarism, plain and simple—as it was when Ben Jonson and Lawrence Sterne did it hundreds of years ago. Authors who introduce themselves as characters in their own works (like Chaucer did) are treated as rule-breaking daredevils. One widely discussed change is the demise of the readership for poetry, once a genuinely popular form. However, almost everyone still consumes poetry in the form of song lyrics—just as people did in ancient Greece. Really, the chief difference between these antique forms and their contemporary versions is that, when they first arose, no one called them new.

A more alarming—and convincing—development is the gathering chorus that proclaims the death of literature. According to this narrative, it is not only poetry that is on its way out. The demise of the novel is also in the works. Meanwhile, serious theater has been driven into spaces so tiny they would be considered inhumane if the audience consisted of cows instead of friends of the actors. Indeed, all around us, we see mounting evidence that the hours young people once devoted to reading are now given to computer games; Facebook; the latest extreme sports (parkour, BMX, wingsuit flying); and starting unwanted companies. It really does appear that our grandchildren may no longer appreciate the subtleties of Flaubert and Cervantes, though they will be able to jump from a fire escape onto a low-flying plane.

Some people dismiss these developments, claiming that the pleasure of a good book will always be with us. Well, that's what they said about smallpox and Kahlil Gibran. Also, don't listen to those people, because it's boring. Listen to me instead, as I entertain you with fun, scare-mongering bullshit.

So here we are, in the world after literature. (Pretend we're in the world after literature. Thanks.) In this twilight kingdom, people have lost the ability to employ critical thinking, to empathize, and to chew with their mouths shut. You can get a PhD in English without learning to read. People speak in mono-syllables, and their idea of wit is using the word "pwn" in contexts where the word "pwn" sounds out of place. If you ask a friend, "But what is it all for?" he can only, mournfully, offer you a Twinkie. All the wrong women are wearing leggings. Also, Kahlil Gibran is back. And what the hell, let's throw in smallpox. There's smallpox. Plenty of it.

Happily, this nightmare world is still many years in the future. Literature is still going strong, and we are all free to enjoy these marvelous artifacts of genius, as long as we remain in a designated area. And as we wind up this tour, let's spare a moment to appreciate the wider social achievements of these writers. Less than a hundred years after *Ulysses* was banned for corrupting public morals, it is now taught in schools and public morals are in the toilet. Thanks in large part to the work of great novelists, people are now fully aware of their feelings—and everyone around them is aware of their feelings, no matter how hard everyone tries to escape. Still, literature remains the best way for intelligent people to amuse themselves without ending up at the helm of an unwanted company, or with a baby. Finally, smallpox has been eradicated, and don't anyone try to tell me that's just a coincidence.

I hope this book has provided you with insights into this great tradition, and with the hunger to read some of the books described here, and that you have been entertained along the way. If it hasn't and you haven't, I feel the least I can do is to save you any further loss of time by writing your negative amazon review for you to copy and paste. Here it is:

"This book arrived after FIVE WEAKS (!!!!) with half of the pages torn out, and water stanes that look like their growing mold. (EW) Also, it failed to provide me with insights into any great tradition, or with the hunger to read any of the books described, and I wasn't entertained along the way. Also, smallpox. Thnaks a lot, amazon!"

Timelines

Great Moments in
the History of Western Literature

Lives of the Great Authors

1200–1 BC

1150–850: BC HOMER IS PROBABLY BORN, PROBABLY WRITES SOME POEMS,
   MAY EVEN EXIST

   Homer

   Sappho (LATE 7TH–EARLY 6TH CENTURY BC)

GREEK TRAGEDY'S GLORY YEARS:

   Aeschylus (525–456 BC)

   Sophocles (496–406 BC)

   Euripides (480–406 BC)

OLD COMEDY ISN'T FUNNY

   Aristophanes (446–386 BC)

MIDDLE COMEDY ALSO ISN'T FUNNY

NEW COMEDY STILL ISN'T FUNNY

   ROME BECOMES AN EMPIRE (27 BC)

   Virgil (70–19 BC)

   Ovid (43 BC–AD 17)

   Horace (65–8 BC)

AD 1–900s

ROMAN EMPIRE TURNS INTO AN EMBARRASSING CLUSTERFUCK (37–177)

   St. Augustine (354–430)

FIFTH CENTURY: FALL OF ROME, YAY! (476)

   Beowulf (700–900)

1200–1400s

MIDDLE AGES SOMEWHERE IN HERE, BETWEEN SOMETHING AND SOMETHING ELSE

   Song of Roland (MID–12TH CENTURY)

   Dante goes to hell (1300)

   Petrarch (1304–1374)

   Boccaccio (1313–1375)

CHAUCER (1343–1400) WRITES *THE CANTERBURY TALES*,
   THE FIRST BOOK CALLED THE FIRST NOVEL THAT WASN'T

1500–1600s

HEIGHT OF THE RENAISSANCE (MEANING "RE-BIRTH" OR "RISE OF THE
   UNDEAD" IN FRENCH) (1525)

> *Zombies terrorize Europe*
>
> *Rabelais (1494–1553) grosses Europe out*
>
> *Let's skip a lot of stuff in here, moving right along*
>
> *1600: Shakespeare! Now you're talking!*
>
> *John Donne (1572–1631)*

1600–1700s

1616: SHAKESPEARE AND CERVANTES DIE ON THE SAME DAY, PROBABLY
   SMOKING-RELATED

> *John Bunyan (1628–1688)*
>
> *Moliere (1622–1673)*

1649: ENGLISH REVOLUTION. NASTY KING DECAPITATED, YAY!

> *This sadly results in Milton (1608–1674)*

1660: KING COMES BACK, ALL IS FORGIVEN

> *This sadly results in Dryden (1631–1700)*
>
> *Alexander Pope (1688–1744)*
>
> *Daniel Defoe (1660–1731)*
>
> *Jonathan Swift (1667–1745)*

1700–1800s

18TH CENTURY: VOLTAIRE, ROUSSEAU, ALL THAT ENLIGHTENMENT STUFF THAT
   CAUSED AMERICA (THANKS, FRENCH ATHEISTS!)

LOTS MORE BOOKS CALLED "THE FIRST NOVEL": *PAMELA, ROBINSON CRUSOE, GULLIVER'S
   TRAVELS*

LATE 18TH CENTURY: THE ROMANTIC POETS APPEAR

> *William Blake (1757–1827)*
>
> *Lord Byron (1788–1824)*
>
> *Percy Bysshe Shelley (1792–1822)*
>
> *John Keats (1795–1821)*

CIRCA 1820: THE ROMANTIC POETS JUST WILL NOT GET A JOB

God strikes them down (1821–1827)

Johann Wolfgang von Goethe (1749–1832)

Henry David Thoreau (1817–1862)

Walt Whitman (1819–1892)

Emily Dickinson (1830–1886)

In these years, the Brontës cannot get laid (1834–1849)

1836: FIRST NOVEL BY DICKENS, LAST MAN TO WRITE A 700-PAGE NOVEL
EVERY YEAR WITHOUT A COKE HABIT

REALISM ARRIVES IN FRANCE, BECOMES TMI ON CONTACT (CIRCA 1840)

1856: Madame Bovary *is pretty good, though*

REALISM ARRIVES IN RUSSIA, JUST SHOOT ME (CIRCA 1860)

1866: *Like, Crime and Punishment, you know what I'm saying?*

1891: *Melville dies forgotten*

1899: Moby-Dick *first read in its entirety*

1900–2000s
....

1900: THE TWENTIETH CENTURY GIVES WRITERS AN EXCUSE TO STOP
MAKING SENSE

1922: *ULYSSES* REALLY TOTALLY DOESN'T MAKE SENSE

1922–1950 AUTHORS STRUGGLE TO MAKE LESS SENSE THAN *ULYSSES*

MID-1920S: HEMINGWAY AND FITZGERALD: "LOOK AT ME, I LIVE IN PARIS"

1962: FAULKNER HEROICALLY DIES OF SOMETHING OTHER THAN ALCOHOLISM

2000–INFINITY
....

1960S–2020: TELEVISION, ADVERTISING, INTERNET, INVENTION OF THE PERFECT
MARGARITA WEAKEN HUMAN CHARACTER

2045: LAST PERSON ABLE TO VOTE RESPONSIBLY DIES

2065: ASCENDANCE OF MAN-DONKEY HYBRIDS

2070–INFINITY: UTOPIA

GREECE

Homer (POSSIBLY 8TH CENTURY BC)
Hesiod (7TH CENTURY BC, *in all likelihood*)
Sappho (LATE 7TH–EARLY 6TH CENTURY BC)
Pindar (LATE 6TH–MID-5TH CENTURY)
Aeschylus (525–456 BC)
Sophocles (496–406 BC)
Euripides (480–406 BC)
Aristophanes (446–386 BC)
Menander (342–291 BC)

ROME

Cattulus, Inventor of the Girlfriend (84–54 BC)
Virgil (70–19 BC)
Ovid (43 BC–17 AD)
Horace (65–8 BC)
Martial (42–102 AD)
Juvenal (60–140 AD)
Lucan (39–65 AD)
Seneca (4–65 AD)
Lucian (125–180 AD)
St. Augustine (354–430)

MIDDLE AGES

Beowulf (APPROX 700–900)
Song of Roland (MID-12TH CENTURY)
Arthur boom starts in EARLY 12TH CENTURY
continues for a couple of hundred years
Gawain, LATE 14TH CENTURY
Abelard & Heloise, LATE 11TH *(him) through* 12TH CENTURY
Romance of the Rose, 13TH CENTURY
Chaucer, 1343–1400
Gawain, LATE 14TH C.
Dante (1265–1321)

THE RENAISSANCE

....

Petrarch (1304–1374)

Boccaccio (1313–1375)

Benvenuto Cellini (1500–1571)

Francois Villon (1431–AFTER 1463)

Francois Rabelais (1494–1553)

Michel de Montaigne (1533–1592)

Miguel de Cervantes Saavedra (1547–1616)

Christopher Marlowe (1564–1593)

Sir Thomas Wyatt (1503–1542)

Sir Philip Sidney (1554–1586)

Sir Walter Raleigh (1552–1618)

Edmund Spenser (1552–1599)

William Shakespeare (1564–1616)

Ben Jonson (1572–1637)

THE PURITANS

....

Robert Herrick (1591–1674)

Richard Lovelace (1618–1657)

Sir John Suckling (1609–1642)

Thomas Carew (1595–1640)

John Donne (1572–1631)

*George Herbert (*1593–1633)

Henry Vaughan (1622–1695)

Abraham Cowley (1618–1667)

Richard Crashaw (1612–1649)

Andrew Marvell (1621–1678)

John Bunyan (1628–1688)

John Milton (1608–1674)

Samuel Butler's Hudibras (1663–78).

Sir Robert Burton's The Anatomy of Melancholy (1621)

Izaak Walton's The Compleat Angler (1653–1676)

THE SHALLOWS

Samuel Pepys (1633–1703)

John Dryden (1631–1700)

Wycherley's The Country Wife (1675)

Congreve's The Way of the World (1700)

Dryden's All for Love (1678)

Nahum Tate's King Lear (1681)

Thomas Otway's Venice Preserved (1682)

Aphra Behn (1640–1689)

John Wilmot, Earl of Rochester (1647–1680)

Madame de la Fayette (1634–1693)

Moliere (1622–1673)

Corneille (1606–1684)

Racine (1639–1699)

La Fontaine (1621–1695)

Mme de Sevigné (1626–1696)

THE AGE OF REASON

Alexander Pope (1688–1744)

Joseph Addison (1672–1719)

Richard Steele (1672–1729)

Daniel Defoe (1660–1731)

Samuel Richardson (1689–1761)

Henry Fielding (1707–1754)

Samuel Johnson (1709–1784)

James Boswell (1740–1795)

Jonathan Swift (1667–1745)

Laurence Sterne (1713–1768)

Thomas Gray (1716–1771)

Frances Burney (1752–1840)

Oliver Goldsmith (1730–1774)

Voltaire (Francois Marie Arouet) (1694–1778)

Denis Diderot (1713–1784)

Choderlos de Laclos (1741–1803)

Jean-Jacques Rousseau (1712–1778)

Marquis de Sade (1740–1814)

THE ROMANTICS

....

Robert Burns (1759–1796)

William Blake (1757–1827)

William Wordsworth (1770–1850)

Samuel Taylor Coleridge (1772–1834)

Robert Southey (1774–1843)

Lord Byron (1788–1824)

Percy Bysshe Shelley (1792–1822)

Mary Shelley (1797–1851)

John Keats (1795–1821)

Johann Wolfgang von Goethe (1749–1832)

Alexander Pushkin (1799–1837)

Alfred Tennyson (1809–1892)

Robert Browning (1812–1889)

Sir Walter Scott (1771–1832)

Victor Hugo (1802–1885)

Alexandre Dumas, father (1802–1870) and son (1824–1895)

AMERICANS

....

Washington Irving (1783–1859)

Ralph Waldo Emerson (1803–1882)

Henry David Thoreau (1817–1862)

Edgar Allan Poe (1809–1849)

Walt Whitman (1819–1892)

Emily Dickinson (1830–1886)

Nathaniel Hawthorne (1804–1864)

Herman Melville (1819–1891)

Mark Twain (Samuel Langhorne Clemens) (1835–1910)

Stephen Crane (1871–1900)

NICE REALISM

....

Jane Austen (1775–1817)

Charlotte (1816–1855), Emily (1818–1848) and
Anne (1820–1849) Brontë

Charles Dickens (1812–1870)

William Makepeace Thackeray (1811–1863)

Thomas Hardy (1840–1928)

Rudyard Kipling (1865–1936)

Oscar Wilde (1854–1900)

Edith Wharton (1862–1937)

D. H. Lawrence (1885–1930)

UNWELCOME REALISM

Stendhal (Marie-Henri Beyle) (1783–1842)

Honoré de Balzac (1799–1850)

Gustave Flaubert (1821–1880)

Emile Zola (1840–1902)

Joseph Conrad (Józef Teodor Konrad Korzeniowski) (1857–1924)

Nikolai Gogol (1809–1852)

Leo Tolstoy (1828–1910)

Fyodor Dostoevsky (1821–1881)

Henrik Ibsen (1828–1906)

August Strindberg (1849–1912)

Anton Chekhov (1860–1904)

THE MESSY TWENTIETH

Charles Baudelaire (1821–1867)

Arthur Rimbaud (1854–1891)

Comte de Lautreamont (1846–1870)

Gerard Nerval (1808–1855)

Tristan Corbiere (1845–1875)

Paul Verlaine (1844–1896)

Jules Laforgue (1860–1887)

Stephane Mallarme (1842–1898)

Alexander Blok (1880–1921)

Guillaume Apollinaire (1880–1918)

William Butler Yeats (1865–1939)

Henry James (1843–1916)

Gertrude Stein (1874–1946)

Franz Kafka (1883–1924)

T. S. Eliot (1888–1965)

William Carlos Williams (1883–1963)

Ezra Pound (1885–1972)

James Joyce (1882–1941)

Marcel Proust (1871–1922)

Virginia Woolf (1882–1941)

Ernest Hemingway (1899–1961)

F. Scott Fitzgerald (1896–1940)

William Faulkner (1897–1962)

About the Author

Sandra Newman is the author of the novels *Cake* and *The Only Good Thing Anyone Has Ever Done*, which won the Guardian First Book Award, and a memoir, *Changeling*. She is the coauthor of *How Not to Write a Novel* and *Read This Next*. She has worked as a professor of literature and writing at Temple University, Chapman University, the New School, and the University of Colorado. Her fiction and nonfiction writing has been published in *Harper's*, *Granta*, and London's *Observer*, *Telegraph*, and *Mail on Sunday*. She currently lives in Brooklyn.